100 JOBS IN
SOCIAL CHANGE

100 jobs in

social change

Harley Jebens

Macmillan · USA

MACMILLAN
A Simon & Schuster Macmillan Company
1633 Broadway
New York, NY 10019

Book design and production by Sandy Bell
100 Jobs in Social Change is produced by becker&mayer!, Ltd.

MACMILLAN is a registered trademark of Macmillan, Inc.

Library of Congress Cataloging-in-Publication Data

Jebens, Harley.
    100 jobs in social change / by Harley Jebens.
        p.   cm.
    Includes bibliographical references.
    ISBN 0–02–861430–5
    1. Vocational guidance—United States. 2. Job descriptions—
United States. 3. Social service—Vocational guidance—United
States. 4. Social change—United States.   I. Title.
HF5382.5.U5J4   1996
361' .0023'73—dc20   96–9074
                                                       CIP

10 9 8 7 6 5 4 3 2 1

Printed in the United States of America

ACKNOWLEDGMENTS

First of all, I would like to thank all the people who took time out of their schedules to talk to me about the jobs they do—the 100 people you will meet in the pages of this book. I would like to thank my sister, who provided me with my first interview; my fiancée, Shireen Razack; Emily and Mike Wethington, Aryani Ong, Jude Filler, Kirby Lindell, Todd Schoonover, JoAnne and Danny Reveles, John Jones, Deann Acton, Sarah Bubolz, Rachel Ganzon, Debra Quintana, Sherri Cole, Kathy Ramirez, Liren Shih, Warren Marr, and all the other people who helped me in my pursuit of this project, either by referring me to people or organizations, or for giving me advice on how best to pursue an undertaking of this magnitude.

And I would like to thank my parents for deciding to have kids.

100 JOBS

CONTENTS

100 JOBS IN
SOCIAL CHANGE

On the Public Payroll

Public Health and Safety—The Criminal Justice System

Health Services Industry

Education

Social Service Organizations

Nonprofit Organizations

Association Work

Labor Union Work

Providing Capital—Funding Social Change

Media Work/Communications

Technology-Oriented Jobs

International Relations/Overseas Work

Other Jobs

INTRODUCTION

- -

WHEN I BEGAN work on this book and started telling people my latest project was something called *100 Jobs in Social Change,* the response I got more often than any other was "Social change, you say. What do you mean by social change?" At first, I really didn't have an answer to that question. Not a good one, at any rate. "I don't want to unknowingly restrict the scope of this project by limiting my vision to any one definition," I would say, for lack of saying, "I don't know." Or I would turn the question around and ask, "How would you define social change?"

As this project continued, however, I settled on a definition that seemed to work—for me, at least.

"What is a job in social change?"

"Well, that's a job that has an impact—a positive impact, you would hope, or at least a positive impact in the eyes of the person doing that job—on society. It's work that helps other people. It's work that does good."

The jobs in this book fit that description, I think.

People's definitions of "good" might differ—and because some of these jobs are on different sides of the political spectrum, those judgments are almost certain to differ—but all the jobs listed in this book have an impact on society in one way or another.

"Do you think there are 100 different jobs in social change?" was another question people asked me. The answer depends on your definition of social change. But for every job description listed in this book, there are hundreds more out there.

It's best not to treat this book as a definitive look at the world of good works, but rather as a source of ideas. Reading through the job descriptions in the following pages will give you an idea of what this kind of work entails. Reading through the interviews in the following pages will give you an idea of how people started on and followed their own career paths, and what decisions and happenstances contributed to their reaching their current positions. Reading through the job search strategies sections in the following pages will give you ideas for organizing your own job search.

I hope these ideas prove useful.

Good luck in your job search.

—Harley Jebens

9

1. Coalition Staffer

AT THE NATIONAL LEVEL

description: Coalition work involves many of the same tasks and duties that working for a nonprofit organization does. Coalitions, though, are alliances of organizations and/or individuals, bound together by their position on a specific issue or series of issues.

Coalition staffers support those organizations or individuals. Workers' specific duties depend on the size of the coalition and the number of its staff workers. Development staff will serve as fund-raisers for the coalition. Program staff will be responsible for developing support materials and for determining the direction of the coalition and which specific programs it undertakes. Administrative personnel will be responsible for the day-to-day operations of the coalition office.

Coalition directors will serve as the organization's chief spokesperson. They will oversee or be involved in the programmatic operations of their office and will supervise the financial and fund-raising end of the coalition's efforts. Depending on the coalition's particular nature, or on the traditions of past directors, directors could find themselves in a predominantly fund-raising role, doing more public relations work, or being more involved in their coalition's programming. In the end, directors will have the ultimate responsibility for their coalition and its efforts.

Depending on the nature of the coalition, staffers could serve as a liaison to the coalition's members, supplying them with research, promotional materials, and other types of support. Staffers may track and prepare reports on legislation affecting their members' interests.

salary: Salaries of coalition workers will depend on the specific coalition for which they work, the constituency of the coalition's members, and the funding level of the coalition. Coalition salaries could start at around $12,000 for entry-level work, rising to as much as $50,000 per year for workers with a legal or professional degree.

prospects: Prospects for work in a national-level coalition vary depending on the nature of the coalition and the cause to which it is attached. Because many coalitions will be involved in issues that are growing in national prominence and support, positions tend to open or be created on a regular basis.

qualifications: Specific qualifications for coalition staffers vary depending on the nature of the coalition and its concerns. Coalition workers should be in philosophical and political agreement with the coalition they work for; they should be in fundamental agreement about their stances on the issues the coalition works on. Good research and writing skills will generally be required, as will a facility for speaking to the public.

characteristics: Someone who is committed to a specific cause will do well working for a coalition devoted to that cause. Social awareness and a willingness to work hard are two other characteristics an able coalition worker will have. Compassion is a quality that also should not be overlooked.

Steven Hawkins *is the executive director of a national coalition operating out of Washington, D.C.*

How did you get the job?

"I came out of law school," Steven says, "and as a young attorney began doing death penalty work, work for the abolitionist movement. It is a movement that attracts all kinds of people—ministers, educators, lawyers, family members of victims, and people with family members on death row.

"The death penalty is banned by various international human rights treaties, but is still carried out in numerous countries. I think that is deplorable. And devoting my life to addressing the death penalty is my mission.

"Young people like myself come in and represent people under sentence of death. When you do that, you realize that so many societal ills could be traced through our clients' lives. Traveling cross-country representing clients, I worked with the NAACP Legal Defense Fund, federal death penalty resource centers that have been around, federal public defender agencies.

"That work led to my ultimately coming to direct this organization.

FOR INFORMATION ON THE ABOLITIONIST MOVEMENT, CONTACT THE NATIONAL COALITION TO ABOLISH THE DEATH PENALTY (FOR ADDITIONAL INFORMATION SEE RESOURCES, PAGE 211). THE NATIONAL COALITION CAN GIVE YOU INFORMATION ABOUT ACTIVITIES GOING ON AT THE STATE LEVEL, AS WELL AS WHO TO CONTACT IN YOUR AREA.

"There are many forms of advocacy, and I have moved from the litigation form to non-litigation work. I came here to help build the national movement and to help further the international movement. I am the only lawyer on our staff. Most of our people here have college degrees, and we welcome people right out of college. At present, we have six people on our staff. Our funds primarily come from membership contributions, special events, foundations, and individual donors."

What do you do all day?

"One thing I do is track executions as they occur in the United States," Steven says, "and determine which cases we should make a national statement on. We take on one to two cases per month.

"I also deal with public inquiries from journalists and academics. I travel to various states working with our local affiliates on outreach efforts.

"Here at the National Coalition to Abolish the Death Penalty we aren't interested in the litigation end of things. But we are interested in addressing the issue of who we are executing, why we are executing them. We are interested in questioning the morality of the death penalty. That's what our work is aimed at doing."

Where do you see this job leading you?

"This is lifework for me," Steven says. "I am committed to the abolitionist movement. I hope to broaden the national coalition and hire more people. "The prospects for a young person finding work in the death penalty movement are fairly good, I think," he says. "As the coalition grows, more positions open up. Each state has something going on, and that provides an opportunity for people to get involved and find out who there is working in the movement. Each state will need to have a state coordinator, and I have seen young people fill those positions. Our office can be a contact organization for people. My advice would be to get involved with the movement, get a position of responsibility, and do it early.

"At the National Coalition to Abolish the Death Penalty, we are asking ourselves, 'How do we bring more young people into the movement?'

"Working in an organization like this gives you the opportunity to learn a whole range of skills and to learn about an issue that is, perhaps, very sporadically talked about in the press. Working here, you learn good organizational skills and good creative skills, because you are thinking constantly about how to bring forth a message. You develop your speaking abilities and your writing abilities."

2. Community Organizer

description: "Politics" can be described as the art of negotiation, dialogue, debate, and confrontation, all leading to a compromise so that people or groups of people can take action together. What community organizers do, at least under Saul Alinsky's Industrial Areas Foundation model, is teach people the art of politics, the art of rebuilding civic culture.

Community organizers typically work with religious congregations or other institutions, such as schools, that are tied to a specific community.

A lot of the work IAF organizers do falls under the heading of "individual meetings." These meetings are the most radical tool of organizing, says IAF organizer Tara Kirkland. Organizers will sit down with members of the congregation, parents of schoolchildren, teachers, and others involved in the church or school. A 30- to 45-minute structured conversation will follow, where the organizers will try to identify issues of concern and, most importantly, whether that person is a leader or potential leader. Organizers could meet with up to 40 people a week in these individual meetings, in which a handful of names are usually mentioned repeatedly—leaders within their organizations, those whom others respect and follow. Next, community organizers attempt to set up "house meetings" with those leaders, in an attempt to identify issues about which people care enough to take action. Once those issues are identified, community organizers will attempt to teach the organization's leaders how they can go about getting those issues addressed.

salary: Community organizers, like so many workers for social change, can expect to make a living wage, but perhaps not much more than that. Organizers can make from $19,000 to $50,000 a year. That wage will depend on the specific organization you're working for and your experience.

prospects: There are close to 30 Industrial Areas Foundation organizations, located in New York, New Jersey, Maryland, Tennessee, Arizona, New Mexico, Louisiana, Nebraska, California, and Texas. The paid staffs of those organizations are likely to be small; and there aren't very many groups doing the type of organizing that IAF promotes. But as IAF and the type of organizing it promotes gain in popularity, opportunities for community organizers should improve, and groups are always looking for good organizers.

qualifications: Community organizers tend to have a breadth of experience. Many have come into organizing from other careers or have become involved with the IAF through their own church, neighborhood, or school communities. Perhaps the primary qualifications for a community organizer are a demonstrated commitment to this type of organizing, and a willingness to "disorganize and reorganize" yourself in order to learn to organize others.

characteristics: Effective community organizers are usually fueled by a sense of anger and a sorrow about the injustices they've experienced in their own lives—these are the catalysts that propel most organizers to do the work they do. Organizers should be willing to learn and should have the ability to handle high-pressure situations. A good sense of humor is also a desirable trait.

Tara Kirkland *works for an Industrial Areas Foundation in Austin, Texas.*

How did you get the job?

"Ever since I was a child, I had a deep concern for others, for the welfare of others," says Tara.

"In college, I needed to write a year-long senior thesis. But by the spring of my junior year, I had no idea what I wanted to do. So I took a year off.

"I then decided that psychology, counseling, was what I wanted to do," Tara says, "so I came back to school to take graduate-level classes in counseling and write my thesis on that. I discovered that I didn't like psychology; I decided that psychology was not part of the answer, but in many cases is part of the problem. I turned my thesis into a critique of psychology, of the culture of individualism that psychology seems to foster and support. We have a problem today in that we view each other as disconnected, autonomous selves. We've all become isolated. I became passionate about that, about how to rebuild civic society and begin to act as citizens rather than as little individualists."

"I began to volunteer at the Austin Interfaith office," Tara says. (Austin Interfaith—a coalition of 30 churches and synagogues of differing faiths

MAKE A CANDID ASSESSMENT OF YOUR OWN STRENGTHS AND WEAKNESSES. FIGURE OUT HOW YOU CAN PRESENT YOUR STRENGTHS TO A PROSPECTIVE EMPLOYER. TRY TO IMPROVE UPON YOUR AREAS OF WEAKNESS, OR AT LEAST KNOW HOW TO COMPENSATE FOR THEM. THAT WAY, WHEN YOU GO INTO AN INTERVIEW, YOU CAN PLAY TO YOUR STRENGTHS, AND DE-EMPHASIZE YOUR WEAKER SPOTS.

and ethnicities in the Austin area—is part of the Industrial Areas Foundation network.) "I was able to get the volunteer position because I had five years of office experience. After working there three or four months, I said to myself, 'Hey I can do this.' I felt that I wanted to make a career out of the kind of work that Austin Interfaith does.

"I came in as a volunteer and was able to negotiate a paid position for myself. There was a 10-day national training seminar put on by IAF. Austin Interfaith said they would match half the payment for that seminar. So I invested $400 and was able to attend. I proved myself there, and the organization here offered me a three-month tryout. After the tryout, I came on full-time. I was the third full-time worker here."

What do you do all day?

"I don't have a 9-to-5 assignment," Tara says. "I work with two schools and two congregations in the Austin area. I try to identify leaders within those schools, and then I start trying to figure out how things are currently organized and how I can disorganize that playing field to create something more effective."

Tara gives one example of the work she's been doing. "In January, we began a series of community meetings with 10 Austin schools. We did a community audit of the different schools to identify problems that those schools and their communities were having. We started working on a plan to address those problems, and in May, the leaders held the Youth Strategies Conference, the cul-

mination of the work we've been doing. The conference was a real success.

"It was six to eight weeks of endless work—this is a very demanding job. You are dealing with people's lives and so you find yourself giving 110 percent. The local organizers agitate us to make time for a personal life, but it can be hard to quit when you know the stakes are so high. I get the most gratification from working with leaders and watching them develop. I feel that the face of Austin is being changed because of my work, and that's very gratifying."

Where do you see this job leading you?

Tara has plans to move on to an IAF group in Dallas, and to continue her community organizing work there.

"The skills you learn in organizing apply to anything, but the IAF doesn't encourage people to come in and then leave. They invest a lot of time in training you, and most people tend to stick with IAF once they find their place here."

3. Contract Lobbyist

description: A contract lobbyist provides information and research to elected officials about issues important to the lobbyist's clients. A contract lobbyist usually works for more than one client, and typically "sells" access to legislators.

"Legislators don't have time to research all the issues they have to cast votes on, and lobbyists provide that research to them" is how Billy Clayton, a lobbyist in Texas, puts it. "Lobbyists have to be forthright and honest with research and presenting information, because, basically, integrity is about all we have to sell."

Part of a lobbyist's time will be spent gathering information—from the client, associations, government committees, and those affected by legislation. The rest of the time will be spent meeting with government officials, and talking to legislators and their assistants—trying to persuade them to vote a particular way on various pieces of legislation. Lobbying work, then, is as much (if not more) about personal contact and persuasion as it is about research and data collection.

salary: "Our clients pay us from $1,000 to $10,000 a month," Billy says, "depending on the complexity of the issue and the work entailed researching it, and presenting our information to the legislators." Contract lobbyists can expect to earn from $30,000 to $120,000 or more per year, depending on their previous experience, the number of clients they work for, and the amount of money those clients have or are willing to spend.

prospects: The lobbying job market can be a very tight one. Many elected officials and government types segue into lobbying after their tenures in office are over, so young lobbyists can be competing with people with years of political and governmental experience under their belts.

The hardest part about finding a job as a lobbyist is likely to be getting the proverbial foot in the door. Lobbying experience tends to build upon itself. Once a person has landed that first lobbying job and gotten some experience, doors should begin to open.

qualifications: The most important qualifications for this type of position are a knowledge of the legislative process and a familiarity with the people involved in the process. That knowledge is typically gained through legislative experience.

"Some of the most effective lobbyists will come up through staff positions with a legislator or through interning with a lobbyist," says one contract lobbyist.

Lobbyists will need to understand the needs of the clients they represent, as well as the needs of the legislators they work with and the needs of those legislators' constituents. A thorough understanding of how the political system works is essential to being effective in this field.

characteristics: An ability to work well with people and a persuasive manner are two of the most important traits for a prospective lobbyist to possess. She or he should be willing to put in long hours—during the legislative session, 80-hour weeks will be a common experience. Lobbyists should also be people who love politics and the political process, and who want to be involved in that process.

Sarah Janecek *works for a contract lobbying firm based in Minneapolis, Minnesota.*

How did you get the job?

You'll find that most lobbyists have legislative experience of some form under their belt, and Sarah is no exception. Sarah's first taste of life in the legislature came when she worked in Washington, D.C., for a semester while in college.

"I came back to Minnesota to go to law school, and met my future business partner at a political event," she says. She began working, along with her future partner, first as an intern. "We decided to break off on our own," she says. "So we did that, and started to get clients of our own."

What do you do all day?

"My job consists of meeting with legislators, checking with governmental offices, and monitoring legislation. I talk to legislators—I'll catch them in the hall or wherever they are and have a moment to chat.

"I help to pass or not pass legislation. I draft legislation in some instances. Sometimes I

THE ELECTRONIC JOB SEARCH REVOLUTION, BY JOYCE LAIN KENNEDY AND THOMAS J. MORROW, CAN FILL YOU IN ON HOW TO BEST CRAFT AN ELECTRONIC RESUME, AND THEN USE IT AND OTHER ELECTRONIC RESOURCES IN YOUR JOB SEARCH.

will form coalitions with other lobbyists and other parties interested in the issues we're working on, people who are interested in seeing certain pieces of legislation passed or, on the other hand, in blocking other pieces of legislation."

This work will parallel the legislative cycle in the state in which you are working. State legislative cycles are usually much shorter than national ones. Some legislatures meet for four to five months every year; some meet only every other year. When the legislature is in session, lobbyists will be working extremely hard, with 12- to 14-hour days being common. During the session, lobbyists will be meeting with legislators one-on-one.

In the interim session, lobbyists will conduct background research on topics of interest to

the concerns that have hired them. During this period, lobbyists will have time to meet with agency representatives, attend commission hearings, and lay the groundwork for what they'll be doing in the next legislative session.

Where do you see this job leading you?

"I don't really plan my life that far in advance," Sarah says.

She adds, however, that legislative experience, or the experience you get working with the legislator as a lobbyist, can be valuable wherever you go. Businesses value that experience, as do nonprofit organizations. Lobbying can be a lucrative business in its own right, and many successful lobbyists choose to stick with it.

4. Coordinator

description: System reform initiatives are attempts to change policies, structures, and fund strategies for serving children and families with programs that serve clients better, or result in more efficient or cost-effective administration. Coordinators help to design initiatives and have to lobby for the changes designated, meeting with government, community representatives, and families to bring those different perspectives together in order to design a system of care. Coordinators push for these reforms at a local, state, and nationwide level.

People in this job represent their program to funders and to the community groups and public agencies for whom the initiative program is designed. They are responsible for developing and working with their own board of directors in some initiatives.

Coordinators have a hand in training workers or volunteers, listening to those workers, and modifying programmatic ideas to fit the reality of working in these new systems on a daily basis.

They are also responsible for overseeing the work of the people under them, and managing budgets and the payroll. They might also have to write grants, as they seek out further funding for their initiatives.

salary: Pay for system reform work can vary from starting salaries of less than $20,000 per year to $40,000. Administrators can expect to make from $40,000 to $65,000 or more. The biggest indicators of salary will be the organization that provides the funding for the job, and the area of the country in which it's located—salaries are generally higher on the East and West Coasts.

prospects: The impetus for these sorts of system reform initiatives comes from many places—community groups, churches, philanthropic organizations, universities, or even with individuals—and the prospects for finding employment are as varied as the many sources calling for change. The most prudent advice for would-be job seekers is to discover a cause or movement to which they owe an allegiance, or a system they feel needs changing, and then do some investigating and seek out the groups working for this type of change. If you cannot find any such groups, form your own.

qualifications: Coordinators of these initiatives have to be part advocate, part negotiator, part teacher, and part administrator. People come into this sort of work from all types of backgrounds. Workers should have experience—either educational or work-related—in the field in which they intend or hope to implement change. Management experience, or perhaps even more importantly, experience in team-building, will prove valuable to this sort of endeavor.

characteristics: If you're going to be involved in system reform work, you should have a patient personality. Strong teamwork and communications skills will also prove essential to the consensus building that makes up much of this type of effort. A strong belief in what you are doing will serve you in good stead. Leadership qualities will prove essential in accomplishing your team's goals.

Sheila Savannah *is a local coordinator and project manager for various systematic reform initiative programs.*

How did you get the job?

"After getting a bachelor's degree in journalism with a secondary area of study in psychology, I came out of the university with the notion that I did not want to work in the majority community. I wanted to start with a community-based organization, doing grant writing for that organization. I thought I could create a niche for myself, doing contract development work, and grant and brochure writing. I worked with a number of community organizations."

Following this, Sheila was engaged in a variety of occupations before being hired by Riverside General Hospital to develop a substance abuse prevention program for schools.

"I became director of that hospital's child and adolescent programs, and began development of treatment programs for adolescents there. We dealt mostly with the children of parents we had in our treatment programs.

"Because of my work at the hospital, I became involved in the application for grants for the program I now work with—

IF YOU'RE INTERESTED IN WORKING FOR THE FEDERAL GOVERNMENT, CHECK OUT THE ALMANAC OF AMERICAN GOVERNMENT JOBS AND CAREERS. THE BOOK PROVIDES CONTACT INFORMATION FOR FEDERAL AGENCIES AND EMPLOYERS, AND SOME HELPFUL INFORMATION FOR PEOPLE LOOKING FOR WORK IN STATE AND LOCAL GOVERNMENT.

the Annie E. Casey Mental Health Initiative for Urban Children.

"Baltimore's Casey Foundation has established several initiatives across the country primarily focused on systems change, impacting the lives of children and their families, and especially aimed at reducing the rate at which children are removed from their home. The foundation is involved in juvenile justice and foster family programs, strategic analysis, and policy projects."

What do you do all day?

Sheila and the Casey Foundation became involved with her state's Health and Human Services Commission to help the commission coordinate the human services agencies across the state, and link them via computer.

"My typical week involves a lot of meetings and one-on-one discussions to help people feel safe putting their agendas on the table," Sheila says. "When we first started out, we had more agency-to-agency meetings and family-to-family meetings, but we found out we get the best results if we mix those groups. My main job is keeping everyone on the table.

"Together we look at the policy and practice barriers at the agencies we work with, and try to develop a streamlined intake process for the social service agencies that people in our community have to deal with. We've helped configure a client-tracking system that should help reduce paperwork for all of these agencies. We've been involved with setting up an integrated database network that connects these agencies.

"I've found that the growth of an organization's development is similar to human growth and behavioral development. My job is to study the pattern of that growth rather than create it, to reinforce the natural supports that are in place, rather than creating artificial supports. I ask, 'What works? What is effective?' and then build on those supports."

Where do you see this job leading you?

"I hope to work myself out of a job," Sheila says. "Once we have gotten the systems changed, have implemented those systems, and have gotten everyone retrained in their work, I will move on to something else.

"I will probably get back to journalism; I see a need for me to get back to writing.

"A lot of people move from work like this into consulting, but I see that market quickly being flooded. I do see a need for people trained in the retraining of staff.

"People have to be what I would call a 'specific-generalist,'" Sheila says. "The minute you say, for instance, 'I'm a juvenile specialist,' you've locked yourself out of potential opportunities outside of that restricted field."

5. Lobbying Director

FOR AN ADVOCACY ORGANIZATION

description: One of the primary goals of any advocacy group is to educate a specific constituency as to the advocacy group's position on an issue or range of issues. Groups work to inform the public about their side of issues; they endeavor to let people know how they can affect, in their personal and professional lives, the course the issue or issues take; they work to educate other groups about their stance, and to form coalitions with like-minded organizations; and they work to educate legislators, and influence how they might vote on specific issues.

Advocacy organizations are, by-and-large, grassroots efforts, and much of the work of an organization's lobbying director will be grassroots mobilizing. They will speak to civic organizations or other interested groups, help organize and speak at conventions or rallies, and organize volunteers to man a telephone solicitation campaign. They will respond to media inquiries, and try to drum up media interest in their issue through press releases, advertisements, and other means. They will write articles and guest editorials about their group's issues.

They will also, in all likelihood, find themselves going to Washington, D.C., or to their state capital to lobby legislators. But generally, those instances will only arise when an issue or bill affecting their group's interests is being debated.

salary: People doing lobbying work for national-level advocacy organizations can expect to earn a starting salary of $20,000 to $22,000 per year, perhaps more depending on experience. Salaries could rise to $30,000 a year or more. Remember that budgets for these sorts of organizations tend to be low, and salary level will depend as much on the nature of the organization and its funding structure as it will on your experience.

prospects: Openings in advocacy organizations can be hard to come by. Applicants with prior experience in the movement, or in working with the state or national legislature, will have the best chance of landing these jobs, especially lobbying jobs. Especially important for lobbying work will be political knowledge or experience.

Keep in mind that certain issues will be propelled into the limelight of media and public attention, and, at those times, organizations fighting for those causes will proliferate and be better-funded. Opportunities will be greater in organizations focusing on these "hot issues."

qualifications: The main qualification for work in this arena will be a passionate drive to be involved in the movement which the organization supports. Somebody hoping to work for an advocacy organization will also need to have a degree in a field particular to the organization, or to have some experience in the movement. Workers involved in the lobbying side of things will need to possess an understanding of, and perhaps experience with, the legislative process.

characteristics: People doing this type of work will have strong convictions and believe in the cause they are advocating. They will realize that they are in the fight for the long haul, be willing to wait to see the fruits of their labors, and realize that success will come in small increments.

Lori Hougens *is the Director of Federal Legislation and Communication for the New York State Right-to-Life Committee.*

- -

How did you get the job?

"My involvement in this movement really began in junior high, when I started to learn about abortion," Lori says, "and it sort of came to the forefront in high school, when I wasn't allowed to give a speech about the topic. I got a communications and public relations undergraduate degree in Rochester, New York, and, for my four years there, I spoke out about abortion, but didn't really know there was an organized right to life movement.

"I moved out to California, where I found out about the movement and, in 1989, I began to volunteer with the Right-to-Life League of Southern California. Then I became the director of education at that organization. I trained people to speak on this issue. I would speak. We would attend conventions and events like Lollapalooza.

"I worked at the Right-to-Life League for three years, then went on to help start an organization called California Collegians for Life. For a program called 'Sex, Love, and Choices,' we went into the schools and talked about abortion and abstinence.

"Then I was offered a job as student activities director at Niyack College, back in New York.

"I spent one year at the college. I was volunteering for Right-to-Life groups at Niyack, and was going to do a speaker-training session there. So I called the New York State Right-to-Life Committee to see about getting some literature I could use in my training session. They asked to see my resume. That's how I ended up here. I've been here two years.

"I took an $8,000 cut in pay to come here," she says. "Anyone hoping to get involved in this type of work should be prepared for a cut in pay."

What do you do all day?

"A typical week here is chaos," Lori says. "We just came to the end of a Congressional session, and that's when a lot of things are happening at once. We were faxing things to every Congressman we might hope to affect. We were contacting all the grassroots organizations with which we are affiliated, trying to mobilize their efforts.

"Last Saturday was our state convention, and we spent a lot of time preparing for that. I was in charge of inviting all the speakers to that convention. We had a whole day full of speakers, and 260 people came to the convention. We sold out and even had to turn people away at the door. People spoke on legislative efforts that would affect abortion.

"I do some speaking myself. I get requests to speak as colleges and schools get Right-to-Life chapters going.

"But legislation is really the thing that takes up most of my time. There is always something going on in the legislative arena that concerns this issue, and if not, I am writing something to affect future legislation. I help put together advertisements.

"For me, October is a busy month. That is Request Life Month. And people are back in school and getting campus chapters organized again for the school year. Work drops off around Christmas, and then spring is also a busy time. Summer can be busy, it just depends what's going on.

"My job entails a lot of weekend work. I don't think anybody here works [less than] 40 hours."

Where do you see this job leading you?

"I have a background in business," Lori says, "and I've had management and public relations experience. Now with this job, I've been a lobbyist. I have no desire to leave the movement, but I can see myself changing my role in the movement."

People with experience in the lobbying department of an advocacy organization can go on to work for other advocacy organizations. They can move back into the legislative arena, working on the staff of a like-minded legislator. They can go to work for a freelance or contract lobbying firm as well.

> **DON'T FORGET THE NEWSPAPER. NOT EVERY JOB OPENING WILL BE ADVERTISED IN THE WANT ADS, BUT PERUSING THEM ON A REGULAR BASIS WILL GIVE YOU A GOOD FEEL FOR THE TYPES OF JOBS THAT ARE AVAILABLE IN YOUR AREA, AND CAN RESULT IN VALUABLE LEADS.**
> - - - - - - - - - - -

6. Lobbyist

description: A lobbyist establishes relationships with members of Congress (or state legislative bodies) and their staffs, so that when issues of importance to the lobbyist and the organization the lobbyist represents come before the legislature, the organization has the ear of that congressional member or legislator and their staffs. They prepare position papers, stating how pending legislation could affect their interests, and suggest amendments or other legislative rewrites that could better affect those interests. Lobbyists might propose legislation and, in some cases, write the bills to which legislators attach their names. They attend committee meetings, visit with committee members, and might set up and/or lead meetings concerning certain issues. Basically, a lobbyist works on networking and making personal connections with legislators and their staffs in order to suggest and influence legislative agendas.

Lobbyists also track legislation and contact lobby members at appropriate moments to recommend what direct action they can take to influence a bill's outcome—calling and writing legislators, phoning in to radio talk shows, etc.

Lobbyists might also have to do some grassroots networking, updating the lobby's members on its efforts. They write reports on the lobby's efforts, and perhaps write for the lobby's newsletter.

Lobbies often engage in coalitions, joining other lobbies with similar positions on particular issues, in order to coordinate and strengthen their lobbying effort.

salary: Salaries for lobbyists can vary widely. A lobbyist just starting out, or working for one of the smaller lobbies, could make $20,000 or less per year initially. Salaries can rise as high as $100,000 or more yearly.

prospects: The number of religiously-based lobbying organizations is quite small, so opportunities there are quite limited. There will always be positions for lobbyists with experience, however. Experience in Washington, D.C., will be highly regarded, even at the state level.

qualifications: The job of a lobbyist is built, perhaps more so than any other, on a foundation of personal connections. A prospective lobbyist is going to have to put in some time in state or national government, or with organizations that do business with the government. Lobbyists will have to have—or acquire—knowledge of the issues with which their organization is concerned. Experience in the political system on the local level, whether paid or volunteer—campaign work, voter registration drives, political party work, or work focused on specific issues—can also prove helpful. If you're going to be involved with a religious organization, you will probably have some relationship or affiliation with that religion.

characteristics: Lobbyists will possess basic political instincts and a willingness to work within and through the political system. They should be at ease meeting with and speaking in front of large groups of people, adept at developing personal relationships, and able to articulate their concerns about issues in person and in writing. They should be committed to making a difference.

Based in Washington, D.C., **Richelle Friedman** *is a lobbyist for a religious organization.*

How did you get the job?

Richelle is a member of a Catholic community of religious women, the Sisters of the Presentation of the Blessed Virgin Mary, based in Dubuque, Iowa. "I taught on the secondary and junior-high levels in Catholic schools for 20 years," she says. "Many of the theology courses I taught were oriented directly towards social justice. I also coordinated service programs.

"At the same time, I did volunteer work at a Catholic Worker house, and at a shelter for abused women. My volunteer work highlighted something I already knew to be a reality—that poor people often have an extremely difficult time breaking out of the cycle of poverty.

"I was aware of NET-WORK—a membership organization with 10,000 members. NETWORK is a national Catholic social justice lobby that attempts to effect systematic change through the national legislative process. One of the organization's basic beliefs is

DETERMINE YOUR FOCUS AND AREA OF INTEREST, AND TAILOR YOUR JOB SEARCH TO THAT FOCUS.

that the character of a nation is determined by how it treats its poor people. NETWORK lobbies for change in three areas: budget priorities, just access to economic resources, and transforming global relationships. Under these categories we work for policies which include: increased progressivity in the tax system, a reduction in military spending, health care reform, welfare reform, affordable housing, and a foreign aid program based on the principles of sustainable development. NET-WORK has nine full-time employees; two of us are lobbyists.

"The organization has a year-long internship program. I applied for the program and was accepted. Partway through my internship, one of the lobbyists left. I was encouraged to apply for that position, and was accepted."

What do you do all day?

"I've worked here six years, and find that legislative activity tends to follow certain patterns. Through the early spring, Congress—and therefore our activities—focuses on the budget process. In late spring through early fall, authorization legislation, which defines programs, and appropriations legislation, which determines program funding levels, are the focuses. During those times, I spend a lot of time on the Hill. After the Congressional session ends in fall or winter, we prepare a voting record that goes to our members. Other activities include responding to member requests for information, attending coalition meetings, and writing issue-related articles for our organization's publication.

"The internal management style at NETWORK lends itself to shared responsibility for the work we do, and shared decision making, which involves organizational meetings. It's a supportive environment in which to work.

"We also focus to educate our members. To that end, I give workshops throughout the country."

Where do you see this job leading you?

"The person who worked in this position as a lobbyist before me went on to do advocacy work for another organization," Richelle says. "As for myself, I'm doing work that is very satisfying. My job is challenging because the political climate in our country is such that there's not a lot of support for poor and working-class people, minorities, or immigrants. It's important for organizations with a perspective such as ours to be involved in the political dialogue, providing a voice that counters what seem to be dominant political themes inside the beltway. Right now, it's very fulfilling work, and I don't see myself doing anything different in the near future."

Lobbying can provide you with experience to work within the government or in the private sector. A job as a lobbyist could lead you to lobbying jobs with other organizations, to a position as a political campaign manager, to a political consultant position, or to work within a legislative think tank. The cliché "it's not what you know, it's who you know" is true, and you'll never get to know more people than you will as a lobbyist.

7. Office Manager

OF A GRASSROOTS ACTIVIST ORGANIZATION

description: As the office manager for an activist organization, you might well be the only full-time staff member of the organization. Your duties will entail the general running of the office—answering phones, making photocopies, keeping the office supplied, gathering information, coordinating schedules of organization members, facilitating networking opportunities for members, scheduling meetings, and other assorted tasks. You'll probably be in charge of the organization's bookkeeping as well. You might also find yourself in the role of fund-raiser.

You will most likely help organize and participate in direct actions, the nature of which will depend on the nature of the organization you work for. You might help in the organizing of media coverage of these direct actions—as such, you'll be a public relations agent as well.

The term "office manager" might lead you to believe that this is a fairly mundane job. Not so, for in this job you may be acting as PR agent, accountant, direct organizer, lobbyist, journalist, and administrator.

There isn't much full-time employment to be had in grassroots and activist organizations, which tend to be volunteer-run and -driven. If you're drawn to this type of work, managing an activist group's office can be one feasible way to do this type of work full-time.

salary: Office managers for activist organizations can expect to make from $16,500 to $25,000 a year. Budgets for these sorts of organizations tend to be low, and salary level will depend as much on the nature of the organization and its funding structure, as it will on your experience.

prospects: These types of jobs tend to be few and far between. Many people are called to activist and grassroots work, making competition for these (admittedly low-paying) jobs quite keen. As certain issues—the environment, or nuclear disarmament, for example—are propelled into the limelight of media and public attention, organizations fighting for those causes will proliferate and be better funded. Opportunities will be greater in organizations focusing on these "hot issues."

qualifications: Activist and grassroots organizations will look for someone with general office experience, as well as knowledge of the issues the organization is involved in. Writing and communications skills will come in handy. If you have experience volunteering, or working with the issues the organization works on, you'll have a leg up on other applicants.

characteristics: Employees of grassroots and activist organizations should be able to work with a variety of people, possess a cool temperament, and be patient and tolerant. A willingness to put in long hours is a crucial trait for an activist.

Bob Brister *is an office coordinator at the Peace and Justice Coalition in a large Southwestern city.*

- -

How did you get the job?

"I did my undergraduate work at Memphis State University, majoring in social work. I went on to the University of Michigan School of Social Work, and earned a master's of social work there," Bob says.

"And then I was out of work for three months. I got a job in Memphis, working in a pre-trial services program. I interviewed folks who had been arrested to determine whether they could be released on their own recognizance. I was there for eight months.

"Then I moved to Florida, where I worked for the American Friends Service Committee for 12 years. I was the director of the Tampa Bay Peace Education Program. I was involved in anti-nuke projects, worked against U.S. involvement in Central America, and showed the connection between peace, social justice, and environmental issues. Our organization suffered from budget cutbacks, and mine was one of the projects that was cut.

"I was unemployed then for one and one-half years. I did some independent organizing projects during that time, developing a Green political party in Florida, and working towards the relegalization of hemp.

"When my savings bottomed out, I set out on an 'economic migrant tour of the United States.' I went to Austin, Eugene, Portland, Arcata (California), and Denver. Before going 'round to cities, I researched the activist groups in these cities. There was an American Friends Service Committee branch here. I checked with them and found out there was an opening with the Peace and Justice Coalition. I was fortunate enough to get the job here."

What do you do all day?

"The Peace and Justice Coalition is comprised of 45 grass-roots peace, social justice, and environmental advocacy groups," Bob says. "We provide technical services for member organizations—a fax program, where we publicize our members' events to a list of media contacts we have. We publish a newsletter once every two months. We sponsor or co-sponsor a number of programs or seminars each year, and do a weekly program on a local community radio station.

> STAY IN TOUCH OR GET IN TOUCH WITH UMBRELLA ORGANIZATIONS. ESTABLISHED UMBRELLA ORGANIZATIONS ARE NETWORKS IN THEMSELVES. PEOPLE INVOLVED WITH THESE UMBRELLA GROUPS WILL KNOW OF OPENINGS IN THEIR MEMBER ORGANIZATIONS.

"I take care of the general running of the office here," he says, "and the occasional organizing of demonstrations, when an issue comes up that nobody can address. For instance, Gary Graham, a prisoner on death row here, came forward with new evidence that would perhaps exonerate him. The state refused to hear that evidence. So we worked with a coalition to abolish the death penalty to organize vigils at the governor's mansion. We helped organize peace vigils when the U.S. military intervened in Haiti, an anti-NAFTA rally at the AFL-CIO building, and we put up tables at events such as gay pride festivals and other events here in town.

"I do the layout of the newsletter on a Macintosh computer using the PageMaker program.

"People principally call on us for media stuff. We've testified before city councils on particular issues in the past.

"This is a jack-of-all-trades job. I do media relations, publications work, radio production, television work—announcements on public access television and things like that, and even computer database stuff."

Where do you see this job leading you?

"I've never been interested in going anywhere else," Bob explains, "so I don't see this job leading my anywhere.

"But this job builds a lot of skills that you can transfer to other jobs, either jobs in the peace and justice movement, or jobs in the general workforce. You get experience in public relations work, public speaking, writing skills. You develop general office management skills—if one is fortunate enough to work in an office instead of out of the house."

8. Program Coordinator
FOR AN ACTIVIST ORGANIZATION

description: As a program coordinator for an activist organization, you'll find yourself faced with administrative, research-oriented, organizational, and public relations-related responsibilities. You could be running an office alone, and thus have to take care of all the office management duties yourself.

Your duties will also include many, if not all, of the following: supervising long-term public education, lobbying, or organizing campaigns, or the programs centering around specific duties or events; organizing a demonstration or public event—rounding up speakers and participants, facilitating press coverage, and putting together supplemental materials explaining the background or context of the event; informing people about the actions they can take in response to certain issues; and public speaking about the goals and methods of your organization.

If you're in charge of ongoing programs, your duties will be much the same, though they will be more developmental in nature.

This type of work will allow you to earn a living while working in an activist capacity, an opportunity that isn't available to many activists, many of whom essentially work as volunteers.

salary: Just because you will be able to earn a living doing this sort of work doesn't mean you'll get rich. Salaries will vary from place to place and from organization to organization, but program coordinators can expect to earn from about $20,000 to $24,000 a year.

prospects: For applicants without a lot of office or activist experience, chances of finding work as a program coordinator for an activist organization are slim. However, if you have skills that the organization is lacking—computer skills, or training in a specific program area—your chances of landing a job like this are much improved.

qualifications: Basic communications skills are important qualifications for a program coordinator. Computer skills are becoming increasingly vital as well, as they are for almost everyone in today's workforce. The ability to convene and conduct meetings is an important skill to master.

characteristics: Program coordinators for activist organizations should possess persistence and an intensity toward their job, and toward the mission of their organization. "People in this line of work need to be intense," one program coordinator says, "but they also need to possess a deep sense of humor. They need to be self-effacing—to take issues seriously, but not themselves. They should be aware that cynicism works against you."

Bill Ramsey *is an area program coordinator for an activist organization based in St. Louis, Missouri.*

How did you get the job?

"I worked in inner city community centers, and did some community organizing work and research while I was in divinity school—that was my first significant work experience with community organizing.

"During the seminary, I was involved in a national caucus focused on the Vietnam War. From 1971 to 1973, I was involved in public activities related to the trials of draft and tax resistors. I handled the media for those trials. That convinced me that I was doing something right, and 'labeled' me as someone who could do press work.

"I did press work for an American Friends Service Committee (AFSC) effort to stop a shipping ordinance [related to the Vietnam War], an effort that eventually led to us closing that port for a time. Then I was offered a job with the Vietnamese Children's Fund, doing fund-raising and education work.

"I spent a year as a Methodist minister in New Jersey, and got involved with the United Farmworkers Union in 1975 in a lettuce, grape, and wine boycott. My wife and I decided to work for the union.

"I worked for the union for two months, and then was offered a job with the AFSC. I was hired as the Peace Education Secretary for the organization's southeast region. I coordinated peace activities for a nine-state service area and stations in six locations. I was involved in a number of projects from 1975 to 1980, ranging from events that rose out of the Vietnam War aftermath— from amnesty for draft resisters and reconstruction aid for Vietnam, to a campaign against the B-1 bomber, to nuclear weapons conversion projects."

In 1981, he moved over to the AFSC office in St. Louis, working for the first year on a half-time basis. Eventually, funding and staffing were increased, and the St. Louis office now supports the equivalent of three full-time positions.

What do you do all day?

"The official AFSC workweek is a 35-hour week," Bill says. "But there are a lot of evening and weekend meetings, so I put in an average of 45 to 50 hours a week.

"What I'm involved in today is an execution scheduled for tonight in Missouri. Our office is facilitating press coverage of anti-capital punishment demonstrations—providing media contacts with information on the case, and on tonight's demonstration.

"I'm also making calls to various organizations involved in the commemoration of the 50th anniversary of the bombing of Hiroshima. Today, I'm trying to line up a Buddhist prayer for that event.

"Our office is involved like this all the time," Bill says.

Where do you see this job leading you?

"People I know of who have left the AFSC over the past 15 years have gone on to other social change positions," Bill says.

"Within the AFSC, there are administrative positions in our regional offices. In Philadelphia, where the American Friends headquarters is located, there are six or seven division-level administrative positions, plus fund-raising positions.

"I've gone from a regional to a local position, which some people would consider a step down. But I like dealing with things on a local level."

> PROGRAM COORDINATORS SHOULD POSSESS PERSISTENCE AND INTENSITY TOWARD THEIR JOB.

9. Program Director

FOR A NATIONAL HUMAN RIGHTS/CIVIL RIGHTS ADVOCACY ORGANIZATION

description: The program director for a human or civil rights advocacy or support organization will take a lot of phone calls. They'll talk to people who feel that they are victims of discrimination or that their human rights have been violated. They will then work to redress those complaints utilizing whatever resources their organization has at its disposal, while keeping in mind the scope of their organization's focus. They could refer the person they're talking with to another agency that might be better able to meet that person's needs, or they might refer the caller to legal counsel. They could also process the complaint, following procedures the organization has established.

Program directors might be called on to give testimony or serve as expert witnesses before legislative councils, caucuses, or committees.

They help facilitate the training of their organization's members by creating training tools, researching information, and putting it into a form that will be most useful to their members.

Program directors can expect to travel in order to get firsthand experience and gather testimony on the causes they're fighting for. They will participate in planned actions and protests, and put on workshops and training seminars.

salary: The primary indicators of salary in this field are experience and education. Program directors of national civil and human rights advocacy groups can expect to earn from $40,000 to $70,000 per year.

prospects: This isn't the best of times to be looking for a position in a civil or human rights organization. Public attention on civil rights issues reached its peak in the 1960s. Now, some of the older and more established civil rights organizations are facing restructuring and cutbacks. New organizations do spring up, however, and these might be the best places to look for work in this field.

qualifications: Program directors should have a management background and experience coordinating volunteers. They should also have a background in the development and implementation of training programs. While it might not be a prerequisite, a pre-established history with the organization for which you hope to work will be a telling factor in many, if not most, instances.

characteristics: Workers in this field should be committed to human and civil rights work. They must be optimists, able to deal with the inherent frustrations of this type of work. And they should be able to work well with many different types of people, from the government official to the victim of discrimination.

John Johnson *is the program director for a civil rights advocacy organization in Baltimore, Maryland.*

How did you get the job?

"I've been involved with the NAACP (National Association for the Advancement of Colored People) since I was a youngster, when I would volunteer in the NAACP youth units in my hometown in Kentucky."

In fact, most of John's work for the NAACP has been in a voluntary capacity. His volunteer work led him to serve as the president of his local branch of the organization, and then as the NAACP president for the state of Kentucky, where he served for 14 years. He was then elected to the organization's national board, where he served for eight years. All of that work was as an unpaid volunteer.

Founded in 1910, the NAACP is the oldest and largest civil rights organization in the country. Today the organization boasts 2,200 local branches—1,700 adult chapters, and 500 college chapters.

When not volunteering with the NAACP, John worked with various community action groups and human rights organizations. He spent seven years as the associate director of the Kentucky Commission on Human Rights, for example.

"I joined the NAACP as a paid employee about 10 years ago," John remembers. "I came here to be the assistant director of another department—the Voter Education Department. I was there for two years. Then, the director of that department left, and that department was merged with the Department of Labor. So I was assistant to the director there for five years. When the director of that department retired, I took over. Then, the director of the Veterans Affairs Department retired too, and they asked me to take over that department as well."

What do you do all day?

"I deal with a wide range of complaints, dealing with discrimination that people in the armed services are experiencing. I process those complaints with the military. I also deal with problems in the workplace. I take phone calls and channel them in the right direction.

"I help put together studies and research materials. This morning I gave testimony to the Congressional Black Caucus on the state of desegregation in the military, from the Korean War until today. Right now, I am putting together materials for our board, which meets next month," John says. "There is a 'get out the vote' rally in Jackson, Mississippi, this weekend, and I've got three boxes of materials ready to go in the mail today for that rally. We're putting on a workshop on Friday in Montgomery, Alabama, on affirmative action, and doing some voter-registration training there. So, I'll fly out to Montgomery Thursday night for that, and then fly on to Jackson for the rally Saturday morning.

"This job does involve a lot of travel, but it also provides you with some freedom of movement. I never have to punch a clock. We don't have the resources that we need in terms of what needs to get done, and that is sometimes frustrating. But in my travels, I get to meet a wide variety of people throughout the country; the decisions I make affect those people positively."

Where do you see this job leading you?

The NAACP is going through a restructuring, and the staff in John's branch is down from a high of around 80 to its present level of about 50 employees. John says, "If I can continue to make a decent living here, I will stay. But the question becomes, 'Can I continue to work for an organization that cannot afford to pay me?' Whatever I do, though, wherever I go, I see myself continuing to work for human rights organizations."

John says that the skills he has built with the NAACP could lead him to jobs in community organizing, or to positions with other equal opportunity groups.

> TARGET YOUR VOLUNTEER EFFORTS. TRY TO GET VOLUNTEER EXPERIENCE IN AN AREA YOU WOULD EVENTUALLY LIKE TO WORK IN. SERVING ON THE HOUSING, EDUCATION, LABOR, PUBLIC RELATIONS, MARKETING, OR FUNDRAISING COMMITTEES OF A NONPROFIT ORGANIZATION CAN PROVIDE YOU WITH VALUABLE EXPERIENCE YOU CAN USE TO LAND A FULL-TIME JOB.

10. Research/ Think Tank Worker

FOR A NATIONAL ADVOCACY ORGANIZATION

description: National-level advocacy organizations are often clearinghouses of information on the cause or causes they serve. They work to get the latest information into the hands of local grassroots advocates in a form those advocates can best use: sound bites that will be good for television or radio interviews; press releases that can be sent out to media contacts; and pamphlets, brochures, and manuals that advocates and their causes' supporters can put to use.

Part of your time will probably be taken up by keeping up to date with what's going on in your movement and related issues. You will comb through newspapers, magazines, legislative updates, and other printed materials to find the latest news that could affect your agenda. You—or the field department, if your organization has one—will be responsible for keeping in touch with local advocates and keeping them up to date on the news you uncover.

You will be responsible for some writing, editing, publishing, and updating the publications your group produces. You'll deal with the layout of the publications, and getting them printed and distributed.

You also might be involved in setting up conferences, meetings, and conventions in areas in which your organization is involved. You'll arrange for speakers, meeting places, hotel rooms, and a myriad of other details.

You may be called on to represent your organization as well, speaking to reporters or giving speeches about your organization and its cause.

salary: Working in the research department of an advocacy organization is not usually an entry-level job. These sorts of jobs usually go to someone who has been working in the movement for a while and who knows some of the players and most of the issues involved. That type of person can probably expect to make from $27,000 to $30,000 per year.

prospects: The primary factors determining your prospects for finding work in the advocacy field are your commitment to the cause and the level of personal investment you're willing to put into the work. There are positions available in advocacy organizations, though you can expect to put in some time as an intern or volunteer before you will find paid employment.

qualifications: A bachelor's degree might not be a requirement for this type of work, but what employers will be looking for are exceptional writing, research, and editing skills. Applicants will also need political knowledge or experience. Experience with the media and in organizing events will be highly regarded, and in some instances will be a prerequisite.

characteristics: Workers in this field should possess a good sense of organization and discipline. You must be able to effectively supervise co-workers when your job demands it. You will be juggling several projects at once, and will need to prioritize them so you can meet all their various deadlines.

Beth Barrett *is an associate director of an advocacy group based in Washington, D.C.*

How did you get the job?

"My interest in this movement stems from my own history—I am a lesbian," says Beth. "My organizational background, though, is in the Jewish community. I also did youth group organizing as an adviser when I was in college.

"Eventually," she says, "I decided I wanted to immerse myself in the gay and lesbian movement, so I moved out to Washington, D.C. and got an unpaid internship for six months with the National Gay and Lesbian Task Force. I assisted the organization's legislative director, and, as a legislative intern, I did lobbying work and learned the ins and outs of this organization and this movement. And, piece by piece, I created a job for myself here at the Task Force."

Beth first delivered publications for the Task Force. She then moved to the media department, where she put together press releases and spoke with reporters, eventually assuming the role of the NGLTF public information manager.

"I worked for eight to 10 months as the public information manager, and during that time began working part-time as a public information manager and part-time as a public policy associate."

What do you do all day?

The National Gay and Lesbian Task Force has been involved in advocacy and grassroots organizing around the issue of gay and lesbian civil rights since it was founded in 1973. Its Policy Institute was formed recently to bring all of the Task Force's research efforts under one umbrella.

"A large part of what I do is organizational research," Beth says. "I commission new

> IF YOU ARE COMMITTED TO A PARTICULAR CAUSE OR ARE PASSIONATE ABOUT RIGHTING A WRONG YOU SEE IN YOUR COMMUNITY, YOU MIGHT WANT TO THINK ABOUT CREATING YOUR OWN JOB.

research, and translate academic research into a form that is useful for activists, squeezing a 30-page paper into three sound bites that activists can use to support their case, for example.

"This job involves a lot of reading and writing and a lot of supervising. We put together several types of publications here. We publish manuals, surveys, and general research papers. Some publications I will simply edit. Some I will write. On some, I will be responsible for the production. And on some, it will be a combination of the three.

"A typical week will involve a couple of meetings with a graphic designer about how a publication is going to look, meetings with staff members to talk about the layout issues of a particular publication, and general staff meetings. I meet with volunteers and interns to discuss and schedule projects. In the fall, typically, I'll be interviewing prospective interns, getting new people in here at the start of the school year. I'm always reading, writing, and editing projects. Talking to grassroots activists and the media, talking to people on the phone, that

also takes up a great deal of my time."

The work is very project-oriented, Beth says, and how busy she is depends on what projects are in the works at any given time—and how close those projects are to their deadlines. She usually works from 40 to 60 hours a week.

Where do you see this job leading you?

"I would eventually like to get involved in nonprofit management," Beth says, "and this job is invaluable experience for that goal. Here, I'm getting exposure to how a nonprofit organization works, how a board of directors works, how hiring works, and how you put together a budget for a nonprofit organization. My lifework is in gay and lesbian civil rights, and I expect to go to law school before too long, and then to move on to nonprofit management work. A lot of us here are on the road to law school, actually."

"I would like to eventually create my own nonprofit organization on the local level. This job is providing me with the supervisory skills, the budgeting and finance skills, and the public speaking skills that will help me out when it comes time to do that."

11. Research and Advocacy Worker

description: Research and advocacy work combines aspects of the work of both the lobbyist and the analyst, the persuader and the information gatherer. One advocacy worker describes this type of work as "in-depth policy research in an attempt to improve my organization's ability to affect policy change through deeper understanding of the issues."

The research you do could involve hands-on research—traveling to the sites of various problems and situations, devising and implementing surveys and other statistical information gathering techniques; meeting with individuals and groups to discuss problems and solutions—or it could involve more scholarly types of endeavors—library or online types of research.

Once you've gathered your facts, you will have to put together a report outlining those facts and suggesting possible courses of action to take regarding the case.

Then you'll find yourself working with coalitions made up of organizations that have similar takes on an issue or series of issues. Your job there could range from coordinating the efforts of the coalition, to chairing meetings, to simply providing technical information that the coalition (and your home organization) needs. You could find yourself making presentations before governmental or private-sector boards or commissions. You might even engage in the hands-on "pressing the flesh" type of work one typically thinks of when the term "lobbyist" is bandied about.

salary: The pay for someone working in the research-advocacy area could range from the mid-$20,000s, all the way up to $70,000 or more for those working in high-level policy think tanks. Salary ranges for nonprofit groups will tend to be on the lower end of that spectrum, with the average salary at about $40,000 a year.

prospects: Opportunities for working in research and advocacy range from nonprofit organizations to high-level governmental think tanks. Though there will always be room for someone with both research and lobbying skills, the opportunities for work in specific policy areas are likely to change as the winds of priority shift. You might find yourself concentrating on one area—research or lobbying—for a time before you're able to find a position where you can combine those two disciplines.

qualifications: Most positions require at least a master's degree. Two to three years experience in the area the organization concentrates on, or in researching and lobbying, is another probable requirement. As in so many other jobs, strong writing and communications skills are paramount to success.

characteristics: A research advocate will need to identify, envision, and carry out projects. Especially in Washington, D.C., where there is so much competition just to be heard, you're going to have to come up with imaginative ways to get your message across, and the facts will have to be there to back up your message. A sense of optimism is crucial to this job.

John Pendegrast *is a policy advocate for an Africa-issues organization based in Washington, D.C.*

How did you get the job?

"I was working for a congressman in the mid-1980s," says John, "and I had a desire to see what was going on in Africa. So I bought a ticket and flew over to Mali, in western Africa, and traveled around the country with different groups there. I thought, ignorantly, that if the United States invested itself more constructively that perhaps we could have a major impact on reversing the hunger I saw there. But as I traveled through Mali, Tanzania, and Somalia, I realized that what the U.S. was doing was more hurtful than helpful.

"At that point, a light went off in my head—I realized that I had to go back to Washington, D.C., to see if we could change the content of our policy, rather than being in the field. I moved from being an aid advocate to being a policy change advocate, I guess you could say.

"I returned to the congressman's office, then I went back to Africa. When I returned, I worked for Bread for the World, an organization that combats hunger throughout the world. I came to the Center of Concern in 1988, and believe I've found a good match. Bread for the

> MAKE SURE PEOPLE ARE AWARE OF YOU AND WHAT YOU ARE DOING. IF THERE IS A JOB OR POSITION OUT THERE THAT YOU ARE INTERESTED IN—EVEN IF THERE ISN'T AN OPENING FOR THAT POSITION AT THE CURRENT TIME—FIND OUT WHAT THE QUALIFICATIONS FOR THAT JOB ARE, TALK TO THE PEOPLE CURRENTLY IN THOSE POSITIONS, AND FIND OUT HOW THEY GOT THEIR JOBS.

World was attracted to me because I was coming from the office of a prominent congressman. And here, I think they took a shot at a young guy who showed some promise. They invested their time in training and developing me."

What do you do all day?

"I'm involved in a number of things," John says. "I deal with public education; I'm coordinating a project to hook people up in the Horn of Africa via e-mail; I work on a task force on Somalia, dealing with academics and people around the world, dealing with the situation extant there after the international troops left; I coordinate an advocacy campaign on Sudan, and I work at combining the forces of a number of international organizations with similar interests—the Coalition for

Peace in the Horn of Africa from the U.S.A., the Horn of Africa Policy Group in Canada, the European Working Group on the Horn of Africa in Brussels.

"I generally do a lot of analysis on what the Clinton administration is doing in the Horn.

"On the research front, I take a number of trips to Africa each year. My research is primarily field-based. I go into a country and conduct interviews. For example, I was doing a study looking at the effect of foreign aid in Sudan. So I went to six or seven villages and interviewed the villagers, aid and medical workers, elders, and chiefs. We talked about the issues I was dealing with. And then I would cross-reference that with the information I got from people in the capital city. I also interview policy makers on higher levels—in the United

States, and at the United Nations. I then put together a report.

"In my advocacy work, I'm not so directly involved in lobbying. I help to put materials together and to develop position papers. I leave the high-level schmoozing to those with bigger constituencies. The Center of Concern is not a huge grassroots organization. What we try to do is develop ideas and combine our research with other groups' advocacy."

Where do you see this job leading you?

John says he sees research advocates go off in many different directions. Some return to school to get doctorates and go on to pursue academic careers. Some go on to policy careers with the United Nations, with the U.S. government, or on the state level.

"People in my position generally go off and work for the administration, the U.N., the State Department, or for nongovernmental organizations," says John. "Some people leave the specificity of what I'm doing and go into more general writing careers. Some of them bounce back to field work."

12. Analyst

FOR A PUBLIC POLICY THINK TANK

description: Public policy think tanks provide research data and suggest initiatives to policy makers. The papers produced and promoted by these think tanks help direct the public policy debate by informing and influencing national legislators and, in turn, help determine the direction in which our nation is headed.

As an analyst, you will most likely be a specialist in a certain policy area—economics, defense, foreign affairs, budget—and your main job will be to produce papers covering that area.

Public policy analysts combine the skills of an academic researcher with those of a political consultant. They identify trends on the horizon, and use their factually-based research to try and sway the debate in the direction that their employers, and like-minded political allies, would like to see it swayed. Though analysts don't have the primary responsibility for promoting their research, they are called on to present their findings in speeches before interested organizations, on television and radio appearances, and in op-ed columns in newspapers. They are also tapped as sources by newspaper and magazine reporters.

Public policy analysts analyze the results of previous policy initiatives, and also suggest new policy initiatives based on their findings.

salary: Junior public policy analysts can expect to earn in the low $20,000s. As analysts get more experience, their salaries can rise into the $40,000 to $50,000 range. At the senior level, they can command from $60,000 to $80,000 a year, augmented by lecture and writing fees which can range from $500 to more than $1,000 per engagement.

prospects: Washington, D.C., is, naturally, a center of political think tanks, but this doesn't mean that you cannot build a reputation outside of Washington that would appeal to policy think tanks in D.C.

"I suspect that the need for analysts will increase in the future," says one think tank analyst. "I think the information age will drive that need. As people get access to more and more information, and as more and more academic and government research goes online, there will be a need for someone to channel that gusher of information into a finely-focused jet."

qualifications: Academic qualifications for these positions are quite high. Prospective analysts should be well versed in a particular area of public policy. Many candidates will be at the doctoral level. It is possible to get your foot in the door with a bachelor's degree, but in that case, you will have to start at the bottom of the ladder and work your way up. Top-notch writing skills are also a prerequisite.

characteristics: A public policy analyst should have an interest in public policy and in shaping the policy debate. Analysts should have an academic orientation, since this is applied academic work. Independent thinkers and self-starters do well in these positions. This is a job that requires someone who thinks pro-actively but can respond reactively when the situation calls for it.

Patrick F. Fagan *is a public policy analyst for a foundation based in Washington, D.C.*

How did you get the job?

Patrick didn't plan to be a public policy analyst. He had set out down the road to becoming a clinical psychologist, but, he says, the move into the public policy debate became obvious to him.

"As I was getting my psychology degree and doing my clinical work, I zeroed in on work with children, families, and marriage," he says.

Patrick later found himself in Washington, D.C., and he eventually moved over from psychology to public policy work. "I wanted to engage myself with the larger cultural forces pulling families apart, the 'bigger battle,' so to speak. At the time, there was only one think tank in town interested in family issues, and that was the Free Congress Foundation. They had a small Family and Child Issues division; I became the director of that division. I became the executive director of the Free Congress Foundation a few years later."

Patrick then joined the staff of Indiana Republican senator Dan Coates, where he developed family policy issues, and later served as President Bush's deputy assistant secretary for Family and Community Policy.

"During the Bush years, William Bennett—the former head of the U.S. Education Department [in the Reagan administration] and drug czar—became a fellow here at the Heritage Foundation. That was the Foundation's first real foray into dealing with cultural issues. That went well, and the Heritage decided to hire a full-time senior analyst to deal with those issues. They knew a fair bit of my work, and so getting the job here, for me, came rather easily."

What do you do all day?

The Heritage Foundation is a conservative think tank, receiving all of its funding from private sources.

"I'm given a lot of freedom to pursue and to write papers on issues I feel need to be addressed," Patrick says. "The main focus of my work is researching and writing papers,

but I will spend time writing op-ed versions of papers for various newspapers, or going on television or radio talk shows and speaking about the papers. For instance, 15 months ago I did a paper that we titled 'Illegitimacy: America's Rising Catastrophe', and that paper made quite a splash. I was doing three to five interviews a day for two months after that paper came out.

"Right now I'm doing an overview of the literature on the effect that religious belief has on a whole slew of family and social issues.

"At any given time, the work I'm doing tends to be preparatory work on the next paper or two I'm working on. I do library searches, gather material, and become familiar with it.

"When Congress begins working on specific areas, they will call on us for research and for a quick response. Our most hectic time is when Congress is in session."

Where do you see this job leading you?

"I see myself staying here, if my career goes where I want it to go," says Patrick. "I'll continue publishing, speaking, and writ-

CHECK WITH YOUR COLLEGE'S CAREER COUNSELING OR GUIDANCE CENTERS. THOSE DEPARTMENTS MIGHT WELL HAVE INFORMATION ON EXCHANGE PROGRAMS WITH WASHINGTON, D.C.-BASED UNIVERSITIES THAT WILL ALLOW YOU TO SPEND SIX MONTHS IN THE NATION'S CAPITAL.

ing. Of course, depending on the political climate on the Hill, a political position always beckons."

There is pretty fluid movement between the world of the public-policy think tanks and that of the Hill—analysts and employees at think tanks will move over to congressional and executive staffing positions, and vice versa. Sometimes public policy analysts will head to the world of academia.

13. Campaign Manager

description: The campaign manager for a candidate running for political office is responsible for the behind-the-scenes organizing of a campaign. Duties will vary depending on the size of the campaign staff, but they will almost certainly include scheduling and planning a candidate's day, from television interviews, to public appearances, to press conferences. Campaign managers finesse all the details of a candidate's public appearances.

The campaign manager will be involved in planning campaign strategy, including researching the district and its wants, needs and opinions, writing speeches, and even designing T-shirts.

Fund-raising could occupy a large or small portion of a campaign manager's time, depending on how fully stocked the candidate's campaign war chest is, and whether or not the candidate is an incumbent. The campaign manager could find him- or herself contracting for an opinion poll, working with an advertising firm or political consultant organization, or coordinating volunteer labor.

salary: Campaign managers' salaries will vary greatly, depending on their employing candidate's campaign fund, the opposition, and whether or not that candidate is an incumbent. Salary level can be greatly dependent on an individual's track record—how many people they have gotten into office, and a history of successful campaigns. For national-level campaigns, salaries will typically start in the $35,000 to $40,000 range, and go up into six figures for "hired guns" brought in to finesse a campaign during a particularly tough race. Salaries for campaign managers on the state and local level will be lower. On all levels, you will also find campaign managers doing their work on a voluntary basis.

prospects: The job of campaign manager will usually fall to someone with a wealth of political experience and connections. Finding work on a campaign as a volunteer coordinator, or in some other lesser capacity, is probably more likely than finding a job as a campaign manager, and such work provides valuable experience that candidates will look for in the manager of their campaign.

qualifications: Know how the political process works, and have connections. One of the best ways to satisfy both these prerequisites is to volunteer to work on a political campaign. Such previous campaign experience will definitely increase your suitability for the job. A candidate usually chooses his or her own campaign manager, so a personal history with that candidate is probably a must.

characteristics: Campaign managers have to be effective communicators. They must be the type of person who is at ease, and skilled, at "working the room" during a fund-raiser—meeting campaign donors and potential donors, finding out their concerns, and conveying how the manager's candidate feels about those concerns. The job has many parallels to a salesperson's job; instead of touting the merits of a particular product, the campaign manager lauds the qualifications of his or her candidate.

To excel at this type of work, the prospective campaign manager will also have to be very detail-oriented.

Eric Snyder *is the campaign manager for a candidate seeking a congressional seat in Minnesota.*

How did you get the job?

Eric graduated from the University of Nebraska with an English and political science degree.

"I interned in Washington, D.C., with a U.S. congressman from Nebraska, during the summer between my junior and senior years of college," Eric says. "As a congressional intern, I did a lot of constituent work, agriculture and health care work. We would get a call from someone in Nebraska concerned about a particular issue or bill; I would research the bill, find out how the congressman felt about it, and then write back with a reply for the person who got in touch with us. I did some minor speechwriting.

"They had a comprehensive program for interns there, where you could hear senators and representatives talk one or two times a week. That was the most fun I had there—getting the exposure to those types of people.

"A lot of people I worked with in Washington, D.C., came back to Nebraska to work on the campaign of Representative Doug Bereuter, who was campaigning to represent the eastern third of Nebraska. I did volunteer work on that

FOR THAT INITIAL FORAY INTO THE POLITICAL ARENA, DO NOT OVERLOOK THE POWER OF A RECOMMENDATION LETTER. RECOMMENDATION LETTERS FROM PEOPLE WHOM A CONGRESSPERSON OR REPRESENTATIVE RESPECTS, OR FROM THOSE WHO CONTRIBUTED TO THEIR CAMPAIGN, WILL PROVE VERY ENTICING TO A POLITICIAN'S EYE, AND JUST MIGHT BE THE FACTOR THAT GETS YOU THE JOB IN WASHINGTON, D.C.

campaign—that is how I got my first campaign experience."

Eric then moved to Minnesota in 1993 to get a master's degree at the Hubert H. Humphrey School of Public Policy.

"Lobbying always intrigued me," he says, "because it was the marriage between politics and policy work. Last spring, I worked as a state lobbyist at the capital, working for a contract lobbying organization.

"Jack Uldrich is a lobbyist, currently with the Minnesota Grocer's Association. I had met him one time previously, but got to know him through our work at the capital. He grew up here in the city; his family is active in politics. He was approached to run for the Fifth Congressional seat this summer. And about a week after he

agreed to run, he came to me and asked if I would be interested in being his campaign manager."

What do you do all day?

"At this point in time, we are in the early stages of the campaign and most of my time has been taken up with trying to generate fund-raising," Eric says.

"Jack will make his official announcement in January and right now we're getting things ready for that announcement, preparing press packets and issue papers.

"Eventually, though, we will be at the point where I will be worrying about scheduling, how to arrange things to get maximum exposure. I will track contributions to the campaign and build up a mailing list.

"We plan on this job becoming full-time in March. Right now, I am a full-time student, putting in about 20 hours a week on the campaign. In Minnesota, the next legislative session runs January through March. I would like to work at the capital next session, and then switch to full-time campaign work after the session is over."

Where do you see this job leading you?

"The best-case scenario," Eric says, "is that Jack is elected. It is a fairly natural progression that I would follow him to Washington and become a staff person. That prospect excites me." This is a common scenario for many campaign managers.

The type of experience—and the connections—garnered as a campaign manager can prove valuable even in the result of a losing campaign. "This campaign will be, in a sense, a crash course in Minnesota politics. By the end of the campaign, I will know most of the Republican heavy hitters in Minnesota," Eric says, "and those contacts will prove helpful when I go about finding another job at the state level or with a lobbying organization. It's important to have those contacts."

14. Legislative Aide

TO A STATE REPRESENTATIVE

description: As a legislative aide, your responsibilities will center on tracking legislation and dealing with constituents and lobbyists. Your specific duties will be defined, for the most part, by the legislator for whom you're working. You will probably be asked to pay special attention to, and watch out for, legislation that could affect the legislator's district or deals with your legislator's pet issues. You'll have to gather information on pending bills.

As a legislative assistant, you will probably take care of scheduling appointments for your legislator. You'll attend meetings in your boss's stead, and report back to him or her on what transpired in those meetings. You might be charged with writing speeches, newspaper columns, magazine columns, or letters in your boss's name. You may also help in the drafting of bills your employer intends to sponsor or attach his or her name to.

Your schedule will closely follow the legislative calendar. When the legislature is in session, expect to spend most of your time in the capital city and most of your day—up to twelve hours a day, seven days a week—in the capitol building.

After the session, you can expect to spend more time in your legislator's district, dealing directly with constituents; helping to put together an overview of the most recent session and the effects that the legislation from that session will have on your district; and helping with fund-raising efforts. If your legislator is up for re-election, you can expect to spend a lot of time working on the re-election campaign.

Legislative aide positions in many states are "at will" jobs, meaning that the legislator you work for can dismiss you at any time if he or she feels you aren't performing up to par. However, there is probably no better position than this one to give you a feel for how state-level government works, to get governmental experience, and to have a hand in shaping governmental policy.

salary: Don't expect to get rich working as a legislative aide. Your salary could range from $18,000 to $30,000 a year.

prospects: The window of opportunity for acquiring a job as a legislative aide is a small one. Political candidates won't be hiring assistants until after the election (when they know whether or not they'll be needing an assistant), and they will have those legislative aide positions filled by, or shortly after, the end of the legislative session.

qualifications: The prerequisites for this job are writing, research, and decision-making skills, and the ability to work under pressure. "It's not what you know, it's who you know" is never more true than it is in politics, however. Perhaps the best place to catch a legislator's eye is working on an election campaign.

characteristics: Legislative aides should be good at following instructions. They should be able to synthesize information quickly and concisely. They should be personable, patient, understanding, and able to work well under pressure.

Gisela Gonzales *is a legislative aide to a member of the Texas House of Representatives.*

- -

How did you get the job?

"When I graduated from college," Gisela says, "I wanted to do something in Corpus Christi, where I was from."

After successfully obtaining a meeting with the director of the Gulf Coast Council in Corpus Christi, Gisela was offered a job—a position that was created just for her. She became an administrative assistant at Gulf Coast Council, oversaw 10 different programs and those programs' employees, and was responsible for suggesting better and more efficient ways to run the council's programs.

After a year, she became coordinator of the GCC's AIDS and HIV education program, and, after funding for that program caused the position to be eliminated, Gisela became instrumental in founding the Texas Young Democrats of the Coastal Bend Area, a group involved in getting young people interested in the Democratic Party. Gisela served as the group's first president.

When the 1994 elections came along, Gisela and her group got involved in area political campaigns.

"I was invited to attend a rally for [then Texas Governor] Ann Richards, and learned that

> HEAD OVER TO THE CAPITOL BUILDING ON THE SECOND DAY OF THE LEGISLATIVE SESSION (THE FIRST DAY IS FILLED WITH SWEARING IN AND OTHER CEREMONIAL FUNCTIONS). LEGISLATORS WHO ARE WITHOUT LEGISLATIVE ASSISTANTS (EITHER BECAUSE THEY HAVE FAILED TO HIRE THEM OR SOMEONE THEY EXPECTED TO WORK FOR THEM THIS SESSION HASN'T SHOWN UP) WILL NEED THEM—PRONTO.

politicians throughout the state were talking about us, talking about our group. Congressman Solomon Ortiz asked me to work with him," she says, "with the understanding that I would not get paid a lot, but I would learn about running an election campaign, and would get to see if this is what I wanted to do."

Following this, she was asked to become a legislative assistant to state Representative Velma Luna. Gisela accepted.

What do you do all day?

"There were two legislative assistants in Representative Luna's office," Gisela says, "and each of us was assigned certain issues. My issues were education, health care, welfare, and environmental issues. I had to read—skim through—all bills that were targeted toward cities

with populations of 200,000 or more—those are the bills that would affect Corpus. Every day, I had to put her packet together, which reported on all the bills that were going to reach the House floor that day. We paid special attention to issues she was concerned with—issues affecting her district of course, but also environmental and health issues.

"I also took care of her scheduling—lobbyists who wanted to meet with her, meetings she had to attend, committee meetings she needed to attend. Actually, we were the ones that mainly talked to the lobbyists—she was in and out of her office so much, she really didn't have time to do that.

"I wrote articles for the local paper for her. I took care of local issues—if members from

the district came in, I would talk to them. The legislative assistants attended meetings when Representative Luna was not able to."

With the legislative session now over, Gisela has returned to Corpus Christi, where she expects to deal more with constituent inquiries and work on issues of constituent concern, attend meetings in the representative's stead, and help push ongoing projects forward.

Where do you see this job leading you?

Gisela has applied to the George Washington University School of Political Management in Washington, D.C., which she hopes to attend in the fall. "In this job, I've made a lot of contacts and have opened my eyes to the opportunities out there. I think I might like to be an expert witness—someone called in to analyze and testify on part of a specific issue. One thing I've learned is that once you're in the political system, you can always move into another area. I do want to stay in politics," she says, "but I don't want to run for office. I want to stay behind the scenes. I think you can be more effective there."

15. Legislative Researcher

description: As a legislative researcher, you will work for a state senate or house of representatives, acting to gather and synthesize information for congresspeople as they go about their legislative duties. You could be a general researcher, or you could specialize in a specific area—education or criminal justice, for example. You will answer to all the congresspeople—either senators or house members, depending upon for which legislative body you work. If a congressperson has a question on how a proposed bill would or might affect his or her constituents, it will be up to you, as a researcher, to find the answer to that question. Constituents will also have questions that you will be called on to answer. You will do background research on matters that are, or have the potential to become, central issues of the legislative session.

You will be at your busiest when the legislature is in session. (In the interim periods, you might have the liberty to pursue research on independent projects, or you could be doing work for committee members.) When a bill that you have done research for, or that falls under your area of expertise, is debated on the floor of the house or senate, you will be down on the floor to help with any questions that might arise. Then, too, you could be called on to write amendments to bills being debated.

You will attend committee meetings—to learn the directions that policies and bills are headed in—and board meetings—to learn the results of those policies and laws.

You will track down how other state legislatures have responded to problems your state is facing and the results of those responses. As a researcher, your tasks will be many and varied.

salary: What you earn will vary depending on the state you're working for, but beginning researchers can expect to make from $22,000 to $26,000 a year. More experienced researchers, or those with a master's degree, can perhaps earn from $25,000 to $35,000 a year.

prospects: Because there are only a limited number of state governments—50, last I checked—the number of research positions within those governmental bodies will always be limited. And with the current trend toward downsizing, growth in this area is not expected. Many municipal governments employ researchers as well—as does the federal government—providing other possible avenues of employment.

qualifications: To be a legislative researcher you must, at the very least, have a bachelor's degree. An advanced degree will better your chances. Writing, researching, and interpersonal skills are necessary for this work. And if you have, or can get, experience in a specific policy area—human services, budgeting, education, criminal justice—so much the better.

characteristics: Legislative researchers should be able to adapt to an ever-changing environment; the political priorities will fluctuate from session to session and even from month to month, and researchers must be able to shift gears quickly. Researchers should also be confident, assertive, and outgoing, as well as articulate.

Anita Fourcard *is a research specialist for the State of Texas Senate Research Center in Austin, Texas.*

How did you get the job?

"I've always worked in the public sector, even if it was a part-time job when I was in college," says Anita, who grew up in Louisiana, where she earned an undergraduate degree in political science.

Anita went on to graduate school, where she earned a master's degree in public administration, specializing in public finance and management.

"At grad school, I decided that if you could develop an expertise in an area—such as finance—where very few people have the expertise, but where such expertise is vital, it could give you an edge over anyone else."

As part of her graduate work, Anita took an internship with the Louisiana governor's office, in the Office of Planning and Budget. "I was considered a special assistant to the deputy budget director," Anita said. "I looked for budget reductions, coordinating meetings between state institutions, budget analysts, government representatives, and other interested parties. I wrote executive orders for the governor mandating budget reductions."

> MAKE AN EFFORT TO BE PLEASANT TO EVERYONE YOU COME IN CONTACT WITH WHEN YOU'RE INTERVIEWING FOR A JOB, FROM THE CUSTODIAL WORKERS TO THE COMPANY PRESIDENT. KINDNESS CAN NEVER HURT, BUT WORD OF A RUDE INTERVIEWEE TRAVELS FAST.

Anita then took a position in the Louisiana House of Representatives' Appropriations Committee, where she was responsible for drafting legislation for representatives, attending Appropriations Committee meetings, and writing amendments to appropriations bills.

Anita spent two years in that position, and then felt that she needed a change. She got a job doing welfare reform policy research with a nonprofit agency, but after three months there, determined that that wasn't the job for her.

She heard about an opening in the Texas legislature's Senate Research Center, which she applied for and was offered the following afternoon.

What do you do all day?

"During the session, I focus on the appropriations bills," Anita says. "Say there will be a hearing, where they are taking up Article 2 in the appropriations bill. The Legislative Budget Board will have already come up with their recommendations for funding, and they will explain their reasons for those recommendations to the committee. I will listen to the discussion and take notes on it, then send out memos to the Senate Finance Committee about what happened at that meeting. I'll do a spreadsheet listing the differences between the House's version of the bill, the Senate's, and the Budget Board's. I get phone calls from senators requesting information.

"During the interim, you can take your own initiative and make your own research projects.

"Once committee assignments are made and projects assigned to committee members

(about three months after the legislature breaks up for the session), things will start to pick back up again."

Where do you see this job leading you?

"I think I am extremely good with people," Anita says. "And I can see myself getting into governmental relations or lobbying work with a private company. My philosophy is to get experience on how government works, and then take that experience to the private sector.

"If I would choose to focus on the public finance side of things, I think there is a lot more opportunity. I could run for public office. I could be a city manager. I could work with state, local, or federal government. I could go on to the U.S. Congressional Budget Committee. I could head a state agency.

"I think you have to carve a niche for yourself. You have to find an area of importance to both the public and the private sector, and then gain expertise in that area."

16. Political Director

FOR A POLITICAL PARTY

description: The main thrust of any political party is to get its candidates elected and thus advance its political agenda. A party's political director will be involved, to a greater or lesser degree, with all the election races and political campaigns the party is involved in.

A political director will work on candidate recruitment—canvassing county chairs and otherwise searching for potential candidates for public office. He or she will work on candidate training—helping party candidates construct a successful campaign. Political directors put together campaign manuals that explain everything from how to make a yard sign, to how to set up a press conference. They will put on weekend or evening seminars where campaign expertise, strategy and tactics, as well as information on issues the party is concerned about, are shared in hands-on settings.

Political directors engage in research—tracking voting records and analyzing voting trends, compiling data, and researching issues of interest to the party. They also may work with interns or other party employees on special projects.

Political directors for a Democratic or Republican party organization are an integral part of the political process. They can feel a real sense of empowerment—that their work and decisions have an impact on how society runs.

salary: Beginning political party workers can expect to make from $15,000 to $30,000 a year. Higher-level workers can expect to earn from $30,000 to $80,000 per year.

prospects: Paid political positions within a political party are limited. If you are persistent, willing to start working with the party on a voluntary basis, and then move up to temporary or part-time work before landing a full-time position, you should be able to work your way into a paid party position.

Remember that there are many third parties—some formed around a single personality, some based on a single issue, and some with a wide platform of issues they address—that can also be a source of employment and job leads.

qualifications: "Communications and psychology—that's how people get elected," one political director says. "People with public relations and human psychology backgrounds will do well in political party work." He notes that political science and related degrees don't really carry a whole lot of weight with party leaders. "People with that sort of background are very good within the bureaucracy, but their training isn't a whole lot of use in the political arena."

characteristics: Political party workers need to be motivated—motivated enough to put in the long hours and hard work it will take for them to be noticed by party leaders. They should be self-starters—willing to take a task and run with it. Party workers should also be able to get along with others; and they should be good at "politicking."

Royal Masset *is the political director of the Republican Party of Texas.*

How did you get the job?

"My first role in politics was as chairman of the Young People for Eugene McCarthy in 1968. I was one of four or five Vietnam war protest leaders in the Austin area. I was then involved with something we called the 'Critical University,' an off-campus university where people would gather and teach each other things they were knowledgeable about. Those experiences taught me how to organize people.

"Gradually, my political philosophy began to change, and I became more libertarian," he says.

Royal attended law school, and, in 1976, headed up the Austin Citizen's League, formed by city business leaders who were displeased with the way the then-mayor and council were running things. Royal's salary at that job was contingent upon the funds he was able to raise, so he acquired fund-raising experience.

"With the Citizen's League, I learned how few people were really involved in the political process. And the Citizen's

League began to change from a lobbying organization into a political organization. We began recruiting candidates to run for the City Council, and I learned that if you help people early, they become your ally.

"I ran a lot of campaigns, about 20 different races.

"Then I resigned from a mayoral candidate's campaign one week before he was elected," Royal says. "I was becoming more conservative, more libertarian, and the city was becoming more liberal, more in favor of government control."

Royal left the Citizen's League and spent six months in Mexico. Upon his return, he read in the paper that the office of the Republican Party of Texas, which had been closed for about six months, was about to reopen.

> ### TRY TO PREDICT WHEN JOB OPENINGS WILL OCCUR AND HOW SOON THEY WILL BE FILLED, AND TAKE ADVANTAGE OF THAT INFORMATION.

Royal knew he wanted to be involved with the Republican Party. So he worked as a researcher (and as a security guard for two years), gradually making himself more and more indispensable to the other party employees. And eventually, he was hired as the party's political director.

What do you do all day?

One of the first things Royal did when he was hired by the Republican Party was to help put together the ORVS (Optimal Republican Voting Strength) method of predicting the outcome of races in various areas of the state, based on those areas' past voting records.

"I knew that something like that—something that could predict the outcomes of election races for the Republican Party within four percent of the vote—would make me indispensable to the party."

Royal says his work follows the election cycle. "In the summer and for the next six months, we do candidate recruitment," he says. "December 4 through January 2 is when candidates can file for office. In the winter, we begin training candidates. We help them

through the primary season. In the post-primary season, we train them how to win general elections. Two months before the election is when we go into crisis management mode.

"And after the election, we train the winning candidates to be legislators. In January, we organize a school for every legislative staffer. We try to demystify the process of what it's like to be a legislator or a legislative aide and build the party that way—we show them how to fill out a bill packet and all the things a legislator needs to know."

Where do you see this job leading you?

"A lobbying position is the big one—that's where a lot of people go after working with the party.

"If you work here or at the capitol, you gain an understanding of how the political process works. You acquire a skill that is invaluable to any company for the rest of your life; you know how the system works. Almost all of the Party's hirings come from our pool of volunteers," Royal says.

17. Political Office Candidate

description: Candidates have to be effective communicators, strategists, and leaders. But perhaps most importantly, candidates have to convince people that they are the best person for the job. And that is the primary goal of a candidate's campaign.

A campaign will unfold in several stages. During the primary or caucus season, a candidate will have to convince party officials and members of his or her suitability for office, and of his or her ability to defeat the opposing party's candidate. If a candidate wins that election and becomes the party's candidate, he or she will then square off against the other parties' candidates. Campaigning consists of making public appearances, giving speeches, talking to reporters and editorial boards, meeting with party members, conceiving and implementing advertising campaigns, raising funds, and perhaps debating with other parties' candidates for the same office.

Generally speaking, the bigger the office, the more time, effort, and money will have to be devoted to campaigning. For most offices, campaigning will be a full-time job for at least the six months prior to an election.

And then, of course, once someone wins a campaign, the even more difficult task of serving in office beckons.

salary: Candidates for office will typically draw no salary while they are running for office. U.S. senators and representatives draw annual salaries of $133,600. Salaries for state legislators are typically much lower, ranging from $100 to $70,000 per year, depending on the state. Salaries for local officials will vary widely, depending on the size of municipality served, and the nature of the duties performed.

prospects: An individual's prospects of winning an elected office will depend on a large number of factors—among them the type of office sought, the situation and political climate in the campaign, and the candidate's own ability to articulate his or her position. For people with the requisite experience, charisma, and drive, the chances of winning an elected office will depend on their ability to build an effective team of supporters and run an effective campaign.

qualifications: Many of the qualifications for elected officials are intangible ones. A politician should possess an understanding of the issues, know why and how to address these issues, and understand who the audience is. They should be able to articulate the issues in a short amount of time—to have an adroitness at coming up with sound bites, in other words. The main qualification for someone wanting to run for office, though, will be an ability to convince voters, through a combination of experience, leadership qualities, charisma, and planning, that he or she is the right person for the job.

characteristics: Optimism and energy are perhaps the two most important personal characteristics that politicians need: energy, to campaign 20 hours a day for months; optimism, so they don't become discouraged by obstacles that are strewn in their path by opponents and circumstances. And politicians should possess a willingness to take a position and stick to it.

Jack Uldrich *is a Republican candidate for the Fifth Congressional District in Minneapolis, Minnesota.*

How did you get the job?

"I have been interested in the political field ever since my undergraduate days at Drake University in Des Moines, Iowa," Jack says.

Jack went on to Officer Candidate School and was commissioned in the Navy as an intelligence officer. He then attended graduate school, was selected for the presidential management internship program, and spent two years in the Defense Department before returning to his home state of Minnesota.

"I became the state director of the Concord Coalition. [The Concord Coalition is an organization founded by former Senators Paul Tsongas and Warren Rudmann with the purpose of building a groundswell of public support around the idea of federal budget deficit reduction.] I was there for one year, and became frustrated with the fact that the Concord Coalition was a nonpartisan organization. I felt that the only way to really affect change was through the political process."

After working on the ultimately unsuccessful campaign of a woman running for the U.S. Senate, Jack became political director for the Minnesota Grocer's Association, a position he currently holds. Jack has also begun a campaign as a Republican candidate for Congress.

What do you do all day?

"About 30 percent of my time at the association deals with building our grassroots support; 30 percent is spent researching issues and legislative matters; and 40 percent is testifying, working and meeting with legislators."

Those skills will play into Jack's campaign, where he will be attempting to build a grassroots following behind himself and the ideas he supports, instead of doing so for an association and its agenda.

"I made the decision to enter this campaign about three months ago," Jack says. "Since that time, I have found a campaign manager. I have been out talking with people who are very active in politics and very active in the Republican Party, exploring the prospects for making a run for office, and then letting them know I am running. My campaign manager and I have been putting together position papers on the issues and identifying key campaign staff—a marketing manager, a treasurer, and a liaison to the university community, which we see as an having an important role in my victory.

"The next stage is preparing for the precinct caucuses. My task will be to educate our party members about how important those caucuses are.

"I am confident that we will win the Republican Party endorsement outright at those caucuses.

> GET INVOLVED IN A POLITICAL CAMPAIGN. YOU WILL LEARN HOW A CAMPAIGN IS RUN, AND WILL MEET AND FORM WORKING RELATIONSHIPS WITH THOSE INVOLVED IN POLITICS AND GOVERNMENT— PEOPLE WHO WILL PROVE TO BE VALUABLE CONTACTS FOR SOMEONE SEEKING TO GET A JOB IN THE POLITICAL ARENA.

"At that point, I will then concentrate my campaign on Martin Sabo, the Democratic incumbent. I will have to start going to neighborhood meetings, attending political events. We'll spend a great deal of time raising funds.

"Right now, my typical day starts very early, at 5 A.M. I am a marathon runner, and I typically work out from 5 to 6:30 A.M. Then I will meet with my campaign manager, staff, and contributors before heading in to work at the association at 8 or 8:30 A.M. In the evening, I shift back into campaign mode, getting on the phone, wooing delegates.

"I will continue campaigning full-time through the summertime, and then, after Labor Day, I will take a leave of absence from the Grocer's Association and begin campaigning seven days a week."

Where do you see this job leading you?

"I would like to stay in Congress six to 10 years and then leave, returning to an academic environment."

18. Staff/Legislative Assistant

FOR A UNITED STATES LEGISLATOR

description: Specific duties of the staff assistant will vary, depending on the legislator the assistant works for and the assistant's own drive and initiative. Duties could include answering the phone, dealing with constituents' requests, scheduling meetings, tracking legislation, reporting on other legislators' positions on issues, and helping the legislator to formulate policy and draft legislation.

Staff and legislative assistants will meet with assistants from other legislators' offices regarding their legislators' positions on issues or pending legislation. They will formulate polls to track public opinion, and will present their opinions to the legislator they work with, saying "This is what I believe, and here is what we should tell our constituents."

salary: Starting pay for congressional staff assistants will typically range from $12,000 to $18,000 per year. Starting salaries for legislative assistants will be slightly higher. The more experience on the Hill a staffer has, the higher the pay will be, up to a high of perhaps $50,000. Members of the House of Representatives and the Senate are limited as to the number of people they can have on their staffs; their total allocations for staff salaries are limited as well.

Work on congressional committees will likely pay a little better, starting at the low- to mid-$20,000s, and rising into the mid-$30,000s.

prospects: A job as a congressional staff or legislative assistant is a good entry-level position in Washington, D.C., and these jobs are excellent preparation for other jobs in the political sector. Turnover rates for these positions are high—the average assistant only stays on the Hill for six to 12 months. That's because the hours are long, the pay is low, and other opportunities quickly beckon. But it does mean that positions are opening on a regular basis.

qualifications: The basic qualification for a congressional staff assistant position will be a college degree. A legislative assistant's position will typically require a law degree or previous political experience (perhaps as a staff assistant). Specific qualifications will vary depending on a particular legislator's proclivities. Many colleges have established internship programs in Washington, D.C., which is one good way to get a foot in the door. But by far, the best way to get a position on the Hill is through connections—knowing someone who knows a legislator or who contributed to his or her campaign.

Another method of getting your foot in the door is by working as a volunteer for a legislator's campaign. If the legislator is then elected and has been impressed by your work, he or she may want to hire you.

characteristics: If you're a schmoozer, adept at networking, and at working a room, then you have already mastered one of the most important skills of a congressional staff person. If your networking skills are somewhat lacking, then you'd be wise to bone up on them—the sooner, the better. A love of politics and of the whole political process will also serve a congressional staffer well. Ambition and aggressiveness are two more qualities that won't be frowned upon.

Rainee Shih *was a staff assistant for a United States legislator in Washington, D.C.*

How did you get the job?

"I was on vacation in Washington, D.C., where my father works," Rainee says. "I was having dinner with my dad, and we bumped into Congressman Solomon Ortiz. He and my dad knew each other through a mutual acquaintance.

"I had graduated from college and was looking for something law-related, since I plan on going to law school.

"We were talking to Solomon Ortiz, and he said, 'A lot of kids work on the Hill. It's a good way to get legislative experience. It's a good place to work with other young people.' He said I should come to his office for an interview.

"Which I did, and was offered the job of staff assistant in his office. I started in Washington, D.C., then took a leave of absence after four months to spend three months working on the campaign trail."

What do you do all day?

"I started out in the front office," Rainee says, "dealing with constituent requests, getting visitors White House tour tickets, and dealing with mail, phone calls, faxes, and press clippings.

> THE BEST WAY TO GET A POSITION ON A LEGISLATOR'S STAFF IS TO MAKE CONTACT WITH THAT LEGISLATOR DIRECTLY. THE HOUSE AND SENATE BOTH HAVE PLACEMENT OFFICES THAT PROVIDE JOB INFORMATION, APPLICATIONS, AND INTERVIEW AND REFERRAL SERVICES FOR STAFF AND COMMITTEE POSITIONS, THOUGH THESE OFFICES DO NOT DO ANY ACTUAL HIRING OF STAFFERS.

"As time went on, I wasn't satisfied doing that, so I asked around for other work, and began writing letters and researching issues. Slowly, they gave me more responsibility.

"During the legislative session, part of the day was spent reading up on all the fliers handed out on the issues. Fliers were put together by lobbying groups and other congresspeople. We would monitor legislation on C-SPAN, where we could watch the House floor and know what the ongoing debate centered on. When your issue would come up, you would stop what you were doing and listen to what was said, putting your thoughts on paper. From all those sources of information, you would prepare a brief to present to the congressman, who would then go off to vote on the issue. You

would keep the congressman abreast of the situation on the floor, and then talk to him one last time before he would go off to vote on the issue.

"I would sometimes draft legislative summaries, and help my supervisor on issues she was working on. I would write up the pros and cons of various issues and positions, and consult with my supervisor before presenting them to Solomon.

"On the campaign trail, I worked as one of Congressman Ortiz's campaign managers. I would help coordinate events, write press releases, and supervise our phone banks. I would make sure Solomon would be where he was supposed to be. I would consult with an outside staff person—a campaign strategist—who helped put together mailing pieces—pro-

motional literature sent out to prospective voters. I consulted with the congressman's campaign director—we talked about what issues we should concentrate on, and where in the district we should concentrate more on; we conducted polls and did research on the campaign's strengths and weaknesses."

Where do you see this job leading you?

"Quite honestly, having experience on the Hill on your resume opens doors to so many job offers," Rainee says. "The fact that you worked on the Hill does make an impression. Whether you want to go on to law school—which many staffers do—or stick with the legislative arena, that experience does stick in people's minds.

"I plan on going to law school. But I want to get some experience first.

"I left the congressman's office and went to the American Seed Trade Association. When I started out, I was doing administrative work. But I told them that I wanted more responsibility, and now I deal with seed arbitration and label laws—I talk to lawyers and seed control officials of various states, and try to answer questions they have."

19. Civil Rights Worker

FOR A STATE OR CITY

description: A civil rights worker's primary responsibility will be to ensure that the civil rights ordinances of the state or municipality are enforced. Civil rights ordinances typically are attempts to legislate against discrimination in the workplace, housing, public accommodation (restaurant and hotel service), and other areas.

Workers in civil rights departments investigate possible instances of discrimination. They prosecute confirmed instances of discrimination, either by taking court action, or by working through other established procedures. They ensure that companies that have contracts with the city or state comply with the civil rights ordinances. They educate companies about the measures they can take to come into compliance. They also present educational seminars designed to let the public know what their rights are, and what legal action they can take if they feel they are experiencing discrimination.

Investigators deal directly with people who feel they have been discriminated against by looking into their claims, and attempting to prove or disprove them. Some workers in a city or state civil rights department might be in charge of public outreach efforts. Others might be in charge of relations with companies.

salary: Starting investigators in municipal or state civil rights departments can expect to make from $16,000 to $28,000 per year, depending on where they work, and the priority and funding levels that particular government places on its civil rights or affirmative action work. Salaries for higher-level workers in the department can rise to $60,000 or more.

prospects: Political and societal realities seem to be working against affirmative action, and that could be reflected in staff cutbacks and curtailed program initiatives. On the other hand, "diversity in the workplace" is a current catch phrase, and the marketplace might drive private industry to invest in ensuring that the goals of governmental affirmative action and civil rights policies continue to be met.

qualifications: Beginning workers in a civil rights department will typically need anywhere from 60 college credit hours to a full-fledged bachelor's degree. To rise to a supervisory position, you will probably need a postgraduate degree in administration, management, or a related field, as well as experience with affirmative action laws and policies. Supervisors will also need some prior administrative experience.

characteristics: Workers in a civil rights department should have the conviction that government policies can make a difference. They should possess hope, optimism, and a sense of humor. Governmental positions—the bureaucracy, the repetitiveness of the job, and the fact that government jobs can, at times, seem to be more about pushing paper or marking time than about making some sort of impact on society—can wear people down, so prospective government workers should guard against that possibility.

Elsa J. Batica *is the deputy director of the Minneapolis Department of Civil Rights in Minneapolis, Minnesota.*

How did you get the job?

Elsa has a bachelor's degree in chemical engineering, as well as graduate degrees in urban planning and community development, and training and organizational development.

She has worked in the quality control department of a brewery as a quality engineer, as a community developer with an international consulting firm, and as a customer service representative for an apparel company.

"I started as a customer service representative there," she says, "and was promoted first to the international marketing department, and then to the manager of the company's legal department. In that position, I learned a lot of what I use in my current position—I learned legal terms; I learned about Equal Employment Opportunity Commission compliance."

From that job, Elsa went on to serve as the associate administrator of a University of Minnesota agricultural research station, overseeing the research fund of that station.

She then took a job as the director of social action for the Minneapolis YWCA.

"And then I was asked by the executive director of the organization I work for now if I would be interested in joining them."

What do you do all day?

"I manage and direct the enforcement of the Minneapolis city civil rights ordinance through the enforcement and investigation of charges of illegal discrimination filed under the ordinance, through education efforts to prevent discrimination, by encouraging voluntary compliance with the ordinance, and by ensuring affirmative action compliance by vendors who do business with the city," says Elsa.

"For example, say you came to our office with an instance of what you thought was discrimination on the basis of race, sex, or class. The city has 13 classes of protection under the ordinance. What we do is collect evidence about the alleged instance of discrimination, analyze that information, and then make a determination as to the outcome of the case.

"As far as compliance is concerned, we monitor the affirmative action plans of companies that do business with the city—anyone that does $50,000 or more of business with the city.

"Our education efforts involve organizing forums on issues related to affirmative action. We are also asked by companies to come in and speak about the ordinance and affirmative action; we refer companies to trainers and consultants to help them conform to the ordinance.

"I manage the day-to-day operation of the department. I develop a developmental training program for our employees and deal with the department's budget. I don't handle cases myself, but I monitor case processing. I work to identify trends, to keep track of what types of cases we're dealing with. I represent the department in meetings and conferences; I prepare reports on the department's activities; I prepare community outreach plans; and I assist the department's executive director in meeting the goals we've set out for the department."

Where do you see this job leading you?

"I think I will be here for three more years at least," she says. "I would like to work in a bigger jurisdiction, somewhere where I can make a bigger change.

"The very least tenure that people have in this department is six years," she says, "and we have people who have been here for 20 years. There is very low turnover in this department."

> **CONTINUALLY RESEARCH THE MARKET TO SEE WHAT SKILLS ARE IN DEMAND. USE THE NEWSPAPERS AND YOUR PERSONAL CONTACTS TO SEE WHICH SKILLS PEOPLE WITH HIRING AUTHORITY ARE LOOKING FOR.**

20. Housing Coordinator

description: A housing coordinator facilitates the implementation of a state, county, city, or other governmental body's fair housing initiatives. Those initiatives may be mandated by a higher-level governmental authority, but the practice of carrying them out will fall most typically on the shoulders of local entities.

Housing coordinators work with government workers, the business community, nonprofit organizations, lending institutions, neighborhood associations, lower-income workers, and community residents to work out solutions to communities' housing problems—solutions that are both legal and equitable to all concerned. They might oversee the allocation of state or national funds, they may work toward purchasing and renovating property, or they may work on updating zoning regulations.

Their job is one of education as much as it is one of management—educating civic leaders and governmental representatives as to their responsibilities under the law, educating businesses as to ways they can be more responsive to the needs of low-income residents, and educating residents of low income housing as to what their responsibilities are under the law.

salary: The salary range for a housing coordinator could range from the low $30,000s to $40,000 per year or more, depending on experience and location.

prospects: Prospects for workers in housing will vary greatly depending on where in the nation they reside or plan to reside. Some states have strong housing regulations, while other states are fairly lax. The political future and fate of the federal Department of Housing and Urban Development could reverberate down to the state and local level. The vagaries of the political wind will have a great effect on opportunities in this field.

qualifications: Housing coordinator applicants will probably need to possess an advanced public policy degree (master's level or above) or an advanced degree in a related field—government, economics, landscape architecture, or geography. They need to be familiar with state and city housing rules and regulations, and probably need at least one or two years of experience with a city, county, state, or regional housing authority or similar body.

characteristics: Housing coordinators need to possess a facility for communicating—both written and oral—as much of their job will entail dealing with the public. They will have to be able to communicate their ideas succinctly and persuasively to decision makers. They should be politically savvy—if they aren't when they start the job, they will be shortly afterward, as they will have to deal with politicians, the business community, and low-, middle-, and upper-income groups, all with their own conflicting agendas.

Heidi Zimmer *is the housing coordinator for the city of Minnetonka, Minnesota.*

How did you get the job?

Heidi was pursuing an undergraduate degree in urban affairs at Michigan State University. Her degree program stipulated that she participate in an internship. This she did, spending four months of her junior year in Washington, D.C., working on a senator's personal staff.

While in D.C., she made connections with people working in housing in Michigan. "I got my first job because of that internship," she says. The job was as a political liaison with the Michigan State Housing Authority. She also did an internship with the authority's executive director's office, and later worked with the intergovernmental relations director.

She then applied to the Hubert H. Humphrey Institute in Minneapolis, to study for a master's in planning. Once she was accepted, she received a packet of scholarship and financial aid information.

"There were four internship positions available," Heidi says, "where you would get your schooling paid for and then work 20 hours a week.

"I sent in my application, and found that the city of Crystal—a fast-growing suburb of

> ONE OF THE "TEN COMMANDMENTS OF NETWORKING SUCCESS" IS TO CARRY YOUR "TOOLS" AT ALL TIMES. THOSE TOOLS INCLUDE A NAME TAG, A COLLECTION OF YOUR OWN BUSINESS CARDS, AND A CARD FILE OR SOME OTHER SUCH HOLDER FOR OTHER PEOPLE'S BUSINESS CARDS. THOSE TOOLS BECOME VITAL WHEN YOU ATTEND A FUNCTION WHERE YOU KNOW THERE WILL BE SOME NETWORKING OPPORTUNITIES. YOU NEVER KNOW, HOWEVER, WHEN A CHANCE ENCOUNTER MIGHT PROVE TO BE AN IMPORTANT CONTACT.

Minneapolis—was looking to hire someone for a housing and planning position. They were looking for someone to rewrite their zoning regulations. I applied for that job and was accepted.

"I updated their zoning ordinances. I helped create neighborhood organizations, starting three neighborhood watch programs. I sent out surveys to get a feel for the neighborhoods that were most interested in programs like that, held meetings with several groups."

She worked with the city of Crystal during the first year she attended the Humphrey Institute, and spent the summer after that working for the Hennepin County Office of Planning and Development,

administering federal housing funds for 43 suburban communities around Minneapolis.

She later worked with the U.S. Department of Housing and Urban Development, drafting a consolidated planning process for these communities.

She then became the city of Minnetonka's housing coordinator.

What do you do all day?

"Minnetonka is one of the wealthiest areas in the metropolitan area," Heidi says, "and they are being targeted by fairhousing advocates to come up with more affordable housing within their city boundaries."

"One half of my workweek is spent meeting with nonprofit organizations, advocacy organizations, human service organizations, state and federal government agencies, and organizations that serve low-income people on a daily basis, talking about additional funding sources, and making sure the city is up to speed on the needs of the residents. Sometimes, I will go into a meeting with businesses in town to see what the city and businesses can work together to accomplish.

"In Minnetonka, land is the biggest obstacle. And we have to use and work with different lending institutions, developers, and property management groups when we get to the building stage of our projects."

Heidi says she typically puts in a 45- to 50-hour week.

Where do you see this job leading you?

Heidi currently works as Minnetonka's housing coordinator on a part-time basis. "If I get hired here full-time, I can see myself staying here three to five years," she says.

Heidi says she will eventually work in either the private sector, or for nonprofit groups. "I could do private consulting for neighborhood development as well," she says.

21. Implementer

OF NEW GOVERNMENT PROGRAMS AND INITIATIVES

description: "Reinventing government" has been a catch phrase since the 1992 election; it is a phrase Bill Clinton rode to the White House, and the Republicans rode to Senate majority two years later. Once all the votes are tallied, however, somebody actually has to go out and do the reinventing. If you're an implementer of new programs or initiatives, you will be handed down policies, procedures, and processes. More likely, however, you will be given a budget and some broad policy goals or directives, and it will be up to you and the people you work with to figure out how to implement these directives. A large part of your job will entail developing policies and plans to implement these programs. You might end up assessing old programs or programs due to be phased out, or you might find yourself evaluating workers due to be transferred to your department, in order to determine which aspects of those programs or which skills of those workers can transfer to what you are doing.

The exact nature of the work you do will depend on the program you're trying to implement. You could end up developing curriculum to train new workers. You could develop programs to serve specific clients or combat specific problems. You could develop hiring policies. Your work could range from rolling up your sleeves and hitting the streets for some direct action, to sitting in an office to develop policies and procedures for your nascent agency or department.

salary: Salary level will depend on the specific program you are working on, your location, and the skills you bring to the job. Beginning salaries for positions like this could start from $18,000 to $23,000 per year.

prospects: Whatever the catch phrase of the moment is—"reinventing government," "getting government off our backs," "returning power to the local level," or some other term—the trend toward change in government looks like it will continue for some time. As the federal government relinquishes its responsibilities, state and local governments will need to reconfigure their programs and priorities as well. And all levels of government will need people to help them in their reconfigurations.

qualifications: Bureaucracy is firmly entrenched in all levels of government, and even attempts to "reinvent" government will have bureaucratic overtones. People brought in to work on teams aimed at re-creating programs will typically be required to have experience either in programs as they have been configured, or in working with programs like those to which the programs will be changing. A bachelor's or master's degree will be another likely requirement.

characteristics: If you're a creative thinker with innovative ideas and a passion for changing the way government works, then this could be the job for you. An ability to work with others, a sense of humor, and patience are other important traits.

Mary Ellen O'Connell *is a curriculum developer and lead trainer for an organization based in New York City.*

How did you get the job?

"I received my education in Russian language and literature in Albany, and did two student exchanges in Russia. I did hospital work and worked with immigrants in Albany, then moved to New York 14 years ago hoping to find work as a translator," Mary Ellen says.

"Instead I got work with a senior citizen's advocacy organization for a short term. I was hired as a caseworker in a welfare-to-work program. I worked for the municipal hospital corporation, and then I got a job with the New York Department of Social Services, in the office of employment services, getting people on welfare to work.

"I started there as a caseworker, then became a field rep, administrative assistant to an agency director, then assistant director for support services, and then worked in the information and communication services department.

"I eventually moved into the procedures unit, where I served as the deputy director of procedures and training."

> **DON'T RESTRICT YOUR JOB SEARCH TO GOVERNMENT AGENCIES AND INSTITUTIONS. CITY, COUNTY, AND STATE GOVERNMENTS NOW CONTRACT OUT A GREAT DEAL OF THEIR WORK; AND THOSE CONTRACTEES COULD PROVIDE YOU OPPORTUNITIES TO ACQUIRE VALUABLE EXPERIENCE.**

The New York City Way Project is a state- and city-funded, and city-administered welfare reform initiative designed to move people from welfare into the workforce in a short period of time.

Mary Ellen, after contemplating leaving civil service after nearly 10 years, soon applied for the project's head of training position.

"They were interested in the fact that I had experience in what they needed to train their incoming staff. My biggest obstacle to getting the job was that I did not have formal training in education. My response? 'I do not have formal experience, but I have taught English as a Second Language; I have worked in refugee camps; I have taught adults. So even if I don't have the theory, I know how to do it.' "

What do you do all day?

Mary Ellen says of her duties as curriculum director and lead trainer for the New York City Way Project, "I assess all the things our incoming workers will have to do. I implement and revise our training programs.

"We're about to begin our first 15-day training program in June, training workers who will serve people on workfare.

"A typical week for me involves attending meetings with city and state representatives and city university personnel, conducting Q-and-A sessions. I'm trying to synthesize information and put together curriculum and materials for our training programs.

"I anticipate implementing changes in policy and procedure, then retraining people who are being transferred to this department from other city departments [necessitated by changing city priorities and the city's ongoing fiscal situation]. After that, I'll focus on staff mentoring and oversight of procedures and training. I'll also be working with our new computer system."

Where do you see this job leading you?

"This position wasn't my plan," Mary Ellen says, "and I look at this as something that will last one or two years. From there, I would like to work as a consultant for a government agency.

"We do have a welfare crisis right now," she says, "but I don't see welfare being eradicated in my lifetime. I think there will be a tremendous need for trainers—as automation continues, as downsizing continues, retraining of the people displaced by these factors will be needed. We'll need analysts, trainers, budget and labor negotiators."

22. Job Coordinator

FOR A "WELFARE-TO-WORK" PROGRAM

description: Perhaps no public program is receiving as much scrutiny and attention in today's political climate as welfare—the combination of programs put into place to serve lower-income families, and people who fall below the poverty level. There is a growing sense that these programs are not working, and movements are in place in many states to radically restructure the manner in which welfare benefits are doled out. Many of these programs include some sort of "welfare-to-work" initiatives.

These new initiatives will typically put a limit on how long a person can receive funds, or will tie the allocation of those funds to participation in a job-training or workforce placement program. It is the duty of a job coordinator or case manager to implement these programs.

A job coordinator will help set up training schemes for these "welfare-to-work" programs. They might work to establish a "jobs resource center" that their clients can use to work on everything from getting their GED, to writing a resume, to preparing for a job interview. They will work with their clients, assisting them in all facets of their movement from welfare recipient to employed individual; the job coordinator will be his or her clients' greatest resource.

In addition, they will serve as a liaison between their office and the public- and private-sector employers who will put their clients to work.

salary: Job coordinators will typically make from $10 to $12 an hour or more, depending on their experience. Job coordinators working for private job services, which concentrate more on the finding of work elements than the training of workers, can make around $25 an hour, or $52,000 per year.

prospects: While "welfare-to-work" programs are becoming more common as the political climate shifts toward an emphasis in this area, there seems to be an increasing de-emphasis on the human service element of this work, with many of these programs being run by private employment agencies, and prerogatives shifting toward getting people off welfare quickly and away from training people to help ensure that they stay off welfare. That said, however, the employment prospects in this area, in both the public and the private sector, are expected to be excellent. The number of human service workers is expected to double between 1992 and 2005, according to the *Occupational Outlook Handbook,* with opportunities expected to be the greatest in job-training programs.

qualifications: "Welfare-to-work" program job coordinators should possess at least a two-year degree and should have social work and/or employment training experience. Management experience will also come in very handy in this occupation.

characteristics: In order to excel in this field, you need to be compassionate and able to empathize with people in social situations other than your own. Realize too, though, that you also will have to employ "tough love" as part of your job. Patience will go a long way toward helping you succeed in this kind of work.

Flexibility and creativity are two other qualities that every job coordinator should possess.

Bonnie Burcaw *is a job coordinator/case manager for a government human services agency in Wisconsin.*

How did you get the job?

Bonnie's initial experience and background was in office management. She and her husband moved to Price County, Wisconsin, and Bonnie started work as a part-time administrator with the Price County Department of Human Services. "I worked with people who came in for general relief and assistance," she says.

Later, her boss applied for and received a $2,000 grant for a preliminary "welfare-to-work" program, and Bonnie was put in charge. The program enabled the county to pay employers $100 to take on employees culled from the ranks of the county's welfare rolls. That program grew, and developed into the Human Service Department's Jobs Program, which Bonnie now oversees.

> THE NUMBER OF HUMAN SERVICE WORKERS IS EXPECTED TO DOUBLE BETWEEN 1992 AND 2005.

What do you do all day?

"One of my job duties has included establishing our jobs resource room," Bonnie says. "We've got computers hooked into NOVA Net, which is a managed system giving people entry onto, and training for, the Internet. People can tap into 10,000-plus training programs using that. We help people train their math skills, and train in circuitry work for entry-level positions. We have job boards where we post job openings.

"We have a job skills class that I teach, where we show people how to apply and search for a job, how to fill out an application, how to match people's interests to jobs, personal grooming, interview skills, computer training, nutrition, budgeting, day care, and family planning. There is a whole array of seminars I've gone to, and I incorporate what I've learned there in these classes. We compile the information from those seminars into booklets.

"I work with clients one-on-one, helping them deal with stressful situations in their lives, as well as helping them with the resources we have available. I act as a mentor and help to facilitate things.

"We have been sending people primarily into public work sites—libraries, the forestry department, the Chamber of Commerce, places like that. But now our work sites are becoming private sector sites. This is something that private sector employers are beginning to try out. So I go out to these employers and try to pitch our program to them, tell them that we can help them develop an employee pool. I talk to employers on a constant basis.

"Right now, I'm also on the state Committee for Job Works Program and two others. So I make frequent trips down to Madison (the state capital) to meet with those committees."

In those meetings, the needs and differences of various areas of the state are brought out.

Where do you see this job leading you?

"This job has helped me build my management skills, my team-building skills, stress management techniques, coordination and facilitation skills, and especially my people skills. In this job, you have to learn to read people—I can now section people in a heartbeat.

"I think I could work very well in a company's human resources department, doing testing and evaluation of potential employees. The skills I've learned here would also be very transferable to real estate work. I think I would also make an excellent sales person—I do sales work constantly. I take a person 'without skills' and sell them to companies."

23. Public Information Officer,

description: Each state has a centralized operation for emergency management, though it may fall under different agencies in different states.

State emergency management offices are responsible for implementing responses to disasters ranging from natural (floods, tornadoes, hurricanes) to man-made (release of hazardous materials, accidents at fixed nuclear facilities), and including riots, and hostile military or paramilitary actions. Comprehensive emergency management is a program designed to help communities prepare for disasters before they strike, respond to disasters when they occur, recover from disasters after they strike, and take action to prevent or lessen the destruction of future disasters.

Each state's emergency management offices are organized differently, depending upon the needs and resources of the area.

Public information officers and their assistants develop awareness campaigns and educational publications, produce publications for emergency managers throughout the state, and conduct media interviews. During a disaster the public information office works with local, state, and federal officials to provide emergency information to citizens in the disaster area. It keeps the press and public informed about resources available to assist disaster victims during the recovery process. It assists in ensuring the lines of communications into and out of the disaster site remain open.

salary: Salary levels vary in each state depending upon the organization. The assistant public information officer for the state of Texas, for example, earns $25,380 annually. For more specific information on salary levels in your state, contact the Office of Emergency Management.

prospects: Emergency management positions on the local and county level will typically be voluntary or part of another job description; larger communities tend to have a public information staff, so the best locations to head to for work of this sort will be the state's capital city. State job banks also are a good source for this information.

qualifications: Public information officers should possess good communication skills, with a background in publications, and in working with the public and the media. They should be able to work well with government officials and employees at all levels. Many local emergency management coordinators wear several hats; these individuals may be police or fire officials, administrators for the county judge or mayor, or may hold part-time or volunteer positions. Experience in emergency management also will serve you in good stead.

characteristics: Public information officers in this type of work must be resourceful and able to pull together resources from a variety of locations. They should be able to shift gears quickly—disasters can strike without notice, and might move them into the field and away from home for weeks at a time. Two other important characteristics: a willingness to travel and (due to the disaster situation) a willingness to put up with very crude conditions, such as lack of running water (or worse).

Caroline M. Guckian *is the assistant public information officer for the Texas Department of Public Safety Division of Emergency Management in Austin, Texas.*

How did you get the job?

Caroline attended the University of Texas at Austin, where she earned a bachelor of fine arts degree. After graduation, she worked in the university's continuing education division's conference coordinator office, where she assisted coordinators with conference activities. While employed by the university, she worked on continuing-education program development, in addition to her other duties. During this period, she also spent time building her portfolio. She later learned of an opening for an illustrator in the Texas Department of Public Safety, applied for the job, and was hired.

"I became interested in the public information field while working as illustrator. Part of my responsibilities were public information officer duties for the Emergency Operating Center. Through that job, I became interested in public information."

She worked as an illustrator within the department for almost three years, before becoming an assistant public information officer.

What do you do all day?

"My work can be seasonal," Caroline says, "because natural disasters tend to follow a seasonal pattern. In Texas, hurricane season runs from June 1 to the end of November; March through May and early fall are when we typically have severe weather; and from December through February the focus is on winter weather. When we're not involved with a disaster, we're typically preparing a handout or brochure that explains what occurs during a disaster, how people should prepare before it strikes, and how to respond when it does strike. In addition, our office is responsible for the Annual State Emergency Management Conference, conducts public information workshops, and heads public awareness campaigns for Texas.

"We start preparing for a disaster before it strikes. For instance, when Hurricane Roxanne was threatening the Texas Coast, we were busy working on press releases, responding to media calls, getting our emergency operating center geared up in case the hurricane did strike. We tried to step up awareness messages. I did a number of radio interviews where I would explain that now—before a storm hits—is a good time to think about disaster preparedness. People should make sure they have a battery-powered radio on hand, that their home is secure, that they have put gas in their car."

Though she normally works an eight-hour day, Caroline says that, "When disaster strikes, my supervisor and I will work 12-hour or longer shifts in the Emergency Operating Center, allowing the media, staff, and informational coordination to run smoothly. If it's a significant enough disaster that it qualifies for federal assistance, we'll set up a local office, where we work with the media and get a hold of our reservists—contract employees who work for us when an area is a federally-declared disaster. We also go into the area and make personal contact with people through our outreach teams to help people get the aid they need."

Where do you see this job leading you?

"Right now, my personal goals are [related to] this job—getting Texas-based resources available for schoolchildren, producing some things that local governments and teachers can use that are simple, and will help explain to children what they can and should do during a severe weather emergency. Special needs populations is another area where informational resources are needed."

"I'm an artist at heart, and I would like to do more with my art. I would also like to be able to spend more time with my children, something that isn't always possible in this job."

> **VOLUNTEER FOR PUBLIC INFORMATION DUTIES WITH YOUR LOCAL EMERGENCY PLANNING COMMITTEE, AMERICAN RED CROSS CHAPTERS, SALVATION ARMY CORPS OR LOCAL EMERGENCY MANAGEMENT COORDINATOR.**

24. Researcher

FOR A HUMAN SERVICES AGENCY

description: Specific job duties might vary, depending on the sources of funding for the agency, but the goal of the research you will be doing will be to justify the agency's existence to its funding sources. It will be up to you and your fellow researchers (if any) to prove that the work your agency is doing is effective, both in financial terms and in terms of human costs.

You will conduct and perhaps oversee research projects that your agency undertakes. You might be called on to compare how clients of your agency fare against clients of alternative programs—more than likely, your programs and initiatives will be considered the "alternative" ones, and you'll be comparing them against status quo programs and systems.

You might be called on to defend your agency's operations to those who control the purse strings. And you might also find yourself writing grant proposals, and working to develop alternative sources of funding. You will also be called on to provide research and statistical support for agency workers in the field.

One of the disadvantages of this type of job is that most of your days might be spent in front of a computer, and you won't have the direct contact with clients that workers in the field have. On the other hand, you will be providing an essential service for the agency and will have contact with workers at all levels—from those working in the field, up to the agency directors and the people who control the money the agency receives.

salary: Salaries for beginning human services researchers can start in the mid- to upper $20,000s per year. Experience will be the most relevant factor in determining salary, which can run up to more than $50,000 a year.

prospects: As government continues to divest itself from much of the human services responsibilities it took on in the past, much of that responsibility will fall to the state and privately funded agencies. Though the need for human services jobs will probably not diminish, the overall number of jobs might well do so. Jobs are out there—it will just take a creative search to find them.

qualifications: Academic training in research strategies and methods will be looked upon favorably, but just as important will be experience in the human services field, whether that be experience in the criminal justice system, in counseling, in fund-raising or grant-writing experience, or in some other aspect of human services. Of course, the closer your area of experience is to the research you will be conducting, the better. Communications skills—the ability to write well and the ability to communicate with people in a variety of conditions and situations—will also be highly prized.

characteristics: A researcher in this field advises that human services researchers should be "detail-oriented, but not so detail-oriented that you can't see the forest for the trees." Someone who is comfortable working in team environments or with other people will do well in this type of job.

Howard Babich *is the director of research for a human services company in New York.*

How did you get the job?

Howard says he has a "government/criminal justice background." After attending a doctoral program in public policy, Howard got a postgraduate internship with then-New York City Mayor Ed Koch, working in his office's community assistance unit. "They kept me on after the summer," Howard says, "and I worked for the city of New York as a research analyst, the last five years within the Department of Correction.

"Once you're employed by the city, it's very easy to move around department to department," Howard adds.

The Education and Assistance Corporation is a private, nonprofit corporation, funded through the public and private sector, that provides educational, vocational, and counseling services for families, youth, the aged, and the disadvantaged. EAC is organized into four divisions: developmental learning programs, educational and vocational services, family services, and a criminal justice division. EAC employs 200 full-time and 80 part-time workers, and utilizes the services of more than 300 volunteers.

> NONPROFIT TIMES: THE LEADING PUBLICATION FOR NONPROFIT MANAGEMENT CAN BE A GOOD SOURCE FOR JOB LEADS. THE NEWSLETTER, PUBLISHED BY DAVIS INFORMATION GROUP, CONTAINS A CLASSIFIED JOB LISTINGS SECTION IN THE BACK.

"A friend of mine from the Department of Correction was working in this position—director of research at EAC. He left to pursue his doctorate and recommended me for the position," Howard says.

"My job description listed a Ph.D. as a job requirement; I didn't have it. But I did have five years of research and supervisory experience. They interviewed a lot of people with Ph.D.s, a lot of academic types, but they went with the person with experience. Some people had much better research skills than I did. I think they went with me because I knew the system, knew the criminal justice system."

What do you do all day?

"I do empirical studies to determine the efficiency of EAC programs." Those programs range from alternative high school diploma programs to counseling for individuals dealing with divorce, separation, and aging. Howard says, "I oversee and conduct all of the EAC's research projects dealing with our alcohol and substance abuse treatment and criminal justice programs.

"For instance, we've done a recidivism study, comparing our clients to offenders who have been incarcerated. We did a cost-benefit analysis and could point to it and say, 'Hey! Putting a nonviolent, substance-abusing offender sentenced to 60 days or more of jail time through a 12-month treatment program costs less than the jail time.' That study came in handy when the state senate threatened to cut our funding. We showed that the state was saving money by funding our programs—most of our money does come from the state.

"I also provide research and statistical support for our field staff, supervise our MIS system, and write grant proposals.

"This is officially a 9-to-5 job, but we're usually here longer than 5 P.M.," Howard says. "For me, a disadvantage is that I don't get out into the field as often as I'd like; I'm often cooped up in front of a computer. We also don't have the research resources we need. Department of Correction information is confidential, so gaining access to that information can be problematic. The big advantage is that I'm working for something in which I believe."

Where do you see this job leading you?

"Counselors in our agency have gone on to become directors of our programs or have gone on to other substance-abuse counseling programs," says Howard. "Wherever people go, most of them still work in the social work field.

"The person who had this job before me went into a doctoral program.

"I don't plan on going anywhere—I've only been at this job for seven months—but if I do go somewhere else, I hope to go to another research position."

25. State Department of Human Services Eligibility Specialist

description: Department of human services programs are funded through a combination of state and federal dollars, and even though potential welfare clients have to meet federal requirements, the programs that administer welfare aid are usually run by state agencies or departments. It falls to human services eligibility specialists to determine whether or not people are eligible for food stamps, Medicaid, Aid for Families with Dependent Children funds, or some combination of the three.

Potential welfare recipients will come into your office and fill out an application. Then they will sit down with you (or other eligibility specialists) for one-on-one interviews where eligibility is determined. Applicants need to verify that they are U.S. citizens and that their income level and home situation (marital status, number of children, where and with whom they are living, etc.) qualify them for assistance.

After that original eligibility is determined, clients will have to return to the human services office to meet with specialists for recertification. Clients are required to report changes in their income level or marital, family, or living status. If they do not receive or lose their benefits, or feel that a change in their funding status is due for some other reason, clients may also contact the office. Clients are also required to come into the office to report a change of address. One-on-one appointments with clients could take anywhere from 15 minutes to an hour or more.

salary: The largest factors determining the wage you will receive are the state in which you will be working, how these jobs are classified, and the salaries allocated to those classification levels. Salaries begin at anywhere from $12,000 to $24,000 per year. Senior eligibility specialists, those with some administrative or managerial authority, can make anywhere from $16,000 to $30,000 or more.

prospects: Despite budget cuts and hiring freezes, openings are expected. Openings will depend on budgets that come down from both state and federal governments—since budgets and funding priorities change every congressional session, if not every year, you should keep in mind that where there are hiring freezes and no openings this year, there might well be positions next year.

qualifications: A college degree is not necessarily a requirement for a welfare eligibility specialist position, but a certain amount of college credit—60 hours or so—is usually required, though human services experience can make up for a lack of college credit in some instances.

characteristics: An eligibility specialist should be able to interpret to clients the department's policies and procedures. He or she should also be able to interpret clients' body language and any evasive behavior to tell whether or not clients are attempting to conceal information. An ability to maintain a pleasant disposition and to deal with people on the lower end of the socioeconomic scale are also important characteristics.

Paul Pfeifer *is an eligibility specialist with the state of Texas Department of Human Services in San Antonio, Texas.*

How did you get the job?

Paul earned a bachelor's degree in English from Southwest Texas State University in San Marcos, Texas.

"An aunt had a friend in the Department of Human Services who knew of an opening there," Paul says. "My aunt's friend showed me how to fill out an application, and I got a job in a Worker I position in Karnes City, Texas, a rural office where we had a caseload of about 180 clients per person. I took care of most of the training of workers there. At that office, I would also interview clients to determine their eligibility for food stamps, Aid for Families with Dependent Children, and Medicaid."

After two years working in the Karnes City office, Paul left that job and spent some time traveling.

"Then I learned that there was an opening in the San Antonio Human Services Department for a verification technician in the recovery unit. I applied for that job and got it. With the state, it's easier to be hired once you've already worked for the state. I worked on recovery of funds; if there

was an overpayment of funds from the state, I sent out letters and tried to recover those funds. I was involved with case research information; I would determine whether or not to send out letters to employers for cases involving wage information that had not been reported or had been under-reported. Cases were then processed to begin payment recovery.

"Then I was hired back on as a Worker. I made the Worker II classification right away, then after a year here applied for a Worker III position and got that."

Paul says, "At the office I am at now, clients are serviced by teams of four: one team leader (classified as a Worker III), two other eligibility specialists, and one certification technician. Each team handles about 1400 cases."

What do you do all day?

Paul interviews clients to determine their eligibility to receive welfare, but, as a Worker III classification, he also has some management responsibility.

"I supervise one technician (which is a position that is a cross between a clerk/secretary and a worker, and involves a lot of clerical tasks). I am a team

> WHEN YOU SEND IN YOUR RESUME AND COVER LETTER, DON'T SEND THEM ALONE. SUPPLEMENT THOSE MATERIALS WITH ADDITIONAL ONES. FOR EXAMPLE, IF ANY PROJECTS YOU HAVE WORKED ON HAVE RECEIVED COVERAGE IN THE PRESS (ESPECIALLY IF YOU WERE QUOTED OR MENTIONED IN THE ARTICLE), SEND THOSE CLIPPINGS ALONG, TOO.

leader—providing guidance and resources for the members of my team. One of my responsibilities is managing the team effectively.

"I am also the chairman of the local office procedure committee," Paul says. "Our building is composed of nine units, with approximately 16 people per unit. We have the Quality Control Unit, the Change Unit,

and the Jobs Unit housed in this building, with six ongoing units of pure eligibility. The committee is looking at new ways to do things and at changes that need to take effect in order for the office to run smoother. Our recommendations go to the unit supervisors for approval."

Where do you see this job leading you?

"Right now, I have five years of social service experience, and finding another job in the social service sphere would basically be a matter of selling myself," Paul says. "But I might want to get into systems analysis or programming—those are interests of mine and I'm starting to get tired of dealing with people. My supervisor has been effective in convincing me to stay with this agency."

Paul says that many people move up within the agency. He has also seen people leave the agency because they couldn't or didn't want to handle the pressure of dealing with such a large number of clients who were all, in greater or lesser degrees, in situations of distress. He has seen workers at the Department of Human Services move on to work in private industry.

26. Court-Appointed Special Advocate Worker

description: The National Court Appointed Special Advocate (CASA) Association explains the work its members do this way: "A CASA worker is a trained community volunteer who is appointed by a juvenile or family court judge to speak for the best interest of children who are brought before the court. The majority of CASA volunteers' assignments are home placement cases where an abused and neglected child has been removed for protection from the care of his or her parents."

Once appointed by the courts, a CASA volunteer will meet with the child or children, parents, foster parents, institutional care workers—all the people involved in the child's life—gathering information to determine what the appropriate next step for the case would be. Then the volunteer recommends that course of action to the court. Volunteers gather materials and do research that other individuals and agencies don't have time to do.

Paid CASA staff recruit, train, and support those people who volunteer to act as advocates in the court system for abused and neglected children. Possible staff positions include administrative/clerical workers, volunteer services directors, program directors, and case advocacy supervisors (people who will oversee the work of volunteer advocates working in the courts).

Executive directors are responsible for the overall management of their organization. They supervise volunteer advocates, oversee the administration of programs that provide services to children, raise funds for their organization, and advocate for change in the judicial system at the state, local, and national levels.

salary: Salaries for CASA staffers vary, depending on the size of the office they work for, the number of clients it serves, and the sources of funding for the office. Salaries for those with bachelor's degrees start at about $20,000 per year. For executive directors salaries could range from $30,000 to $50,000 per year.

prospects: CASA has grown tremendously since its inception in 1977. There are now 610 programs in the U.S. utilizing the skills of more than 37,000 volunteers, and helping an estimated 25 percent of the nation's abused and neglected children in their court proceedings.

With a growth rate like this, positions do come open on a regular basis. But specific prospects will depend on a prospective worker's experience, and where he or she lives.

qualifications: For paid work at a CASA office, a degree in social work, psychology, family law, or business will likely be required. Prospects should also have an understanding of the dynamics at work within a family in crisis, and a minimum of two years of experience in direct service, in a voluntary or paid capacity.

A graduate-level degree, and some minimum supervisory or management experience in community service or within the court system will likely be asked of those aspiring to the director's position.

characteristics: An effective CASA director or staff member should be outgoing, yet be a good listener. They need to have a tough skin, as many times the advocate's position will not be a popular one, and it will be rigorously attacked.

Ann Peterson Jones *is the executive director of CASA of St. Louis County in Missouri.*

How did you get the job?

"I got my undergraduate degree in merchandising and marketing," she says, "and when I got out of school I did some promotion and advertising work. I began to get interested in nonprofit management, and I went on to get a master's degree in consumer behavior and marketing at Louisiana State University. All along, I was interested in serving families.

"After earning that degree, I worked with the Cooperative Extension Service (part of the Department of Agriculture) as the assistant area agent of New Orleans, an area that included five parishes.

"I had the option of going on to work on my Ph.D. or going to law school, and I decided to go to law school. While at law school, I worked for the American Arbitration Association, and got some nonprofit management experience.

"Then I moved to Florida and worked in a private law practice. I practiced family law there.

"I took on a position as the part-time attorney for the Guardian Ad Litem program, which is the Court Appointed Special Advocates program in Florida. I really, really liked it and could see that CASA volunteers made a big difference.

"I had the opportunity to move to St. Louis, and I called the CASA program here. It just so happened that the executive director was leaving. I applied for that job, and got it."

What do you do all day?

"Here, I have been able to utilize my business background and my legal background. I administer this grassroots program. I deal with accounting,

> **YOU MUST BE CREATIVE AND BE ABLE TO RE-ENERGIZE YOURSELF FOR WHAT, AT TIMES, CAN BE GRUELING WORK.**

bookkeeping, payroll, insurance, and workers' compensation. I handle the organizational management of this CASA office, which I look at as a business. I create a budget. I will write grants. I will do fundraising. I will go to corporations. I do a thorough evaluation of our programs. I do public relations and community relations work.

"I do a lot of policy advocacy work. Because we work as a grassroots organization, I can advocate for change on a statewide level," Ann says. "That is very challenging work. For instance, I just sat on a panel at a symposium on children and the law sponsored by the Missouri Bar Association. I serve on a number of task forces and committees. I chaired a committee to create Guardian Ad Litem standards for the state of Missouri; we just submitted our standards to the Supreme Court for their approval. I tried to keep the needs of the children paramount in those discussions. What I see is that people tend to stop their efforts at the level of what is best for the professional worker in that arena,

and forget that what we're trying to do is serve children. Participation in these activities entails a critical time commitment. But it is crucial that I participate in these committees so that I can press our commitment for children.

"And then there's the telephone, telephone, telephone. I just received a call from an organization asking me to review a grant proposal."

Where do you see this job leading you?

"I've been here three years and I see myself staying here for some time," Ann says. "No matter where I might go, I think I would do something in child advocacy. I might go on to do something policy related on the state level, go on to an organization whose efforts are more focused on policy.

"My predecessor wanted to move to a part-time position and is now the director of a foundation. That is one place I'd like to go. Another option is consulting work, which would give me a more flexible schedule."

27. Home Detention Caseworker

description: Home detention programs have grown due to the continuing decrease of space in juvenile detention facilities, and in the number of foster parents equipped to deal with problem children. These programs are designed to help parents learn how to deal constructively with, and set limits for, their offspring. Juvenile offenders sentenced to these programs by the courts will gradually receive more privileges if they meet the restrictions of their sentences. They will start out with zero privileges, and gradually work up to the point where they are let out of the house one or two nights of the week. These programs can be restrictive to parents as well, since parents must be home to watch over their children.

Home detention caseworkers work in concert with social workers and juvenile probation officers. They are the ones who ensure that those sentenced to home detention programs are meeting those programs' requirements. Home detention caseworkers will check in with the juveniles sentenced to these types of programs on a regular basis—usually at least once a day. (Since these programs are typically of short duration—five weeks to two months or so—more frequent contact is required of their caseworkers than would be of, say, a juvenile probation officer.)

Home detention caseworkers file any and all paperwork required by the individual cases. They also meet with judges, attorneys, and social workers to go over the status of their cases.

salary: Full-time home detention caseworkers can expect to make between $15,000 and $25,000 per year, depending on experience. Many of these positions are not full-time, however, and the pay for those positions, of course, will not be as high.

prospects: Prospects for home detention caseworkers—indeed for all workers in the field of human services—are expected to be quite good for qualified applicants. The ability to find work as a home detention caseworker will depend on whether or not the community in which you reside, or wish to reside, has a home detention program in place, and on how high a priority that program is in your community.

qualifications: Home detention caseworkers will almost certainly be required to have some experience in the law enforcement or human services fields, or in working with children. A bachelor's degree in criminology, social work, education, or some other related field will be another likely prerequisite.

characteristics: Persons aspiring to home detention casework should relate well to youths, especially to those who are troubled. They should be able to work well with others, but be able to pursue their job duties independently.

Home detention caseworkers work odd hours. The work might not even be full-time employment. Prospective caseworkers should acknowledge those factors and be prepared to live with them. They should also be willing to travel.

Mike Johnson *is a home detention caseworker for the social services department in Phillips, Wisconsin.*

How did you get the job?

Mike started on his career in law enforcement as a patrolman with the Chicago Police Department. He had attended the University of Wisconsin-Madison, then went to Chicago and attended the police academy there.

He then worked as an investigator, part of a tactical undercover force, and later served on the police department's youth division. "I spent most of my time in that job making arrests," he says. "I made a lot of referrals to juvenile homes, and to housing where offenders would spend time before their case went to trial."

He ultimately served as the sheriff in Price County, Wisconsin.

Soon after he left that job, "the social service department of the county started a home detention program, and I started doing some investigation of welfare fraud."

What do you do all day?

"In the home detention programs, I have to check up on the kids in the program three times a day," Mike says. "One of those times will be a face-to-face contact. During the school year, making those contacts is easier, because you can drop in on them at school. It's harder in the summer, when the kids are all out and about.

"I am a game warden in the sense that I try to get these kids to follow the rules. If they don't, I tattle on 'em to the social workers. If home detention doesn't seem to be working—the really naughty kids—they get sent to group homes. They'll be there for three or four days, and then they will come back home. If that doesn't work, they go on to shelter care. We gradually increase the security of the places they are sent to. Sometimes the kids are taken away from their family for good—but those instances are rare.

"My job requires me to meet with the social workers one time a week. Social workers will have 70 to 80 cases under their jurisdiction. They try to meet with the kids too, but because of their caseload, they can't do that

> ONE OF THE "TEN COMMANDMENTS OF NETWORKING" IS: SET A GOAL REGARDING HOW MANY PEOPLE YOU WANT TO MEET AT ANY GIVEN SOCIAL EVENT OR NETWORKING OPPORTUNITY, AND DO NOT LEAVE UNTIL YOU HAVE ACHIEVED THAT MARK.

as much as I can. I am the eyes and ears of the social workers, and report back to them the progress of the kids they are assigned to.

"I am a contract employee. Other counties use mostly in-house people, but I don't want a 40-hour-a-week job. This job is nice because I'm out all the time. I like the job because I like to do different things every day. This is a job where you have to work seven days a week, and not many people want to do that."

Where do you see this job leading you?

"I have recently taken on more responsibilities," Mike says. "The Price County Sheriff's office cannot handle the service process part of their job—they're too busy with other tasks to serve papers to people—so I have taken on some of that work.

"In order to progress any further in the human services field, I would have to have some sort of additional education or training," he says. "Most people who work in social services have to have a background in that field, to have taken behavioral problems courses and classes like that. For myself, most of what I have learned, I've learned on the job—how to deal with people, how to handle different situations. There was a training division in the Chicago Police Department, and we learned about all these things, but on the street things are completely different. You learn from experience when you handle these things for the first time."

28. Investigative Assistant

FOR A POLICE DEPARTMENT

description: Investigative assistants help patrol officers with their casework. They file reports for officers on the street, and take care of a lot of paperwork that would otherwise fall on an officer's shoulders. They research cases on which officers are working. They take complaints from people involved in incidents, and record statements from witnesses. They go to court with victims if necessary. Their basic role is to help officers in the investigation and prosecution of their cases.

In many cases, it will be misdemeanors and minor offenses that the investigative assistants will deal with, leaving officers free to tackle major crimes.

Investigative assistants work in tandem with a team of officers—patrol officers, detectives, sergeants—and get their input on cases, since those officers will, in many instances, be the people with whom the victims first interact. They also work closely with the public.

As part of this job, you might get the opportunity to take classes in police work and investigating, though at times, it might still feel like you're inadequately trained for the job you're doing. This is one way to get a real feel for the way the criminal justice system works, and it is a good avenue to find out more about police work.

salary: Civilian police department employees should expect to make less than commissioned police officers. Beginning salaries can start from $11,000 a year to $17,000 or more. Salaries for experienced workers can rise into the $20,000s.

prospects: Prospects will depend on the political reality of the city you're looking for a job in. Safety is an issue of public concern, which usually leads to demands for increased police department staffing; however, trimming government spending is also an issue of public concern. There are more likely to be openings on the night shift and in data-entry or clerk-type positions than in the investigative units—and those jobs are also basic entry-level positions in the police force for applicants without law enforcement backgrounds.

qualifications: Candidates for investigative assistant positions in the police department will typically need five years or more of experience with law enforcement or related work, along with computer skills. Educational training (through criminal justice or related programs) could substitute for some of this experience. Though a bachelor's degree will not always be required for these positions, it is becoming a more common requirement.

characteristics: Persons going into police work should have a good attitude, and be able to separate themselves from their job. You will often encounter people at their worst, and the kind of person who is going to let that environment get to him or her probably isn't cut out for police work. Patience is a virtue, in this type of work especially, as you'll be dealing with people who are rude, angry, or violent at times, or who simply want someone to talk to. The ability to put yourself in someone else's place will also come in handy in this job.

Susan Saldana *is an investigative assistant in the Investigative Services/Family Violence Unit of a police department in Arizona.*

- -

How did you get the job?

Susan heard there was a data-entry opening at city hall, so she went downtown and applied for the job.

"I really thought that I would be hired in the city's personnel department," Susan says, "and my first reaction was 'the police department?' So I came in for an interview and got the job. And I've been in the police department for 21 years now."

During her first six years there, she worked in the data entry department serving people who came into the police station, selling collision reports (which people needed for insurance purposes), and releasing cars from the pound. From there, she moved up to a receptionist position with the department's criminal investigation bureau, a department that dealt with theft, burglary, homicide, robbery, assault, and youth services.

After a year in this position, she became the secretary for the general assignments bureau. She was in that unit for 10 years.

"At that point, I was not getting any more merit increases, and had really come to a standstill. An opening came up in the sex crimes unit, and the supervisor there asked if I would be interested. So, I worked as a secretary in the sex crimes unit."

> **GOOD WORKS: A GUIDE TO CAREERS IN SOCIAL CHANGE IS A HELPFUL RESOURCE FOR PEOPLE LOOKING FOR JOBS THAT MAKE A DIFFERENCE. THIS MORE THAN 600-PAGE TOME LISTS CONTACT INFORMATION FOR MORE THAN 1,000 ORGANIZATIONS ACROSS THE UNITED STATES, ALL INVOLVED IN SOME ASPECT OF SOCIAL CHANGE WORK.**
>
> - - - - - - - - - -

"This unit (the Investigative Services/Family Violence Unit) was forming, and they told us that whoever was interested in the investigative assistant positions should apply."

What do you do all day?

"We take reports from officers on the street," Susan says, "and we take reports over the phone—for example, criminal mischief cases or cases that are filed mostly for insurance purposes.

"In criminal mischief or harassment cases, we tend to do the investigating because we have to sign the report, not the victim.

"We get cases assigned to us each day, normally 20 to 30 cases per day. On Mondays, though, you know you're going to get a big caseload—30 cases at least. All those cases have to be cleared. The majority of them you can clear immediately. Some of them you can suspend—we're waiting for the victim to contact us, and so we leave those cases open. Or we try to get in touch with the vic-

tims by sending out contact cards asking them to call us. We take statements from victims, and then we'll send contact cards to suspects when we want to file charges against them. We always try to contact the suspect. A criminal history check on a suspect is the only type of investigating that we try to do.

"When a suspect is named, we fill out an affidavit—a warrant of arrest. Then we take that warrant before a judge, who approves and signs it. And then we fill out a disposition sheet, which is sent to the county attorney's or to the D.A.'s office, depending on the severity of the crime. Once charges are filed, once the warrant is in the attorneys' hands, it is out of our hands."

Where do you see this job leading you?

"I don't intend to go anywhere else," Susan says. "This is the highest civilian investigative position one can rise to in the department."

29. Manager

OF ALTERNATIVE-TO-INCARCERATION
PROGRAMS

description: When criminal justice offenders are sentenced to minimum jail time—from 1 to 60 days—for offenses ranging from nonviolent criminal larceny or possession of stolen property, to domestic violence or criminal possession of controlled substances, they can be offered the opportunity to serve in alternative programs, rather than serve their prison time. Many of these offenders will be facing substance abuse problems, and the programs they will be referred to will be treatment programs, which will be charged with screening offenders and placing them in programs with which you have connections.

The program's referrals will come from the criminal justice system—judges and lawyers. As the manager of such programs, your function will be as a liaison between administration and line staff.

You will oversee daily operations of your program and its staff. You'll do the hiring and firing of program workers and will supervise the program staff. You will have to report to the program's funding sources, and will network with criminal justice officials and treatment providers. You'll also find yourself intervening with clients on an as-needed basis.

As an administrator, you'll have a lot of control over your position, and will be able to implement your own ideas more effectively. You'll have the opportunity to develop programs and watch them grow. On the other hand, you'll have to deal with the bulk of the bureaucratic red tape in which these types of programs can become mired. Acting as a go-between between your line staff and your administrative overseers can also be a difficult balancing act.

salary: Directors of projects like this can expect to make from $40,000 to $50,000 a year. Caseworkers (those who help place clients in programs, and act as liaisons with program managers, clients, probation officers, and the courts) can expect to earn between $21,000 and $25,000.

prospects: Employment prospects for those working in all aspects of the criminal justice system are expected to improve through at least the year 2005. An increasing inmate population will mean an increasing number of programs either to deal with released inmates or to help lessen the number of inmates going into incarceration. Correctional institutions and criminal justice programs have traditionally had difficulty attracting qualified applicants, so opportunities for talented individuals are excellent.

qualifications: Caseworkers will usually need a high school diploma plus several years of experience, or a college degree with one or more years of experience. Program managers will, of course, need several years of experience beyond that, plus management experience or training.

characteristics: Workers should be flexible, open, conscientious, and organized. Workers in this field suffer from a high rate of burnout, so those anticipating working in programs like this should prepare themselves for that.

Jayme Delano *is the project director of an alternative-to-incarceration program for criminal justice offenders in Brooklyn, New York.*

How did you get the job?

"I received my B.A. in criminal justice," says Jayme. "After graduating, I thought I wanted to work in the field for a while, then apply to law school.

"I started in a TASC [Treatment Alternatives to Street Crime] office as a case manager/court liaison. A professor of mine got me that first job. Once I started working, I decided that maybe law school wasn't the way to go.

"I spent one year in the Nassau TASC office. Then a Queens TASC office opened and I transferred there to help start that program. I was there for two years.

"Then I took a job with the New York Office of Corrections, working as an assessment officer at Rikers Island. From there, I went to the Vera Institute of Justice, where I was offered a job as a project director of one of their outlying agencies, the Nassau Bail Bond Agency. The Vera Institute of Justice gets involved in community and criminal justice programs, develops and tests those programs, and then spins them off into their own agencies. I worked in a pre-trial, intensive community-supervision program.

> **MAKE SURE YOU DRESS APPROPRIATELY FOR THE INTERVIEW (AN OFT-REPEATED PIECE OF ADVICE, BUT ONE THAT BEARS SOME LISTENING TO). GOING INTO A SITUATION DRESSED TOO CASUALLY CAN PUT YOU OUT OF THE RUNNING, NO MATTER HOW STUNNING YOUR CREDENTIALS MIGHT OTHERWISE BE.**

"After one year, I transferred to the Bronx, and spent two years there. Then I spent four months with the Women's Prison Association.

"Through all this, I was attending New York University night school, where I attained a master's degree in social work. I started work at a mental health clinic in the evenings.

"I worked for a while as an intake coordinator, a position where I had less responsibility, so I could develop my skills as a therapist. But I wasn't happy there, so when the Brooklyn Bridge Project began, I applied for a job there and got it. Our project director was unhappy and left, so I took over that position."

What do you do all day?

"I oversee and do case management for a vocational-educational unit—the Brooklyn Bridge Project. We try to address substance abuse problems that criminal justice offenders face that are not otherwise addressed by the normal criminal justice system. I approve all new applicants to the program; I review the screening packets that our case management unit puts together to use in the screening of applicants. I oversee the coordination of documentation that all clients need to enter the program.

"I put together quarterly and monthly reports, and report on a weekly basis to my boss.

"I'm a hands-on manager. I deal with clients—that's just the way I operate. I deal with difficult clients—mentally ill clients, etc."

Jayme estimates that she has more than a 9-to-5-type job. During the startup phase of this project, Jayme says, people were typically working from 7:30 A.M. to 7 or 8 at night. "We're off to a smoother run now," she says, "and things aren't quite that bad."

Where do you see this job leading you?

"For people who would like to get involved in the criminal justice system," Jayme says, "there are really two sides to get involved in—the human services side and the law enforcement side. I'm not into the law enforcement side.

"A lot of people I work with are recovering addicts and are personally drawn to this type of work. The field is very small—there are basically pretrial release programs and alternative-to-incarceration programs. People tend to jump from program to program.

"People come in with social-work degrees, and go on to get certified in alcohol and substance abuse counseling. It's a young field, so there's room for new workers, but I don't see executives going anywhere for a long time.

"My ultimate goal is to teach criminal justice and do clinical work on the side."

30. AIDS and HIV Services Counselor

description: AIDS (Acquired Immune Deficiency Syndrome) and HIV (the virus that causes AIDS) are a scourge that has left no community untouched. Virtually unheard of in the United States in the early 1980s, today AIDS is something one cannot help but be aware of, perhaps because it often strikes the young and because its effects can be so harrowing. Just because most people know about AIDS, though, doesn't mean they know the facts behind the disease and its transmission.

Fighting against the mountain of misinformation about the disease is one of the less tangible tasks facing the AIDS services counselor. But that is the least of the emotional hurdles with which workers in this field are confronted. Part of their jobs entails telling people whether they have tested positive or negative for the HIV virus, with a positive pronouncement being seen as tantamount to a death sentence.

AIDS services counselors administer the HIV tests and take their clients through pre- and post-test procedures. Should the tests prove positive, they help line their clients up with social service and health programs that aid in the treatment of the disease. They help guide their HIV-positive clients through the maze of social service and health care regulations to try and ensure that they receive the best possible care. They work to educate their clients on how they can best treat the disease and its ramifications.

salary: Salaries for HIV counselors vary from state to state, but in general, HIV testers and counselors will make from the low $20,000s to the low $30,000s. Administrative positions start in the low $20,000s and rise into the $50,000s or $60,000s, depending on the experience the administrator brings to the job, and the responsibilities the job entails.

prospects: Unfortunately, AIDS is not about to go away. The nature of the disease serves to keep many people out of this field, and because incidence of burnout is high (dealing with victims of AIDS is highly traumatic work), opportunities are constantly arising. And, as an AIDS services counselor says, "For administrative positions in some agencies, they want a master's degree, but I run three programs and I don't have a master's."

qualifications: Specific qualifications vary from state to state, but AIDS services counselors usually have to go through some sort of training course. Contact your state's department of health or the human resources department of a nearby hospital for information about training programs and qualifications in your area. Employers typically require program administrators to have some management training or experience, as well as experience in the AIDS field.

characteristics: People interested in pursuing work in the HIV and AIDS services fields should, first and foremost, be committed to doing the work. People faced with HIV and AIDS are faced with death, and some of the trauma of that situation can spill over to the person counseling them. AIDS services counselors should also be caring and patient individuals.

Alexis Dominguez *is the project director for three HIV and AIDS awareness and education programs in New York City.*

How did you get the job?

"Blind fate brought me to the position I now have," Alexis says. "I was working as a clerk in the clinic here at the hospital, and I saw the way other clerks dealt with patients with HIV. I saw how those patients were red-flagged. The clerks had no sensitivity training for how to deal with these patients. And our hospital is at the epicenter of the AIDS epidemic.

"There's a five-day course available through the state that certifies you to be an HIV counselor. You receive training in pre- and post-test counseling. I received all of my HIV-counseling experience through an organization called AIDS-Related Community Services, which was founded as a community service organization for people who were HIV-positive. I worked at the hospital for about a year and a half, then heard about AIDS-Related Community Services and went there to receive my counseling training.

"I came back to the hospital as a pre- and post-test counselor," Alexis says. "I had bilingual skills, and they needed someone who was bilingual.

"I took on the teen and adolescent program. Then the

> THE AIDS TREATMENT DATA NETWORK CAN PROVIDE INFORMATION ON HIV AND AIDS COUNSELING, CASE MANAGEMENT, REFERRAL, AND OUTREACH PROGRAMS. ACT UP, THE AIDS COALITION TO UNLEASH POWER, A NONPROFIT GROUP ORGANIZED TO FORCE PUBLIC AND GOVERNMENTAL FOCUS ON THE ISSUE, CAN ALSO BE A USEFUL SOURCE OF INFORMATION.

director of the program left, and I was the only one here with HIV case-management experience. I took over her job, which included the substance abuse program. I later took on the teen and adolescent program as well."

What do you do all day?

"Each of the programs I oversee has a staff of about five," Alexis says. "For the Project for Better Health, I deal with all the administrative tasks. I verify schedules and oversee staff. I do a lot of general management stuff, and take an active part in budgeting, protocol, and procedural issues. I am a liaison for the Department of Health's testing lab. I track the tests we do, and screen our testers once a month. I oversee and review our charts, making sure that everyone who comes in to get tested for HIV is referred to the right place and is followed up on—I make sure they are referred to the correct clinic; I make sure they make their appointments; I try to make sure that no one falls through the cracks.

"For the substance abuse program, I deal more with the program end of things. I make sure all our clients fit into the program—they all have to be HIV-positive and be substance abusers. I oversee the counseling of these clients. I work with the clinical supervisor of the program, who reviews prospective clients for proper documentation, and makes sure they are getting the proper kind of help. I complete all the reports. I prepare the strategic part of the reports, and work with the fiscal department for the budget of the program.

"For the teen program side of things, I make sure that we are doing sexually transmitted

disease prevention, and hygiene workshops out in the community, where we introduce proper care to these adolescents, talking to them about getting to the doctor, coming back for treatment, and promoting abstinence. We do HIV testing and pregnancy testing, and referral for social work. We do these workshops in the community, and in our facility. I coordinate with different agencies. I'm a liaison with all the different agencies we work with."

Where do you see this job leading you?

"Working in the AIDS services arena, you feed into a huge mass movement," Alexis says. "You have the opportunity to be a pioneer; you can get recognized for what you do. I'm looking at becoming a physician's assistant. I'm only 25, and I have been running three programs for New York City—that is excellent experience."

Work in this field is excellent preparation for any career in the health care or health services field, because all aspects of the health care field are affected by this disease. Work in this field could also be a good experience for people hoping to get into psychology or counseling work.

31. Certified Nursing Assistant

description: Certified nursing assistants can find themselves working in a variety of locales—in hospitals, in nursing homes, or in the homes of outpatients. They are typically workers with some medical training who perform routine tasks of physicians and nurses, and prepare patients for treatment or therapy.

Nursing assistants will help with patients' basic care. They take patients' temperatures; they give patients baths; they make beds for patients; and they move patients from one room to another, or from their own room to an examining or operating room.

If nursing assistants have specialized training, they will perform other duties as well—setting up traction for patients, performing CPR, and other tasks. They typically work 40-hour weeks—or less, since many of these jobs are part-time.

Many hospitals will pay for their nursing assistants' certification and continuing education classes. The opportunity to have your education—or part of it—paid for is one advantage to this job.

salary: Work as a certified nursing assistant is fairly low-paying, with a salary of $12,000 to $18,000 a year. Workers in the home health field typically earn the highest per-hour wages, but they won't receive the benefits that hospital and nursing home workers do.

prospects: Health care is still a growing field, and openings for nursing assistants are expected to remain prevalent. As the elderly population in this country increases, the need for trained workers to take care of those people will likewise increase. The prospects for trained nursing assistants will also improve as pressures to keep down the rising costs of health care remain constant (and since paying assistants is so much cheaper than paying nurses and doctors).

qualifications: People hoping to become certified nursing assistants should possess a high school diploma, and they should be in good physical shape, as the job requires lifting of both patients and equipment. Your prospects will improve if you are CPR-certified—you will be required to get certification as part of your nursing assistant training. Hospitals and home health care agencies will also be looking for someone with previous C.N.A. experience.

characteristics: Certified nursing assistants should be patient—in many cases they will be dealing with people whose physical and perhaps mental capabilities have been temporarily or permanently damaged.

C.N.A.s should also be caring; in many cases, it will be up to them to provide the bedside manner that was formerly the province of the doctor.

Mark Phillips *is a certified nursing assistant at a nursing home in Tennessee.*

How did you get the job?

"I lucked out," Mark says, "when a friend who worked at a nursing home told me that they were taking C.N.A. applications, and were also offering C.N.A. training in exchange for working a predetermined amount of time for them.

"I trained in that nursing home for one year, and then got a position as an orderly in a hospital in Johnson City, Tennessee. I took classes on setting up traction for patients when I was at that hospital.

"Then I moved to Knoxville, and worked at a couple of nursing homes before getting the job at Baptist Hospital here. They needed a C.N.A. or someone with equivalent experience, and they needed someone with orthopedic experience, experience setting up traction."

Currently, Mark works as an orthopedic traction assistant at

> FOR INFORMATION ON HOW TO BECOME A CERTIFIED NURSING ASSISTANT, CONTACT THE AMERICAN HEALTH CARE ASSOCIATION IN WASHINGTON, D.C., AS WELL AS LOCAL HOSPITALS, NURSING HOMES, PSYCHIATRIC FACILITIES, AND STATE BOARDS OF NURSING. FOR GENERAL INFORMATION ON HOME HEALTH AIDE TRAINING, REFERRALS TO STATE AND LOCAL AGENCIES FOR HOME HEALTH OPPORTUNITIES, NATIONAL CERTIFICATION, AND A LIST OF RELEVANT PUBLICATIONS, CONTACT THE FOUNDATION FOR HOSPICE AND HOMECARE/NATIONAL CERTIFICATION PROGRAM. (SEE RESOURCES, PAGES 210-11, FOR BOTH ORGANIZATIONS.)

Baptist Hospital, as a certified nursing assistant at a local nursing home, and, on the weekends, as a home health assistant for a home health care agency.

What do you do all day?

"At the hospital right now, I'm on a schedule where I work eight days out of every two weeks," Mark says. "As an orthopedic traction assistant, I help the couriers take patients to be X-rayed. I call to set up traction and check on all the patients in traction every shift.

"Regular C.N.A. duties include helping the nurses help the patients with daily living. You wash patients. You help patients get up in a wheelchair, things like that.

"At a nursing home, your daily activities include things like helping with meals, helping set people up to eat, keeping patients dry if they're incontinent, giving them baths. Right now, I work at the nursing home one or two days a week at most.

"And I work weekends for a home health care agency, where I see five patients on Saturday and five on Sunday. I typically spend 45 minutes to an hour with each patient. I go into the house and I check the patient for changes in his or her condition—see how well their skin is cared for, looking for tears or bruises on the skin. I take each patient's vital signs. I clean them up, give them a bed bath. Basically, I get them ready for the day. It's the same type of care that you would give in a nursing home setting except that you do one-on-one patient care for a limited time."

Where do you see this job leading you?

"I'm using my C.N.A. experience to go on for my registered nurse's (R.N.) degree," Mark says.

"Nursing assistant certification gives you a base from which to further your education in the nursing field. You can go on from this to become a doctor, an X-ray technician, or a medical technician," he says.

32. Chemical Dependency Counselor

description: People check themselves into a chemical dependency treatment program for a variety of reasons: some come in of their own volition, some are brought in by family members, and some are brought into such programs because of medical problems caused by their dependency. Counselors will typically not have to deal with checking a patient into a facility or program—medical staff most often take care of those duties. Counselors see patients after they have sobered up or gone through the withdrawal process.

Chemical dependency counselors engage their patients in therapy sessions, most often patterned after the 12-step recovery program developed by Alcoholics Anonymous. Group and individual therapy sessions, plus sessions that get family members involved in the healing process, are the most common forms of therapy.

The length of time a patient can stay in a treatment center is most often determined by their insurance company or the type of insurance they have through their employer—10 days is the most common length of stay for a patient at an inpatient facility.

Part of the chemical dependency counselor's job is to prepare patients for the next step in their treatment, whether that be an outpatient program or a stay in a group home.

salary: You can expect to make from $15,000 to $25,000 a year as a chemical dependency counselor. Education and experience will play a factor in salary negotiations, but where you are working will perhaps play a more important role; hospitals are likely to pay the highest salaries, while wages at outpatient and stand-alone facilities will tend to be smaller.

prospects: Prospects for finding a job as a chemical dependency counselor can depend a great deal upon the area of the country in which you are looking. Some areas will be saturated with counselors, while others will lack them. Different states have different qualifications for counseling licenses, so the experience and education you possess can play a big factor in your eligibility for counseling positions in that state.

qualifications: Chemical dependency treatment facilities require that their counselors have gone through some sort of counseling certification program. More and more states are requiring a bachelor's degree in addition to such certification (and in many cases, a bachelor's degree is a prerequisite for getting a counseling certificate). Counselors also need to have at least three years of sobriety behind them.

characteristics: If you're a good listener, you possess one of the characteristics of an effective chemical dependency counselor. You should have empathy for the people you're counseling, but also respect your own boundaries—know when you won't be able to work effectively with a patient—and guard against patients who try to "push your buttons" to get a reaction out of you.

Tracy Schultz *is a chemical dependency counselor at a hospital in a medium-size town in Minnesota.*

How did you get the job?

"I have a family background in chemical dependency," Tracy says, "and have my own chemical dependency issues, so when I went to college, I sought out a B.A. in psychology. I worked with a student group that dealt with chemical dependency."

After earning her bachelor's degree in psychology, Tracy furthered her education through a certificate program in chemical dependency counseling, which entailed 10 courses, 1,000 hours of internship work, and an extra year and a half of schooling.

"I was working with conduct disorder adolescents—emotionally and behaviorally disturbed adolescents, those who were truant, had problems with alcohol, drugs, or theft—while I was getting my certificate," she says.

"I was lucky enough to get a job through my internship," she says. As part of her 1,000 hours of interning, she worked in Fairview Southdale Hospital's inpatient and outpatient programs. That experience—and the relationships she had developed with her peers—helped her to land the chemical dependency counseling job when that position opened.

What do you do all day?

"My workday begins with an assessment of the work I have in front of me," Tracy says. "I will do what paperwork there is that needs to get done. I'll update our patients' charts. I'll do discharge summaries on patients who are about to go off to other facilities. I look at our caseload and get a handle on where I will send people. I'll work on after-care planning. I will see who I have coming in for family therapy. I interview new patients as they come in to our facility and do a brief diagnostic of what is compelling their chemical dependency.

"I have three hours of group therapy sessions a day," Tracy says. "We have an average of 10 adults, males and females, in our facility at any one time. I will meet with them in groups, for an hour at a time. In group therapy sessions, I try to draw their emotions out, and find a link—similarities—to other members of the group. Those similarities can facilitate breaking down a patient's defense mechanisms. I try to help group members see how they are in

denial about their problem, get members to help each other with their problems, and get the group to work on their own problems.

"Lots of times, people want one-on-one sessions, and I try to facilitate that. Oftentimes, I will do a family session.

"Sometimes, I will do an intake assessment. Someone will come in off the street and ask me to assess their dependency. I try to see if they have problems with addiction or dependency or if they don't have a problem at all.

"I spend part of my day dealing with insurance companies," Tracy says, "trying to haggle where we can send a patient for treatment after he or she leaves our facility. I have to fill out

insurance forms as well. The insurance game takes up a good one or two hours a day."

Where do you see this job leading you?

"In the long run, I would like to open a private practice," Tracy says. "But that's several years away. In the short range, I would like to work at a mental health clinic.

"I'm not going to focus on chemical dependency counseling," she says. "I'm lucky, though, in that the chemical dependency counseling certification I have makes me more marketable. I want to use my chemical dependency work as a background, and focus on women's issues and depression.

"Right now, I am working on a master's degree in counseling psychology."

Many chemical dependency counselors follow Tracy's path and go on to further their education. Some will go into private practice after putting in a number of years on the staff of a hospital or outpatient clinic.

> **TRY A TEMPORARY EMPLOYMENT AGENCY. TEMPING CAN BE AN EXCELLENT WAY TO BUILD UP YOUR SKILLS AND EARN SOME MONEY WHILE YOU'RE LOOKING FOR THAT "REAL JOB."**

33. Health Care System Manager

description: Health care system managers work with their system's board of directors, providing them with operational reports, recommending policy changes, and generally serving as their communications channel by telling them what's going on within the organization. Managers also work with their system's medical staff, acting as a liaison among those staff members, other system employees, and patients. They have a fiscal role, reviewing capital expenditures, helping to formulate budgets, and involving themselves in fund-raising efforts. Managers have a human resource role as well, doing some hiring and approving the hiring decisions of administrators under their supervision. They make provisions for staff members' managerial and professional development. Managers also have a role in the community; they may be expected to involve themselves in community organizations, or to represent their employer through public speaking engagements.

Health care system managers make sure that all aspects of their operation comply with state and federal standards. Part of their role will involve monitoring evolving legislation to see what regulations could affect their operation in the future.

salary: Health care system managers can expect to make from $40,000 to more than $175,000 per year, depending on experience, education, and the size of the system they work for. Salary levels will vary widely based on geography as well.

prospects: Prospects are very good for finding work at all levels of the health care field. However, the trend of health care organizations merging and affiliating is expected to continue; this trend will eliminate the need for many positions, especially at the administrative and middle-management levels. Despite this trend, the Department of Labor estimates that through the year 2005 openings in this field will grow faster than average.

qualifications: Health system managers generally have previous administrative experience as well as experience working in the health field—nursing experience or work in the home health or hospice industry. A degree in business or health care administration is usually required.

characteristics: As with any administrative position, "people" skills are essential for this job. Organizational ability and the skill for juggling many tasks will come in handy. An effective manager will have an even-tempered personality, especially when people he or she must deal with are not so even-tempered.

Karen Jeselun *is president and chief executive officer of a convalescent center in Wisconsin.*

- -

How did you get the job?

"I earned a bachelor of science in nursing," Karen says. "My first job was as a staff nurse in Medford, Wisconsin. My husband was in the forest service, and we ended up moving to Salem, Mississippi, to a rural community on the edge of the Ozarks. Three R.N.s were trying to run the hospital there. I knocked on the door, and have been in public health nursing ever since.

"I started out at this organization—Dr. Kate Newcomb Health Care—when I took the position of home health manager.

"Two years later, I was promoted to administrator, which was basically the same job with a new title. The position did entail some additional responsibilities, more budgeting responsibilities.

"My newest position—president and CEO—came to be in July of this year. Now, I'm not only responsible for our home care and hospice operations, but also our nursing home, community-based residential facility,

---

THE AMERICAN ALMANAC OF JOBS AND SALARIES CAN HELP CLUE YOU IN ON THE PROSPECTS OF FINDING WORK IN A NUMBER OF DIFFERENT FIELDS. THE BOOK PROVIDES A LISTING OF JOBS AND THEIR AVERAGE SALARIES, AND INDICATES SOURCES OF FINDING WORK FOR EMPLOYEES IN THE PUBLIC SECTOR, THE MEDIA, SCIENCE, TECHNOLOGY, HEALTH CARE, AND A NUMBER OF OTHER FIELDS. THOUGH NOT PARTICULARLY FOCUSED ON CAREERS THAT HAVE A SOCIAL IMPACT, IT DOES PROVIDE A NICE LOOK AT THE OVERALL EMPLOYMENT PICTURE.

- -

---

low-income housing unit, and a durable medical equipment company."

What do you do all day?

"My management style is one of employee contact," Karen says, "and I believe that my job goes better if my leadership team is doing well. So I meet with my leadership staff every week, and help with problem-solving, or provide guidance, or listen.

"Much of my time is spent in meetings. I spend a lot of time working within the system and working with the other executive staff members. We are also in the midst of a big strategic planning session right now.

I am trying to involve line staff and everyone else in that process.

"We've recently done two employee surveys. Come January, I will do a lot of time doing staff meetings, giving the results to our staff, and telling them what we plan to do as a result of those surveys.

"Another part of my job is dealing with complaints. Thankfully, that doesn't happen all that often, and my leadership staff handles many of those complaints.

"We also have taken on a humongous project, training all 900-plus people on our staff in 'total quality management.' I'm part of the team we put together to plan that initiative. Here at Dr. Kate, we have been using those principles for the past three years, but our parent corporation has not. So we have done a couple retreats to introduce this concept to other managers, and will begin implementing it shortly. It's a whole culture shift, a whole new way of thinking about your work, and I will be working to implement that."

Where do you see this job leading you?

"With my work experience," Karen says, "I could step from here to a larger health care system.

"My boss went to a hospital system, and moved up a notch to do that. She had a master's degree in health care administration; she had the educational training to make that move."

34. Social Services Director

FOR A HEALTH CARE AGENCY

description: Social services directors for health services agencies are liaisons with the clients those agencies serve; another term for social services director could be "resident advocate." Social services directors visit people in the agency's nursing homes and hospitals, and communicate with homebound or home-based patients. They apprise patients and residents at agency facilities of their rights. They take part in, or at least supervise, patient and resident intake and discharge procedures. They help set up care plans for patients and residents who are being discharged or are being switched to home-based status.

They also deal with the families of patients and residents, attempting to answer concerns that those people have, and explain to them the role and responsibility of the agency in their family member's care.

Paperwork consumes a good portion of a social services director's time, as Medicare and Medicaid paperwork, insurance forms, and year-end surveys need to be filled out. Supervisors have to make sure that patients' medical charts are being filled out correctly.

They will meet with other managers to determine the future direction of the agency, and to work at solving interdepartmental problems.

salary: Salaries for people working in the social services department of a health care agency can start at around $8 an hour (equivalent to $16,640 a year). Workers with master's degrees or equivalent experience can expect to earn higher salaries, from around $11 an hour ($22,880 a year) to $14 an hour ($29,120 per year).

prospects: Despite talk of Medicare cutbacks (or maybe in part because of those cutbacks), the health care field is a growing one. As the population ages, there will be an increasing need for nursing homes and similar facilities to care for that population, and an increase in the variety of groups serving that population's medical needs. Community-based residential facilities and assisted-living facilities are the wave of the future, while the more expensive nursing homes will be places of last resort. All of these facilities will have social services departments.

qualifications: Social services director positions almost always require a bachelor's degree in social work, social services, or a related field; many of them require a master's degree as well, though that qualification might be waived in light of an applicant's work experiences. Experience in hospital or nursing home social work is another likely requirement, as is prior supervisory experience.

characteristics: Social service providers should be good listeners; they should be able to recognize people's wants and needs, even if the people they are talking to are unable or unwilling to articulate them. They have to be good speakers as well, as their persuasive abilities—to present alternatives and their consequences without appearing judgmental, for instance—are called into play on a regular basis. They deal with confidentiality issues on a regular basis.

Linda Rinne *is the director of social services at a medium-size organization in Wisconsin.*

How did you get the job?

"I graduated from NMU in Marquette, Michigan, with a bachelor of science degree in social service," Linda says. "My first job was at St. John's Hospital in Springfield, Illinois, where I worked for one year, primarily in the area of geriatrics.

"Upon my husband's graduation, we moved to Phillips, Wisconsin. I was offered a job at Taylor County Memorial Hospital in Medford, Wisconsin. I worked there for only eight months. My responsibilities included doing discharge

> A RECOGNITION OF THE IMPORTANCE OF CONFIDENTIALITY IS A REQUESITE CHARACTERISTIC OF SOCIAL SERVICE PROVIDERS.

work in the hospital and being the social worker for the long-term care unit in the hospital, as well as the social worker for the nursing home.

"After staying out of the workforce for about one year, I was given the opportunity to work at Pleasant View Nursing Home in Phillips, where I stayed for three years working two to three mornings a week.

"With the advent of our children going to college, it was once again time to think about re-entering the workforce. In 1991, I was offered an opportunity to go back into my field. I was hired as a second social worker at Parkside Care Center in Little Chute, Wisconsin.

"After having worked in the social service field for quite a few years, it seemed logical to take the next step professionally. I was hired as the social services director at Good Shepherd Home in Seymour, Wisconsin."

What do you do all day?

"My typical week involves numerous activities," Linda says. "My work starts with the assessment process, which is conducted by the director of nursing and myself. We complete this process for everyone who is admitted to our facility to determine whether or not we can meet their needs, and whether or not they are appropriate for our facility. I am responsible for completing admission paperwork with either the resident or family member. Another responsibility I have is to talk to patients about who comes to our rehabilitation center for outpatient therapy.

"Social workers in nursing homes participate with the multidisciplinary team in formulating a plan of care for each resident. The resident and family are encouraged to be actively involved in formulating their plan of care. We do histories for each resident, which provide a

wealth of information about each person's past and give the staff insight into who this person is and was. Each person is evaluated as to their discharge potential."

Where do you see this job leading you?

"Nursing homes and other health care facilities are great places to get experience for those contemplating or starting a career in the health field."

Social services directors can make a switch to the administrative side of their agencies or similar agencies with additional education or training, or can take their experience into other social service agencies.

35. Charter School Manager/Teacher

description: One method of education reform gaining support and attention in many quarters is the movement to "privatize the public schools" or develop charter schools. A school board contracts out the management of a school or schools in their district to a private company. The company is responsible for running the school, including the hiring and training of teachers, and overseeing employees and students.

Most of the companies involved in managing charter schools are new or startup companies, because the charter school movement is a relatively young one. Some work involved in charter school management might actually include forming the managing company.

Part of the work is political as well, working with school boards, reporters, lawyers, politicians, and other workers in the public policy arena, making sure all of the rules and regulations are followed and that all of the parties involved are satisfied with the arrangement, and mobilizing public opinion in support of the idea of charter school management.

A teacher's job in such a situation is likely to be similar to that of a public school educator. While the curriculum will likely be dictated by a state board of education or some similar entity, there will be differences in how the school day is organized, the manner in which teaching is done, and the way in which teachers are evaluated.

salary: Charter school teachers should expect to make salaries equivalent to those of public school teachers, with starting salaries in the $20,000 to $26,000 range. Raises will likely be tied to performance in charter schools, more so than in regular public schools.

Administrative salaries vary widely, depending on the nature of the relationship formed between the school's governing body and its management team. Administrators can expect to make $40,000 to $60,000 per year.

prospects: Most of the charter schools being formed are being created by parents and groups of teachers; some of them will be created by school boards. All of them will require faculty to fill new positions in the school. For applicants with the proper experience and an interest in exploring this form of education, jobs should be plentiful.

qualifications: Charter school teachers should be certified teachers and should have experience in subject areas in which the school has openings. Administrative staff should possess management and business experience, as well as some experience in education.

characteristics: Bill DeLoache, who helped found Alternative Public Schools, Inc., and has helped establish a charter school in Pennsylvania, says, "In my case, we needed to have two things. One, we had to have resolve to see what we were doing to its conclusion, because the obstacles we faced were horrendous. There were political difficulties in getting this done in the face of opposition from the teachers union. We failed to get a contract twice. Two, it was important to be even-tempered. We were placed in many situations where the tendency might be to get very angry, and we constantly had to remind ourselves not to get too excitable."

Prospective teachers should be open to new ways of doing things, and should be extremely committed to helping their students learn.

Bill DeLoache *is a partner in a private Tennessee firm that helps establish charter schools.*

How did you get the job?

Bill is a graduate of Nashville's Vanderbilt University and of the University of Chicago Business School. He started an investment and venture capital business, where he managed stocks and bonds.

"When my child started school," he says, "I developed an interest in education. I and others tried to get legislation passed in Tennessee that would provide for charter schools, that would allow for a contractual relationship between a for-profit company and some authority—the local school board or some other authority—to provide children in the district with an education.

"This company—Alternative Public Schools, Inc.—was formed as a result of the venture to get that type of legislation passed in Tennessee.

"A school board in Wilkinsburg, a suburb of Pittsburgh, decided to pursue contract management of one of their schools. It is a low-income part of town, with 80 percent of the students, approximately 400 kindergarten through sixth-grade students, on free or reduced lunch. Test scores were abysmal. The culture of the school was not what it needed to be. The school board decided to do something radical.

"Ours was one of five proposals for charter management that was considered.

"In our model, we go into a school and use our own employees. We think education is a model that hinges on its employees. Our model is to recruit energetic people, give them ownership in the company, and then provide them with autonomy in doing their job."

What do you do all day?

"During a typical week, I will spend one or two days at the school, handling some of the administrative tasks there, dealing with personnel matters, meeting with school board members, meeting with reporters there. And I spend some time here in Nashville, dealing with mundane administrative tasks, making sure the payroll is correct, budgeting. I talk to public policy people, I talk to students doing research on charter schools. I talk to school board members and other officials considering doing this in other places."

Where do you see this job leading you?

"I would like to see this corporation grow steadily," Bill says. "I would like to see us get additional contracts based on the job that we've done."

Charter school teachers could take their experience into other, more traditional methods of schooling. Or they could move on to other jobs in the field of child development. Administrators could parlay this experience into management or administrative positions in other types of businesses.

TO FIND OUT MORE ABOUT CHARTER SCHOOLS OR COMMUNITY-BASED SCHOOLING, GET IN TOUCH WITH SUCH ORGANIZATIONS AS THE ANNENBERG INSTITUTE FOR SCHOOL REFORM AT BROWN UNIVERSITY, THE ASSOCIATION FOR COMMUNITY-BASED EDUCATION IN WASHINGTON, D.C., THE NATIONAL ALLIANCE FOR RESTRUCTURING EDUCATION IN WASHINGTON, D.C., OR THE CENTER FOR EDUCATIONAL RENEWAL AT THE UNIVERSITY OF WASHINGTON IN SEATTLE. YOU CAN ALSO PERUSE EDUCATION WEEK, WHICH OCCASIONALLY FEATURES ARTICLES ON COMMUNITY-BASED AND CHARTER SCHOOL EDUCATION.

---

36. Educational Researcher

description: As an educational researcher, your job will really be twofold: First, you will work to conduct research and synthesize information that will help various players in the American educational system make their educational efforts more effective; second, you will work to implement the programs created as a result of your research.

Research efforts include visiting various schools and talking to all the players involved; observing what goes on in the classroom and administrative offices, before, during, and after school; poring over academic research to see what information can be drawn from those documents; and maintaining contacts with others in the educational research and developmental field.

The implementation part of the job entails visiting schools, presenting the materials that have been developed, and training others in how to use (and train still others in the use of) those materials and programs that have been developed. Work will range from hands-on training, to serving as a support person when programs go astray or aren't having the intended results.

Part of the job might also entail securing funding for the projects being worked on, so grant-writing skills may definitely come into play.

salary: Salary level will vary greatly, depending on what agency or entity employs you, and the sources of funding for that agency. Education and experience level will also play a role in the salary you can expect. Educational researchers, though, earn between $25,000 and $45,000 per year.

prospects: Both federal and state-level governmental entities seem intent on budgetary belt-tightening, at least in the short term, and with fewer funds available for educational efforts of all types, educational researchers will face competition. It remains to be seen whether private funding sources will take up the slack of public institutions. On the other hand, there seems to be growing awareness that our educational system is due for a change, which could result in improved educational research opportunities.

qualifications: Prospective educational researchers should, first and foremost, be familiar with teaching and the issues involved in contemporary education, whether this be through hands-on teaching experience or by dealing with these issues in an academic context.

Research and training experience will also be very highly regarded. Prospects with an advanced degree stand the best chances of finding work; you can expect a master's degree to be a prerequisite for most educational research positions.

characteristics: Educational researchers should be committed to education, and addicted to learning.

Researchers should be good synthesizers of information, with a facility for recognizing the commonalities between disparate programs and situations. They should be creative, able to come up with new programs and methodologies. And they should be flexible, able to roll with changing program prerogatives brought on both by changing governmental and educational emphasis, and by funding changes.

K. Victoria Boyd *is the senior training and technical assistance associate for an educational development laboratory in the Southwest.*

How did you get the job?

"I left teaching after 12 years, and went to a an Educational Service Center. I did training there, developing math strategies and working with schools who were having problems getting their achievement scores up—I worked with targeted schools. The center I worked in worked with small schools in the region."

From there she became involved with the Southwest Educational Development Laboratory (SEDL), a nonprofit corporation committed to educational research and development work.

"We're a link between educational research and practice," Victoria says. "We take research and turn it into products that educators can use."

What do you do all day?

"I am very interested in technology and how you can use technology to improve teaching," Victoria says. "The Department of Education funded a teacher-networking program we call Arkansas Adventures in Networking.

"Seven rural schools are involved in the Ventures in Education project, funded by the National Science Foundation. That is an effort to change the method of teaching from having a teacher stand up in front of the class and talk to them, to a problem-resolving method of teaching.

"At Arkansas Adventures in Networking, we try to get all teachers connected to the Net, get them using e-mail to talk to one another.

"We help teachers use the Net to access the resources they need for problem-based learning—the Library of Con-

> WHEN YOU'RE TALKING WITH A PROSPECTIVE CONTACT, SOMEONE WHO MIGHT BE ABLE TO HELP YOU IN YOUR JOB SEARCH, REMEMBER TO LISTEN TO THE PERSON YOU'RE TALKING TO AND TO ASK THE FIVE "W" QUESTIONS— WHO, WHAT, WHEN, WHERE, AND WHY.

gress, things like that. We get teachers to talk to each other, to see what other teachers are doing.

"I write reports and respond to our funders. Every three months I archive all the e-mail we receive, and analyze the topics that were discussed. I take phone calls, responding to people needing information or technical assistance with their programs. I'm designing an on-line training program. I work on planning and delivering that training. I monitor the listserv that the teachers belong to. I help teachers overcome their technophobia."

Victoria says she typically puts in 40 to 60 hours a week.

Where do you see this job leading you?

"I have a couple of years left on this project. My goal is to continue to help teachers learn how to use technology. I could do that at a university, a corporation, or I could stay here if SEDL continues to remain viable."

37. Elementary School Teacher

description: In general, the role of the teacher is to help children learn, to help them prepare themselves for what lies ahead of them.

A teacher's time is primarily spent guiding his or her class through the day's activities and lessons, helping students when necessary, and preparing for the next day's class. Teaching is very planning-intensive; you will plan activities for the class, gather materials to carry out those plans, lecture before the class, work with them on certain subjects, and grade papers and tests.

Other duties will come under the banners of "dealing with the administration" and "dealing with the parents." Both groups will have expectations of you as a teacher, and some of those expectations might conflict with how you feel you can best teach your class. You will engage in parent-teacher conferences. You might be called on to attend board meetings, prepare reports for the principal or school board, or otherwise work with the administration.

The job will keep you busy eight to nine hours a day; even if school lets out at 2:30 P.M., you will have enough to keep you busy until at least 5:00 in the evening. The nice thing about a teaching job is the vacation time—even if you teach in a year-round school, you will still have approximately three months off every year. On the downside, pay for public school teachers is, as always, despicably low. For private school teachers, the pay can be even worse.

salary: The most recent average salary for elementary school teachers was $34,800, according to the National Education Association. Starting salaries were around $21,500.

prospects: Job growth is expected for all levels of teachers through 2005, especially for those teaching special education. Specific prospects will depend on population growth in your area, the number of teachers who reach retirement age, and taxpayer pressures to spend more or cut-back on educational concerns.

qualifications: The primary qualification for a public school teaching job is a teaching certificate. The specific qualifications for earning such a certificate will vary from state to state, but they will include a bachelor's degree in education or some related field, as well as teacher training courses and substitute teaching experience. Most states require prospective teachers to pass a competency test before they are allowed to teach in the classroom. Requirements for substitute teachers are less strict. Some states also feature alternative certification programs for those embarking upon teaching as a secondary career or who cannot attend the regular certification classes.

characteristics: Teachers tend to take their work home with them. If they are not grading tests or working on lesson plans, they are worrying about their students' problems or are trying to figure out a way to reach that particularly unresponsive student. Prospective teachers should be prepared to carry that emotional burden.

Janet Krebs *is a third-grade teacher at an elementary school in California.*

How did you get the job?

Janet earned a bachelor's degree in human development. She went on to earn a master's in clinical psychology, with secondary degrees in career counseling and organizational development.

She took a job with the personnel department of the city of Pittsburgh. "I worked in that department's human resources department as a job counselor," she says, "working with the unemployed, helping them gain the skills they needed to transition themselves back into the world of work. I worked with military wives. I worked with corporate executives, trying to help them market themselves."

After five years working with the city of Pittsburgh, she went back to school to get her teaching credentials. When she was done, she took a job with the Antioch School District, teaching third grade.

What do you do all day?

"The role of teacher is very different today than what it was when I was in school," Janet says. "You no longer stand in front of the room and talk to the kids. Now teachers are more facilitators of knowledge. But you're not just that, you're also a social worker, a psychologist, an administrator, lead hugger, a peacemaker with parents, and a parole officer.

"In elementary school, we have a self-contained class—the kids only leave my classroom for classes like physical education. In this district, it's not until the sixth grade that kids start moving from teacher to teacher for different classes.

"We concentrate on thematic instruction—integrating all the different things that we are teaching at any one time. For instance, when I was student-teaching, the children grew sunflowers. But they didn't just grow sunflowers. They measured the flowers; they drew sunflowers; they wrote about sunflowers. That's not the way we used to teach.

"I went into this thinking, 'They'll never want me,' but I have found that my counseling degree has helped me a great deal. It helps me deal with parents—parent-teacher conferences are not an issue at all. It's important to learn to work with parents," Janet says. "In teaching, in a sense, you are your own boss. You have guidelines and principals, but you can always close the door to your classroom and do your own thing. You don't have a boss in that respect, but you do have 30 parents, which can be worse than a boss. If the parents are in your corner, though, you've got it made.

"Posturing and dealing with the administration—that's something you evolve into as you progress in your job. That's something that teachers come in and learn the hard way—how to politic.

"One of the favorite pastimes of teachers is labeling—they get into 'I had so-and-so last year and …' I'm not going to put my kids in compartments. I'm not going to have any preconceived expectations for them.

> SMILE. IT'S A SIMPLE THING, BUT ONE THAT PEOPLE OFTEN FORGET. WHEN YOU SMILE, YOU GIVE YOURSELF A POSTURE OF SELF-CONFIDENCE.

What I am going to have is high expectations."

Where do you see this job leading you?

Janet has just recently earned her teaching certificate, and she says it's too soon for her to tell what she will do next. "I love what I'm doing, and love the kids, and I do know that I will be in education, in one way, shape, or form, until I retire. I can see myself burning out on teaching 32 kids a year after about 10 years, but I can see myself writing curriculum for a school district when I'm 70. Or I could use my public speaking skills to give lectures on education or do curriculum trainings.

"Maybe I'll go on to administrative work at a school site or at the district level. Many teachers do go into administration. Many teachers will also tell you that that is selling out, but I think it's a logical progression. When you start in a classroom and work your way up, it is usually into some form of administration.

"You could also go into curriculum management, where you review pilot math, science, or other programs."

38. Instructor

IN ENGLISH AS A SECOND LANGUAGE

description: English as a Second Language (ESL) instruction will be different from typical classroom instruction; instead of attempting to help the students achieve mastery over a certain subject or helping them prepare for an upcoming exam, the ESL instructor's main emphasis will be on enabling the students to speak and use English.

ESL teachers act things out for their students and get their students to do the same as a way to increase their retention of words and concepts. Teachers set up scenarios where students have to use English. There will be a lot of group work involved.

At higher levels, students write book reports and essays, and engage in activities that more closely approximate other class environments.

ESL instructors work with other teachers in their schools to integrate lesson plans and activities with what is being taught in other classes, and to tie in vocabulary with what students are studying in their other classes.

salary: ESL teachers make the equivalent of what other teachers with their experience and credentials are making in the same school district, though ESL instructors may receive a bonus of some sort if they are fluent in a foreign language. Novice teachers can expect to start at between $20,000 and $30,000 annually, depending on where they are teaching and the resources from which their school district has to draw. The best salaries for teachers, according to *Jobs '95,* are in Alaska, New York, and Connecticut.

prospects: Employment prospects look to improve over the long term. Budget shortfalls and cutbacks may temporarily curtail the number of teaching openings, but more children entering the educational system translates into a need for more teachers. Most positions will be filled just prior to the beginning of the school year, but teachers leave their positions at all times, so openings can occur throughout the year. Bilingual candidates will be more attractive to many school districts than those who speak English only; but being bilingual isn't necessarily a prerequisite for finding ESL work.

qualifications: Qualifications for attaining a teaching certificate or some other form of teaching credentials vary from state to state, and lack of a certificate from a certain state (or of one that is accepted in a certain state) may bar you from entering the teaching profession in that state. Qualifications for a substitute teaching position are typically less stringent than those for a certified teacher, and one option—especially if there is a specific area of the country you wish to live in—is to substitute-teach while you pursue your certification. That way, by the time you are certified, you will have made contacts in the district and will, if you have done a good job, have references to call on and professional contacts who might advise you of openings.

characteristics: ESL teachers need to be flexible and open-minded with students from other cultures. Teachers should be excited about getting familiar with the community in which they're teaching.

Dave Carr *is an English as a Second Language teacher at a school in south-central Los Angeles.*

How did you get the job?

Dave earned an undergraduate degree in literature, but he says, "I always knew I wanted to teach, and I knew I wanted to teach in the inner city.

"I was accepted into Teach for America and underwent six weeks of intensive training. I did my student training with sixth graders.

"My first interview was with Compton [Unified School District], and I came here to teach English as a Second Language at the high school level.

"This is my third year here. I have what are called emergency credentials—that's the level of certification that Teach for America gets for you [because TFA volunteers are sent to school districts that have problems, for one reason or another, hiring teachers with standard credentials]. TFA is a two-year commitment, and once you're out, you have to find a job, take classes, do what it takes to get 'clear credentials.' Los Angeles is cracking down, and wants all its teachers to have clear credentials.

"I also went back this summer to help train new corps members."

What do you do all day?

"The Compton Unified School District follows a block schedule, where I will have kids for two hours a day, twice a week, and then see every class for 50 minutes on Monday," Dave says.

"Once the kids get into the classroom, they all read silently for 20 minutes," Dave says. "I stress reading in my classes. Then we'll go into our daily routines. I'll read a book to them, and act stuff out as I read. They read while I act out. Then they will act out while I read. Then we'll pair off in groups of two, and they'll read to each other.

"You have to use something to hook them in to what we're doing. For instance, I was getting ready to read a story about graduation. It was about a kid who didn't want to wear these shoes to his graduation. So I had the kids talk about words that have to do with graduation, words that have to do with shoes. We talked about what they wanted for graduation. Then we hit the vocabulary. Then we hit the story. We read the story again. I asked them questions about the story. We drew pictures and talked about those pictures.

"The job itself goes from 8:10 A.M. to 3 P.M. And after that, at least two or three hours at home, grading or lesson planning. The classes require a lot of preparation—one to one and a half hours of work for every class. You phone someone's home. You get materials. You line up guest teachers. And on the weekends, you go to fairs and festivals to meet people in the community and look for materials that might prove useful in the classroom."

Where do you see this job leading you?

"A lot of people go on to grad school after their time with Teach for America," Dave says.

"As for me, right now I am taking the three courses I need to get my clear credentials in California. I have my preliminary credentials right now. Once I have my clear credentials, I think I might want to go on to get a master's in education. Then I would like to come back and teach in the Los Angeles inner city, still at the high school level, still in ESL, though with maybe one English course besides."

39. Public School Guidance Counselor

description: Public school guidance counselors work in a single school, in a number of schools in a single school district, or, in the case of very small or rural districts, in schools in a number of different districts.

On the elementary level, a guidance counselor job will be to support students so that they are academically successful. Elementary school counselors may deal with a child's separation anxiety or with children who develop a school phobia. They might have to test students for learning disabilities, or deal with problems stemming from divorce, alcoholism, or other problems in the family. Sibling and classmate rivalry are other problems that might arise. Helping children cope with adversity is also a big part of the guidance counselor's job.

At the junior high level, most children are in transition from a small school to a larger one. They begin to have to make elective choices and vocational-technical choices as well. Part of the counselor's job is to help students with those choices.

High school-level counselors focus much more on helping students with the post-high school transition.

salary: Salaries for public school guidance counselors, as for most teachers and administrators, is based on years of experience. Counselors can start at around $24,000 a year and might make $45,000 on the high end. Salary levels may vary depending on school district.

prospects: Prospects for work as a guidance counselor will depend largely on where you live. Since counseling is one way of advancement above the teacher level in public schools (going into administration is another way of advancement), these jobs can be highly coveted. Still, if you're in the right place at the right time, and you have the necessary qualifications, you should be able to find work.

qualifications: In most states, you will need a master's degree before you can apply for a school guidance counselor position. Some states also require that a guidance counselor applicant also have some classroom teaching experience. In order to receive state certification as a guidance counselor, you will probably have to spend a pre-specified number of hours interning with, and working under, a certified counselor. Primary- and secondary-level certification will generally consist of two different programs.

characteristics: Guidance counselors should be self-motivated. They must be able to manage their time in order to complete daily tasks. A guidance counselor should be able to keep the confidentiality of a student. Good communication skills are another important asset for a guidance counselor. Guidance counselors must also be able to handle the frustration that they won't be able to "reach" every student they work with, nor "fix" the home situation in which some children live.

Brenda Schoonover *is a guidance counselor for an elementary school in Pennsylvania.*

How did you get the job?

Brenda received a bachelor's degree in secondary math education, and then taught in a local junior high school for 10 years.

"After you've reached a certain level as a teacher, in order to achieve any advancement, you have to go into guidance or administration. I knew I didn't want to be an administrator so I went on to get a master's degree in guidance and counseling.

"I spent eight years as a high school counselor, then I moved on to this job. I've been a counselor at the elementary level for five years."

What do you do all day?

"My district has six elementary schools," Brenda says, "and four of them have full-time counselors. The other two schools share one counselor. The size of the schools varies from 300 to 500 kids. There are about 330 kids in my school in kindergarten through sixth grade.

"My district is involved in a developmental guidance curriculum, which has a preventative focus more than being reactive. It's a model that has been gaining popularity in the past 10 or 15 years. Our district adopted this model about five years ago. Under the developmental guidance curriculum model, instead of reacting to each crisis as it comes along, we try to provide all the students with the skills to handle life experiences. We try to teach the kids coping skills, stress management, peer relations, and decision-making [processes].

"We tailor what we do to what the kids and their teachers need. At the elementary level, there's a lot of consulting with teachers and parents, and I have lots of interaction with the principal.

"I'll monitor classes to see if students' grades are slipping, and if they are, I'll try and work with those students to get them back on track. If there is a discipline problem, I try to talk to the disruptive student to see if there are any unresolved problems. I try to be in each classroom at least once a month.

"At the beginning of the year, I work to wean kids away from their parents. And throughout the year, various kids will develop school phobia, and we'll try to deal with that.

"Some counselors hold group sessions for, say, children who come from divorced

> SUBSTITUTE TEACHING CAN BE A GREAT WAY TO GET YOUR FOOT IN THE DOOR OF A SCHOOL DISTRICT YOU ARE INTERESTED IN WORKING IN FULL-TIME (OR EVEN IN A SCHOOL DISTRICT YOU THINK YOU MIGHT BE INTERESTED IN TEACHING IN FULL-TIME).

homes," Brenda says. "I haven't done one of those here. In my school, marriage is not a prerequisite for partners. Sometimes we'll have small groups of students working on peer relationships, where we'll partner kids without friends with those who have good peer relationships. We may do sessions with kids who come from alcoholic homes, or work with kids on anger management. Those group sessions can last from about six to 12 weeks.

"Throughout the year, we'll deal with many different situations, the death of a relative, parents separating, families moving, a new kid coming to school, boyfriend/girlfriend things. In the five years I have been here, I've had three suicidal students. When that happened, we contacted the parents and took the students to a mental health facility. At the end of the school year, we do a lot of wrap-up activities. We have a large graduation ceremony for our sixth-graders, and I work on the planning of that celebration."

Where do you see this job leading you?

"I've just finished getting my certification to be an elementary principal," Brenda says. "I think a counselor can impact more students, but an administrator is more of a change agent; the administrator sets the tone of the building.

"Now that I've got my principal degree, I'm not sure I want to go on to administrative-level work.

"Most counselors do stay on until they retire," Brenda says. "Some guidance counselors go back to being classroom teachers, and when they do go back, they go back with a new perspective. Some counselors do go on and get administrative degrees."

40. Remedial Education Teacher

description: As a remedial education teacher, you will be working with children who have not been successful in traditional classroom education. These are students who have problems—for one reason or another—with traditional subjects like reading, math, or science. While remedial education teachers work to get those students up to speed on those subjects, they also find themselves working on building their students' self-esteem, and working on a host of other issues—the root causes of their students' educational dysfunction.

In some cases, you might have to give a student the support his or her family does not give. You'll have to work to impress the value of education on your students, and will face frustrations in having to deal with the issues spilling over from the students' home lives, without being able to do anything to change what is causing those issues.

Your day will probably be structured differently from that of teachers in traditional classrooms. Your class size will likely be smaller, but you might be seeing a larger number of students from a wider age and grade range.

Your curriculum will be dictated by what other teachers are doing, and by the educational problems of your students.

salary: The average salary for elementary and secondary-level remedial education teachers is around $34,500 a year. Beginning teacher salaries start at around $22,000. Experience and, more importantly, location will play a large role in determining the salary level you can command.

prospects: Employment opportunities for teachers—especially those who can adapt to and embrace the possible coming changes in our educational system—are expected to increase faster than the rate of growth for most other jobs. Prospects will vary depending on location, level of training, and educational specialty, but most school districts employ some remedial education teachers.

qualifications: Remedial education teachers will almost certainly be required to possess remedial education certification, as well as a teaching certificate. Districts might also look for someone who has an affinity for working with troubled or disadvantaged students.

characteristics: Remedial education teachers should be people who can work with children, not talk at them; people who can see beyond all the factors inhibiting a student from achieving academic success and who can recognize the real person behind all those barriers; people who can reach out and embrace children and make education relevant to them. Remedial education teachers might also be on the forefront of change in this country's educational system, and so must be prepared for possible changes in their programs and responsibilities with each new school year.

Jean Morris *is a remedial reading program teacher for a school district in Colorado.*

How did you get the job?

"At first, I wanted to work on my language skills and become an interpreter for the United Nations. In college I was a Spanish major, and minored in German and philosophy. I became certified in foreign language education. I student-taught Spanish in a small town in Ohio. I was asking myself, 'How can I unite my dreams and my goals?' and, almost by default, I ended up in education.

"I went to the local district—I had my certification—and I applied for work there. The only way I would have been able to teach a foreign language was on a part-time basis, but I didn't want a part-time job. They offered me a job teaching second grade in a rural school in the district. I spent two years at that school."

Later, Jean became a reading specialist at a vocational high school with the understanding that she "would go back to school and get a reading specialist degree and training in teaching students to read and in working with students who had problems reading," she says.

"I was with that district for five years. Then my family moved to Colorado, and I have been a Chapter One teacher on and off ever since."

What do you do all day?

"Every year, it seems that what I do changes. I've been teaching in a Chapter One reading program, a remedial reading program, which, in our district, gets a lot of kids graduating from an English as a Second Language program. Here in the district, our Chapter One program has been expanded to encompass kids not being successful in the standard program. Almost one-third of our kids are in alternative programs by the time they hit middle school.

> **PASSION SELLS, AND IF YOU CAN CHANNEL YOUR PASSION INTO A POSSIBLE CAREER PATH, YOU MAY FIND THAT VERY PASSION ALONE OPENING DOORS FOR YOU.**

"Our district's junior high has about 1,050 students in eighth and ninth grade. In March of last year, we had a school board meeting because it looked like about 100 kids weren't going to be going on to the ninth grade the next year. We had to figure out what to do about this situation. A police officer came up with a program for this next year that we're calling the 'Futures' program for repeating eighth-graders.

"This program will be more than simply teaching students what they didn't pass the first time. We'll have a community service component. We'll work on self-esteem, goal-setting, drug and alcohol education, and finances. We'll work on their reading, but we will also pre-teach science and technology so that when these kids go into their regular classes they will have an idea of what they're talking about.

"We'll have two teachers, two aides from the local university, and counselors working with us on this project.

"We'll spend the first half-hour of the day doing educational activities interwoven with what the kids are doing in their regular classes. We'll do a lot of small-group activities. And we'll

spend one or two days a week out of the building, doing field trips or performing community service. We plan to work with the elderly, to take our kids over to the elementary school, to teach kids over their computers and reading. We'll all work to landscape this new building.

"We also plan a lot of parental components in this program. The kids are going to help plan a back-to-school barbecue for the parents. As much as possible, we want to relate what is going on inside the classroom to out-of-class experiences, to relate what we're doing to real life.

"Aside from this work, I am teaching one class a day at an alternative high school, and working at an alternative middle school."

Where do you see this job leading you?

"I could move on to the administration or college-teaching level," Jean says. "I would make more money at those levels. But in education, moving up means moving away from the kids. A great administrator and a great teacher are two different things. There really is no step up from where I am at."

41. School-to-Work Coordinator

description: A school-to-work coordinator typically works within a public school system, assisting schools in identifying the skills that business and industry need for high school graduates to possess, and then helping the schools modify their curriculums to address those needs. A school-to-work coordinator also works with students, exposing them to job opportunities that exist, and helping them see the kinds of skills called for in different jobs.

To that end, school-to-work coordinators set up classroom programs for students from kindergarten through 12th grade. The specifics of these programs will vary from school district to school district, but they will usually begin with classroom instruction—exposing students to the various career opportunities that are out there, and the skills needed for various jobs. You'll help establish programs that let students (high school students, most likely) "shadow" workers in local industries and businesses to see what those jobs are really like. You'll work with teachers to help them tailor their curriculum to help students develop "real world" skills. You will work with local businesses and industry, mapping out the details of these programs, and devising ways for schools to better prepare students for postgraduation realities. And you will have to go before the school board to press for curriculum changes and special program funding.

As a school-to-work coordinator, you will find yourself working out in the community more than a traditional classroom teacher. In a very real sense you will be the liaison between the school district and the local business and industrial community.

salary: Salaries for full-time school-to-work coordinators will match those of starting teachers—about $21,000 a year.

prospects: Different states and school districts will place a different emphasis on school-to-work programs, but the general trend throughout the U.S. is an increased attention to such programs. School funding, however, is dependent on political whims, and when a budget crunch comes along, newer and more innovative programs are among the first to be cut.

qualifications: Districts look for someone who has experience in both industry and education when they're seeking to fill a school-to-work vacancy. They want someone who can understand the realms of both business and academia, and can act as a translator between the two. A demonstrated commitment to bridging the gaps between these two worlds will make your qualifications sparkle. Writing and communications skills are also vital for this job.

characteristics: School-to-work coordinators should be risk-takers, unafraid to walk into a company and meet with the head of that company—or into a principal's office to meet with a principal—in order to get programs off the ground. An ability to put yourself in a lot of different shoes is also a trait that you should desire and cultivate.

Ron Cerveny *is a school-to-work coordinator at a school district in Wisconsin.*

How did you get the job?

"I earned a graduate degree in physics. After working for a time in industry, I started teaching young people. I taught for a while in Rockford, Illinois.

"I saw that there was an opening in Phillips High School for a chemistry and physics teacher and became familiar with the situation here. Phillips had all the ingredients that were important to me. It was a community with a sense of community. So I came here and taught physics and chemistry at the high school.

"My physics class became involved with a local industrial company for an engineering project, which gave my students the opportunity to design physics experiments, and then receive feedback from industry.

"I had been teaching at Phillips High School for seven years when Carl Marschke [the president of the company that had worked with Ron on the class engineering project] called me up and said he had an idea." That idea came to be called the Young Scientists of America, of which Ron serves as the vice president.

"Our objective is to enhance interest in math, technology, and science in people ages 8 to 18."

Ron works in a volunteer capacity and says, "My duties are to execute programs, and to oversee, schedule, assist, do whatever it takes to keep things going. I repair machines. I make phone calls."

And now he's serving as the school-to-work coordinator for the Phillips School District in a part-time capacity.

What do you do all day?

"I was aware that for this program [school-to-work coordination] to work, teachers must be involved," Ron says. "So I got a grant that will supplement teachers' salaries this summer and allow them to visit different industries and retail operations, to spend a day with these companies, and then come back armed with suggestions for changes, and reinforcements of ideas they've already had, to the school climate and the educational curriculum. We've set up objectives and will measure the results of the program, but it should help teachers develop awareness of what businesses need and expect from students entering the workforce."

Once the school year starts, Ron's job begins in earnest. He works with children on all levels, from kindergarten to high school students. "When high school students come back in the fall, they participate in a program where they shadow businesses in their areas of interest for one or two hours a day. There are a series of evaluations that students and their mentors in the business community fill out. There is a job application that all students must fill out before they take part in this program. This is the first time many of them will have ever filled out a job application.

"In junior high and elementary school, it's not that type of experience. Things start out more in the classroom, and by the time students get to high school, most of the learning opportunities are outside the classroom." Ron's duties are to set up such learning opportunities, to evaluate the students and volunteer mentors in the community, and to oversee such programs.

Where do you see this job leading you?

"My security is in myself," Ron says, and to that end he has started his own company. "I see myself continuing to participate in Young Scientists, which I see as a program that can help students develop a sense of worth in what they do."

> TAILOR YOUR INTERVIEW TO THE EMPLOYER. WATCH THE INTERVIEWER TO TRY AND PICK UP CUES AS TO WHETHER OR NOT YOU ARE ANSWERING THE QUESTIONS CORRECTLY, AND PROVIDING THE INTERVIEWER WITH THE INFORMATION HE OR SHE NEEDS.

42. Teach for America Teacher

description: Teach for America (TFA) teachers are sent to school districts that cannot find teachers through more usual hiring channels. People who come into teaching through TFA haven't gone through the credentialing process that state-certified teachers do; they are given their certification on an "emergency" or temporary basis. TFA teachers typically are posted to inner-city school districts or to small, rural school districts.

They will have all the duties of "regular" teachers in that district—preparing for classes and leading them through daily activities; preparing, administering, and grading tests; counseling students and parents; and other duties the district or principal might assign.

As TFA teachers, they have obligations above and beyond those of their contemporaries. They will be obligated to perform community service projects as part of their TFA "tour of duty," everything from painting bathrooms in their school and planting trees around the school to putting together a career fair for students in their district.

salary: Salaries for TFA teachers will depend on the region to which they are posted. Those sent to schools in the larger cities, where the cost of living is higher, can expect to bring in more money, perhaps up to $30,000 per year. Teachers posted to rural districts can expect to make closer to $20,000 annually. Their salaries will be paid by the school districts for which they work, so their pay will tend to be in line with what other first- and second-year teachers make in their district.

As of 1994, Teach for America became affiliated with the Americorps program, so (for the moment at least) an educational stipend is part of the TFA package.

prospects: TFA has grown every year since its inception, and expectations are that this growth will continue. In this case, there should be more opportunities in the program for qualified applicants.

qualifications: Teach for America candidates need to have a college degree, but it doesn't necessarily need to be in education. In fact, TFA looks for candidates who have degrees in fields other than education. TFA will help its workers get their emergency teaching certification, for those credentials aren't necessary for applicants for this type of work. TFA looks for people who wouldn't normally go into teaching; candidates who can demonstrate their commitment to education have as good a chance as anyone of being selected. If chosen for the program, candidates will have to commit to a two-year term of service.

characteristics: TFA teachers need an extreme commitment to teaching. They will be posted to schools that won't be rich or in the most glamorous of locations. Candidates should be able to draw on an enormous well of self-confidence and should be self-reliant to boot. Open-mindedness, flexibility, and adaptability are all talents that come into play in this job.

Tiffany Tidwell *is a high school French teacher in a public school in Arkansas.*

How did you get the job?

"In college, at the University of Kansas, I took French courses," Tiffany says. "I was a sociology and American studies major, and coming up on my fourth year, I decided to go abroad. I studied in France and learned enough French there, enough credits, to earn a French degree.

"In late fall of my senior year, I was looking around at what to do once I graduated. Teach for America was right up my alley.

"The Teach for America application was due in January. I had an interview with them in April. I wanted to do this desperately. So I wasn't picky at all as far as where I wanted to be sent or what I would be doing.

"The letter came in early May, telling me that I was accepted and that I would be teaching fifth-grade social studies in the Mississippi Delta. I began getting psyched for elementary school.

"I went to the TFA Institute—a four-week-long training course—in the summer, in Houston. All 400 people

accepted that year from around the country went through the training. We worked with the public schools in Houston.

"While I was at the Institute, I got the word that I would probably not be teaching elementary school or social studies, but that I should prepare myself to teach high school French."

What do you do all day?

"The daily challenges here can be daunting," Tiffany says. "We have students who are brilliant and students who are barely literate in the same classroom. A lot of students in the district drop out before they get to high school. We have a high absentee rate—there are kids that come to class about every 10th day And the teen pregnancy rate here is very high; it's one of the highest in the country. And there is only one small prenatal class set up to deal with the situation.

"Kids walk in the door here at 7:40 A.M. I'm at the school by 7 A.M. One thing you'll notice about TFA teachers—theirs are often the first cars in the parking lot and the last to leave. Every night is crazy—there is always something to be done. You regularly work until midnight, then crash, and get up

again the next day to be at school by 7 A.M. again. I did that seven days a week last year." (Tiffany is in the second year of her TFA contract.)

"When you walk into your classroom, you need a complete

**CONTACT TEACH FOR AMERICA FOR MORE INFORMATION AND AN APPLICATION PACKAGE.
(SEE RESOURCES, PAGE 212.)**

lesson plan plus 10 alternatives in case the first plan doesn't work. If I didn't do that, I would be massacred. There are kids with behavioral problems, and you need to be 100 percent on top of what's going on, or it could turn into a riot. . . .

"It can be very frustrating, because the work never stops, but when things do go well, there is no other feeling quite like it. One of my biggest triumphs last year was when I and two other TFA French teachers took a group of students to France. We fund-raised like

crazy and were able to bring an opportunity to these kids who otherwise never would have had an opportunity like that."

Where do you see this job leading you?

"Many of the second-year TFA teachers here are contemplating remaining for a third year," Tiffany says. "We had 26 people come to this region last year. One of them left by Thanksgiving; two more left at the end of the year; 38 new people came to the region this year. And the school districts here are asking for more. So they like the job we are doing.

"I think I will eventually go back to school," she says, "with this experience in the forefront. I don't see that I could ever get away from education. This is a field I feel I can contribute to. I'm not sure exactly where I will go from here, but wherever I go, I will be a lifelong supporter of public education."

43. Teacher

description: Teachers in the American Schools network work all over the world. Teaching conditions will vary depending on the country you are in, the school you are posted to, and the age of the children you are teaching. You might be teaching different groups of children at different times throughout the day, or you might have one group of kids for the entire day. Regardless of where you are teaching, you will be teaching in English. And, more than likely, you will be following an American curriculum. One of the focuses of the American Schools is to prepare students for admission into American universities. American Schools teachers teach subjects such as English, math, science, and history.

American Schools contracts are most often two-year contracts. Those contracts can be extended at the end of the two-year period, based on the discretion of the school administrators.

salary: Salary levels can vary widely, depending more upon the country and school you're teaching in than on experience. Salaries can range from $10,000 or less per year up to $36,000 or more. The more experienced teachers, of course, will be recruited by the higher-paying schools. Usually, housing and airfare between the United States and the foreign country at the beginning and end of your contract will be paid for by the school. There will also typically be a monetary bonus awarded to teachers completing their contracts.

prospects: The prospects for getting a job as an International School System teacher are good for those who have earned a teaching certificate from any of the 50 states in the U.S., or from Canada. Most of the hiring is done at international job fairs, sponsored by the International School Service, Search Associates, and other organizations. The trick is finding out where and when those job fairs will be; that information can be garnered from the newsletters of these organizations, and through collegiate education departments. Married teaching teams are also highly sought after.

qualifications: The main qualification for employment as a teacher in the American Overseas Schools is a teaching certificate from any of the 50 states in the U.S., or from Canada. Getting a teaching certificate usually requires an undergraduate degree, plus a year or more of teacher training and substitute teaching. More and more programs are seeking candidates with two or more years of experience in elementary and secondary school teaching. Interviewers also look for international teaching experience—prospects with such experience will be favored over almost all others.

characteristics: Teachers abroad should have the same characteristics as those teaching in the states—energy, creativity, and a commitment to education and to the children you're instructing. But as an overseas teacher, you'll also need to have an understanding of, and patience with, the culture you find yourself working in. Flexibility is another important asset.

Teachers in the American Schools network should also be comfortable at surviving alone. Although there probably will be other American teachers working with you, you all will be living in a foreign country for two years, which can get pretty lonely at times.

Alex Ross *is a social studies teacher in the American Schools network, and is currently teaching in Kaohsiung, Taiwan.*

How did you get the job?

After obtaining a degree in Middle Eastern Studies and trying unsuccessfully to enter two different fields, Alex decided to become a teacher, and enrolled in his local university's program that prepared students for getting their teaching certificate. "I learned absolutely nothing in that program.

"Lots of the teachers there were worksheet teachers. It seemed like the teachers were out to make history boring. I didn't want to do that. So I would parade the kids out to the football field, and make them pray to Allah when we were studying Islam. We were studying the Vikings, and I made the kids lie down and close their eyes as I described the Vikings marching into battle.

"I saw that most students' grasp of geography was mediocre at best. Now how can you teach history if someone doesn't know geography? I got excited about the idea of coordinating history with geography.

"At the end of the student-teaching period, I received excellent recommendations from my supervisors. The stu-

> FOR INFORMATION ON TEACHING OPPORTUNITIES ABROAD, CHECK WITH THE U.S. STATE DEPARTMENT OR WITH ORGANIZATIONS LIKE THE INTERNATIONAL SCHOOLS SERVICES. (FOR ADDITIONAL INFORMATION, SEE RESOURCES PAGE 211).

dents seemed to like what I had done. There were openings all over the state—I applied for them all, and was shot down all over the state.

Alex attributes his lack of success in landing a job to several factors. One is that social studies and history teaching positions often are given to people who also coach athletic teams. Another is that although male teachers are highly sought after on the elementary school level, on the high school level, they aren't nearly in that high a demand.

"I called the U.S. State Department and had them send me a list of all American schools overseas. I checked out the International School Service newsletter. I applied to about 100 of the schools listed in those places."

Alex took a job in Durango, Mexico, where he taught geography and world history for two years. He is now teaching in Kaohsiung, Taiwan.

What do you do all day?

"I was hired to be the geography teacher, but I also served as the homeroom teacher, library assistant, and coaching assistant, and was expected to help run school activities.

"I probably put in 60-hour workweeks. We weren't provided with a curriculum in Durango, so we had to write our own.

"Probably 10 hours a week were spent in prep time. You were allotted preparatory periods throughout the school day, but you would spend time after school as well, grading papers or preparing lessons.

"You had to get used to doing without things. There were times when we wouldn't have chalk. We had to do without textbooks. All the books in the library were hopelessly out of date."

Where do you see this job leading you?

"You can use experience in overseas schools to keep going overseas, to move on to other American Schools," Alex says. "A lot of people do two years in an American School and then go back home, to get back into teaching in the United States, or to go and get a master's degree in education or in another field. Some schools will offer a master's program overseas. Teaching in an American School is definitely good for getting into graduate programs back in the States.

"I think this is good preparation for working in a multicultural school district back in the States. I've heard of people in Mexico City that transferred to teaching in GM plants there, doing what they call 'instruction for technology.' I've heard of people opening up their own import/export store after teaching somewhere for a couple years. Some people have gone on to start their own schools. In Guatemala, a couple of teachers started an action group with the Indians there, and gradually that became their job instead of teaching."

44. Teacher

ON A NATIVE AMERICAN RESERVATION

description: Teaching on a reservation closely resembles a public school teaching job ... at least on paper. You will generally be following accepted public school curriculum, and your day will be structured like that of most other public school teachers.

Certain aspects of reservation education separate it from public school education, however. For one thing, reservation schools are typically run by the Bureau of Indian Affairs or are grant funded, so facilities tend to be better kept, and budgets tend to be more generous than in many public schools. Your school will draw students from across the reservation, where students and families may live miles apart from each other. A high percentage of your students could suffer from fetal alcohol syndrome or could be special education students. You can expect to have a better student-teacher ratio than in public schools, or at least to have more assistance in the classroom.

Your job duties will consist of preparing and carrying out classroom instruction, grading papers and tests, attending teacher-parent conferences, and meeting with the principal and school board.

salary: Teaching on a reservation will earn slightly higher pay than public school teaching jobs. Salaries will start at around $20,000 and could increase by $1,500 to $2,000 a year for every year you remain teaching on the reservation. Housing will usually be provided, or will be extremely cheap.

prospects: Good. Reservation schools tend to have a hard time attracting people, and there is usually a steady turnover among the school staff.

qualifications: To teach on a Native American reservation, you'll need a public school teaching certificate. For many reservation teachers, it is their first job outside of student teaching.

characteristics: Understanding of and patience with both the kids you will be teaching and the culture you will be working in are crucial to success in this field.

Julie Morris *was a teacher in the Ramah-Navajo Reservation School in New Mexico.*

How did you get the job?

"My mom was a teacher," Julie says, "and teaching just seemed the logical thing for me to do. I always wanted to be a teacher.

"I didn't want to teach in a regular school, though. That seemed bland.

"I was doing my student teaching," she says, "and I was just about finished doing that. I went to a teaching job fair. The lines were long for everything except for reservation jobs. Despite the higher pay, nobody really seemed to want to work there.

"I had a few interviews, and the Ramah-Navajo Reservation School wanted me to come there. This was in New Mexico, about two hours west of Albuquerque.

"I was hired to teach second grade. I went there with a friend, lived in a trailer, and stayed there for two years."

What do you do all day?

"The school I worked at was pretty small. There were about 400 kids there, ranging from Head Start kids to grade 12. There was a lot of federal money coming in, and the school itself was wonderful. They paid for a lot of professional training. We had unlimited materials.

"There were 18 kids in my class," she says. "I team-taught second and third grade, working with two other teachers, two special education teachers, and one music teacher. Our curriculum was the same as other schools. We had a Navajo culture class taught by aides from the Navajo tribe. They taught for half a day and were not certified teachers.

"Working with the kids was a little rough. A lot of the kids suffered from fetal alcohol syndrome. They had no idea of cause and effect and were very hard to control. There were a lot of abused kids in the class as well. Kids would go crazy and start beating on kids or teachers for no reason. Thirty percent of the kids in our school were in special education classes.

"A lot of the kids also lived in a dorm the Navajo ran, and there were problems we had to deal with because of that.

> **ATTEND JOB FAIRS. THEY ARE GREAT PLACES TO FIND OUT WHAT OPPORTUNITIES ARE AVAILABLE AT DIFFERENT COMPANIES, AND WHICH COMPANIES ARE HIRING. LOOK UPON THEM AS OPPORTUNITIES TO HONE YOUR NETWORKING SKILLS.**

"The kids needed a lot of attention. But thanks to our teaching situation, the kids had a lot of small-group work and did receive a lot of individual attention.

"There was no community where the school was located," Julie says. "There was the school, the business office, and a clinic—that was all there was in the vicinity of the school. The isolation was a bit much after a while, a little too much."

Where do you see this job leading you?

Julie parlayed her reservation job into a job teaching overseas in the American Schools system. "I attended an international schools fair in Carmel, California," she says. "Interviewers there seemed impressed by my two years of reservation experience—almost as if it were international teaching experience."

Most people go from teaching on a reservation to jobs in the public school system. Because financial incentives to stay on at reservation schools tend to be greater than in the public school system, however, some teachers elect to stay.

45. Administrator/Caretaker
OF A RESIDENCE FOR PERSONS WITH AIDS/HIV

description: A caretaker at an AIDS residence is responsible for seeing to the health and well-being of the residents under his or her supervision. Residents are likely to be at different stages in the disease's progression at different residences, so the level of care you will be required to provide will vary from job to job, and indeed from residence to residence.

Your responsibilities will range from helping your residents into and out of the bathtub, to distributing medication to them, to helping with meals. You might be responsible for interviewing prospective residents. You'll have to enforce the rules of the residence, and might find yourself addressing problems such as drinking and drug use. You'll be responsible for running the house, dealing with paperwork (of which there is likely to be a lot), buying groceries for the house, and dealing with other day-to-day duties that may arise.

salary: AIDS residence caretakers aren't likely to make much money. Starting salaries could be at or slightly above minimum wage, and could rise to $10 an hour or slightly higher, depending on the organization you work for, and how that organization is funded. Salaries can start at around $11,000 a year and can rise into the $20,000s. However, in most instances, room and board will be provided, as the job is a live-in one.

prospects: The need for long-term residences for HIV-positive persons and those suffering from AIDS far surpasses the number in existence. Since the need for facilities of this nature is only going to rise, unfortunately, opportunities to work in such residences are also going to increase.

qualifications: To run a residence for persons with AIDS or HIV, you will need to be a certified nursing assistant for the state you plan to work in. Experience dealing with people with AIDS or HIV will be helpful. You'll need management skills and experience.

characteristics: An AIDS residence caretaker should possess compassion in abundance, as well as patience and good humor. You might have to face some distressing, gut-wrenching situations in your tenure as a caretaker, and you'll have to prepare yourself to handle those sorts of situations and to provide comfort to friends and family members who might be devastated by those same situations. Prepare for a lot of paperwork in this job.

Joy Celyn Hayes *is the founder of Our House, a residence for persons with AIDS or HIV, located in Colorado.*

- -

How did you get the job?

Joy has been working for the past five years to realize her dream of Our House, a residence for persons with AIDS or HIV. It all started with her son. "My son brought home someone without any place to live, without any money," she says. "I took him in. Then my son brought home another person in the same situation. I realized that there wasn't any place for people in these situations to stay. So I formed a nonprofit corporation to do something about it."

Joy didn't have any experience such as this prior to founding Our House. She learned pretty quickly, though.

"Our first problem was finding qualified people to serve on our board of directors," says Joy, "finding accountants, people with political connections, people with money, people with clout. We needed someone to help us with development, so we found a developer to sit on the board. We needed a lawyer, so we found one.

"We had to incorporate, so we got incorporation papers from the state and filed those."

> THE NATIONAL DIRECTORY OF CORPORATE PUBLIC AFFAIRS CAN BE A BOON TO THOSE SEEKING JOBS IN THE FIELD OF CORPORATE-SPONSORED PHILANTHROPY. THE BOOK INCLUDES LISTINGS OF CORPORATE PUBLIC RELATIONS AND COMMUNITY AFFAIRS DEPARTMENTS, CORPORATE-FUNDED FOUNDATIONS AND CONTRIBUTIONS DEPARTMENTS, POLITICAL ACTION COMMITTEES, ISSUE MANAGEMENT AND RISK ANALYSIS DEPARTMENTS, AND MORE.

If Our House was to be an ongoing concern and not a failed pipe dream, Joy discovered, her nascent nonprofit corporation was going to need to raise money. "We started doing fund-raisers," she says. "We put on a Chinese auction, a little show, and raised $700. A movie theater in town was showing the film *Paris Is Burning,* and that was our next benefit. We raised $8,000 in two weeks.

"At that time, some HUD money had been set aside to help pay for AIDS-related housing projects. Most of those projects were apartment buildings. Certain people can't live alone, though, and that's where Our House will come in."

Once completed, the facility will house seven residents at a time. "We're hoping to create a model project in Our House, something that can be stamped out like cookie cutters throughout the country," Joy says. "In nursing homes, which is where many AIDS patients end up when they can no longer care for themselves, it costs a minimum of $2,500 a month to care for a patient. At Our House, care will cost $1,000 a month—half of that will be paid by the client, and half will come from Medicaid."

What do you do all day?

"The house as it is now is an independent living facility; the guys who live here are still physically able to take care of themselves," Joy says. "I charge them $200 a month, all bills paid.

Each resident contributes an additional $50 per month.

"The guys and I will make crafts. We'll sell them and use the money to help support the house.

"I do the basic running of the home," Joy says. "I interview prospective residents, guys who think they might want to live here. I help supply volunteers. I enforce the rules. We all take turns cooking meals.

"Running this house is just like having a bunch of roommates. Once in a while I'll have to jump up and put my foot down. We'll have occasional disciplinary problems—people will move in and find out they can't live with others, or someone will come home drunk and in that case will get to live somewhere else. Our problems are drinking and drugs, mostly."

Where do you see this job leading you?

"Once the Our House residence is up and running, I plan to phase this one out," says Joy. "I'll still write grants and help raise money. But the next time I try to do something, I'll do something easier," she says with a laugh.

46. Child and Youth Protective Services Worker

description: Workers in children and youth protective services departments will typically be state or county employees whose job duties will include working to protect victims of child abuse and neglect, to counsel youth and juvenile delinquents, to try to reunify families that have been separated or, if the best interests of the child or youth dictate continued separation, to work towards finding a stable living arrangement for those youths and children.

Child and youth protective services workers endeavor to address problems perpetuated by child abuse and neglect, and juvenile delinquency. Specific job duties will entail initiating and supervising home detention programs; providing therapy, family and parenting skills, and independent living training; conducting court-ordered custody studies (typically undertaken during contested divorce proceedings); licensing and working with foster care providers; placing children and youth in appropriate "alternative care" centers—juvenile correction facilities, residential treatment centers or group homes, for example; and managing all the cases under their watch.

Workers will typically put in 40 hours a week, but overtime might often be required, and schedules will, out of necessity, be very flexible, with home visits after typical working hours making up a normal part of a caseworker's "routine."

salary: Salaries for beginning child and youth protective services caseworkers will typically start at $16,000 to $25,000 per year, and can rise to $30,000 or more, depending on experience and educational training. Salaries for casework supervisors can range from $23,000 to $38,000 or more.

prospects: Despite government cutbacks to social services (and threats of cutbacks), the need for workers in the field—which includes child and youth protective services—is not about to go away. Indeed, the government itself projects a 40% growth rate for social work and human services jobs over the course of the next decade.

qualifications: Applicants for child and youth protective services positions should possess a bachelor's degree in social work or some other related field. Most states will require that applicants be licensed social workers—you can discover what that process involves by getting in touch with your state's department of regulation and licensing, or with your local county's department of human services.

Applicants with volunteer experience—especially with Big Brothers/Big Sisters, Special Olympics, or other organizations that give volunteers experience working with families or children—will be highly regarded.

Good written and oral communications skills will also come in handy.

characteristics: Child and youth protective services workers should possess an understanding of human behavior and childhood development. They have to be open to new ideas, open to beliefs different from their own, and to the different ways that families live.

The ability to handle crisis situations, to think under fire, and to deal with people screaming at you, are things you will possess coming into the job, or will quickly develop.

Marilyn Schreuder *and* **Sherry McGee-Wirth** *work in a human services children and youth department in Wisconsin.*

How did you get the job?

"When I was in high school, I didn't know what a social worker was," says Marilyn Schreuder.

"In college, I became aware of the profession, and earned a bachelor's degree in social work from Kansas State University in Manhattan, Kansas.

"I spent a few years as a child protective services worker in Dodge City, Kansas. I then moved to Wisconsin and was hired by the county's human services department as a social worker, with more general duties. I spent seven years doing that, and then became a supervisor of this department."

Sherry McGee-Wirth earned her bachelor's degree in psychology. Hired as a secretary in a human services department in 1986, she applied for a social work caseworker position when a job came open two years later. She has been an "ongoing social worker" ever since, she says.

What do you do all day?

"One of the services I provide is in-home family treatment, what we call 'intensive treatment'," Sherry says. "We receive referrals from law-enforcement personnel, from people who do (child abuse or neglect) investigations,

or from self-referrals. The cases are transferred to me, and I take them from there through to the end of the case.

"We try to provide our therapy in the home because family members are more likely to be comfortable there than they would be in a mental health clinic setting. Our treatment is flexible, based on fitting a family's needs. We work with the family to prioritize what the underlying causes of the problems are, the core issues, and where to go from here to address those causes.

"I deal with a variety of issues in the therapy sessions: communications, boundaries, marital issues, unresolved divorce issues. I set goals with the family, and then develop a treatment plan. I meet with families once a week, two times a month, whatever the situation calls for."

"Our typical day is often not what we expect it to be," Marilyn says. "A crisis can arise and change our entire day; one phone call can mean a child's in

> **THE JOB INVOLVES A LOT OF NETWORKING WITHIN THE COMMUNITY.**

immediate danger, and we have to respond to that. We could receive a child abuse or neglect referral from one of the schools—we'll get a call telling us that a dad has hit a kid, that this kid has come to school with a black eye. Or a foster parent will call us at 4 P.M. to tell us that a child is destroying his or her room. Or the police department will call and tell us they picked up two juvenile boys from Milwaukee, driving a stolen vehicle, and we'll have to begin processing that case.

"Different people in our office are on beeper duty on different nights, and if someone receives a call for a client that is not [his or hers], he or she will drop information on that client off on that client's caseworker's desk. And so that caseworker will have to deal with that client once they come in in the morning.

"Or we'll have a foster child who has left a foster home or is a runaway, and we'll have to try and find those people. Or a runaway will have been found, and we'll have to process that case.

"We spend some of our time carting kids around. Workers in our juvenile intake positions will spend a lot of time in court. Tem-

porary physical custody cases, for instance, will have to go before a judge within 24 hours.

"A lot of work is done in the homes, a lot of our work is done at night."

Sherry adds, "Our job also entails a lot of paperwork, and a lot of phone calls. We work to coordinate services and monitor court orders."

Where do you see this job leading you?

"What you do in this field depends on your main interest," Marilyn says. "Some people go on to become supervisors, but in that capacity, you don't have as much contact with the clients.

"We're a county agency, administered by the state, and sometimes the state will hire social workers, and those people are more involved with establishing policy.

"Sometimes people will move to different departments within the human services field," she says. "It is quite stressful to work in this unit; we deal with a lot of tragedy. It can be pretty threatening to people when you tell them you're removing their child. And so some people choose to work with a population where things are less threatening—the elderly, for example."

47. Community Service Project Coordinator

description: As a community service project coordinator, you will most likely work to support or supplement existing social programs. That work will entail assessing community needs, developing programs to fill those needs, procuring funding for those programs, and then working to implement them in your community.

The job will involve networking among social service agencies, governmental agencies, funding sources, your supervisors, and your organization's board of directors. You will write proposals and present your ideas to your board, and then work on securing funding from potential donors. (For ongoing projects, part of your job will be to appease people representing the various entities that support or oppose your organization's work.) Some of your presentations will be to the community at large.

You will craft budgets, compile reports, and document your efforts. You will be involved in the design and creation of fund-raising and outreach plans. You will oversee the implementation of your organization's community service programs; you'll supervise the work of staff members, too. The job might also entail taking some direct action—everything from preparing and/or serving food at a soup kitchen to delivering services to members of your community. And you will be constantly looking for means of creating new programs or initiatives to further serve your community's needs.

Your particular priorities will in all likelihood depend on the priorities of the organization for which you work.

salary: Salaries can vary greatly, depending on experience and the agency or organization for which you work. Beginning salaries can start at around $20,000 per year; for supervisory-level employees, those salaries can rise as high as $50,000 to $75,000.

prospects: This type of job calls for a varied yet specific skill set. People possessing the skills that this type of work requires, and the desire to coordinate community service efforts, should be able to locate this type of employment, depending on how hard they want to look. As government funding for nonprofit and social service types of work perhaps becomes more scarce, other types of organizations will step in to "fill the gap" or to supplement existing social service programs. Colleges, private businesses, business improvement districts, and other organizations can be places to look for this type of employment.

qualifications: A master's degree in a related field is a possible requirement, but more important will be an understanding of government and how it works, an understanding of how social services are provided, and a demonstrated ability to develop and implement projects. Good communications skills—both writing and public speaking—are also a must for jobs in this field.

characteristics: Exemplary community service project coordinators will be the type of people who talk to everyone they meet and have a knack for meeting others on their own terms—"the ability to move with different constituencies," as a community services director puts it. They will also be able to work independently on projects, yet be a team player when the situation calls for it.

Janelle Farris *is the director of community services for a business improvement organization in New York City.*

How did you get the job?

"I have an eclectic background," Janelle says, "which oddly enough made me perfect for this job. I have worked for the state legislature. I did economic development work for another agency, writing grants and working with small businesses. I worked on affirmative action, and served on the loan review committee of the New York State Urban Development Corporation. I worked for the New York City Charter Revision Commission, where I got experience in public speaking, and learned in minute detail how New York City government actually works. At the Manhattan borough president's office, I worked on economic development and job creation initiatives, and dealt with tourism."

The Times Square Business Improvement District is a non-profit organization comprised of businesses and community leaders in the Times Square area. Established to help make the Times Square area "clean, safe, and friendly," the approximately 90-employee organization funds sanitation pick-up, safety patrols, and services for visitors to the area. Homeless services and other community-oriented activities also fall under the organization's purview. (It is also responsible for organizing the Times Square New Year's Eve festivities and other cultural activities.)

"I got this job because of my previous job experience working with small businesses and communities, and because of a demonstrated ability to learn quickly and create and implement programs that a community desires."

What do you do all day?

"The main focus of what I do is community service," says Janelle. "I develop and implement programs designed to serve both the constituents (the property owners who pay our bills) and the target population.

"We have programs in place on a number of fronts," she says. "On the homeless front, we have created the Times Square Consortium for the Homeless, made up of seven social service agencies and Times Square BID.

"Another project is Times Square Delivers—a donation transportation program that connects local businesses with social service providers, and has brought in more than $800,000 worth of donations to social service agencies in the Times Square area. A third project is called Times Square Wishes, where we put together a catalog which lists local service organizations and their wishes. People and organizations look at that catalog and make donations off of that list.

"There really is no typical day in this job. Today I got to the office by 8 A.M. I had letters to get out to businesses regarding Times Square Wishes. Then I went downtown to meet with a social service agency that administers one of our homeless projects to talk about a new contract. Then I came back to the office to deal with problems that have arisen over getting the Times Square Wishes catalog printed.

"I have days when it's one meeting after another. Later this week I have to meet with the 42nd Street Association, then come back and do some letter writing and phone work. Then I have to talk to a hotel in our area committed to becoming a good social-service neighbor. Then there's a staff meeting. I frequently go to city council and government meetings too.

"Then there are days when I'm happy to simply sit at my desk and catch up—not that those days come along very often."

Where do you see this job leading you?

Janelle says that she doesn't know where she wants to go after this job. "I'm eclectic," she says. "The idea of going to Japan and teaching pottery sounds exciting to me. But, as far as becoming a director of a business improvement district—more than any other job in our organization, my job prepares you for doing that because it is so varied. I could also go on to be the director of a social service agency or the head of a social service unit. Going on to economic development jobs is another possibility."

> REMEMBER TO SEND THANK-YOU NOTES TO EVERYONE WITH WHOM YOU INTERVIEW—OR AT LEAST TO EVERYONE WHO INTERVIEWED YOU FOR A JOB WHICH YOU ARE STILL INTERESTED IN, AND FEEL YOU HAVE A SHOT AT, AFTER THE INTERVIEW.

48. Counselor

FOR A HIGH-RISK YOUTH VIOLENCE PREVENTION AND MENTORING PROGRAM

description: These sorts of violence prevention and mentoring programs will vary depending on the specific nature and goals of the program, but generally, counselors will oversee the activities of program participants. They could be in charge of specific activities or areas—computers, or arts and crafts. Or they could be responsible for overseeing the activities of a specific group of participants.

Coordinators (or, perhaps, directors) will be responsible for their programs' overall development and supervision. Staff supervision, of course, will come under their purview. Coordinators will be the public face of their program—they will be responsible for their program's outreach efforts, visiting with members of the community, presenting the program to youths and their parents, and working with police anbd other social service providers in the community.

salary: This is another of those positions that will never make the people working at it rich. Starting salaries for counselors in these sorts of programs will range from $15,000 to $20,000 per year, depending on education and experience. Workers who come to the job with niche skills, computer experience, or fluency in a second language, for example, will be able to start at the upper end of that range. The type of organization funding the program, how that organization comes by its funding, and the area of the country staffers are working in could serve to modify those salaries.

prospects: The need for violence prevention and mentoring programs for high-risk youths has perhaps never been greater. And programs to serve those youths are cropping up at various sites throughout the country. But when hard policy choices have to be made between incarceration and prevention programs, government funds typically go toward incarceration and punishment. Funding for most of these preventative programs will come from private foundations and corporations. Though counseling and administrative positions within these programs are out there, they can be difficult to find.

qualifications: Specific qualifications for counselor and coordinator positions in those programs will vary, again depending on the nature of the program and its specific goals. The needs of the program will dictate what type of worker they are looking for—they may need someone who can supervise their computer activities, say, or they could have a gap in their arts and crafts staff.

In general, though, workers should have experience with the type of clients the program serves, having worked with them in a residential program or public school context, for instance.

Program coordinators should have previous management or supervisory experience, above and beyond the qualifications for a counselor.

characteristics: People hoping to work in these types of programs should possess perseverance, patience, reliability, and integrity. You will need to be a role model to the clients you work with as much as you will be a supervisor to them, and all of those qualities will be essential to being a positive role model.

Ernest McMillan *is a program coordinator for a youth center in a large Southwestern city.*

How did you get the job?

"I was working as the project manager of an agency called Communities in the Schools, working in elementary schools on a dropout protection program. My work was noted by the director of a clinic in our city's Fifth Ward. I was invited to sit on a panel investigating ways to help prevent teen pregnancies, and ways to extend those prevention initiatives to boys.

"The Fifth Ward Enrichment Program started out of that panel. The program was started to take a holistic approach to problems young boys face in this community, and to provide a mentor approach to solving those problems."

The Fifth Ward Enrichment Program (FWEP) was founded as a pilot project, with funds coming from the Hogg Foundation for Mental Health. The program has grown from servicing boys at a single middle school in the area to the point where it targets two middle and two elementary schools, and serves around 150 students each year.

Boys come to the FWEP center after school and during the summer months. There,

> **IF YOU SEE A NEED IN YOUR COMMUNITY, AND HAVE AN IDEA FOR A PROGRAM THAT COULD ADDRESS THAT NEED, MAKE AN APPOINTMENT WITH THE DIRECTOR OF A COMMUNITY SERVICE AGENCY IN YOUR COMMUNITY. COME TO THE MEETING WITH AN AGENDA IN MIND. PRESENT YOUR PROGRAM IDEA, AND ASK WHAT THE DIRECTOR THINKS OF IT.**

they participate in activities and projects designed to help them succeed academically and developmentally, and to provide them with male role-socialization opportunities. Program activities are also devised for parents of boys participating in the program.

What do you do all day?

Cultural, educational, and recreational activities are all part of the FWEP regimen. Field trips, arts and crafts, drama, chess, karate, camping trips, and organized sports are a few of those activities. Other FWEP programs include community service projects and leadership development retreats and seminars.

"I usually arrive here between 7 and 9 A.M., depending on what's up," Ernest says. "I'll work on coordinating activities for upcoming events or supervising of staff. I'll get on the phone. I'll develop curriculum and programs with staff members and members of the community. I supervise our staff members and evaluate their performances. I coordinate activities with other agencies. I'll try and put a stop to crises. Or I'll work with our planning committee, correspond with parents, organize reports. I do everything from cleaning off tables and making coffee to meeting with the mayor's representative.

"During the summer, we put on an eight-week program, which entails a community service project where we engage up to 150 boys. A typical day during the summer involves checking the boys in, then getting them motivated through exercise. Then we get the young men out in the field. We all do lunch together here. After lunch, we engage in cooperative learning and role-playing exercises where the boys participating in our program learn about leadership and violence reduction. Those sessions are over at around 2 P.M., at which point we organize the boys into teams for competitive sports activities. At the end of the day, we have our "Yack to Snack" session, where we get together with the boys and talk about the events of the day.

"Our older boys, ages 15 to 17, are involved in our teen enterprises programs, where they work in silk-screening, computer repair, newspaper delivery, filmmaking, and working as vendors in the Astrodome."

Where do you see this job leading you?

"Some of our counselors end up going back to school," Ernest says. "People can move from here to positions of elected office.

"From an administrative position here, you could move from a program like this to an administrative position in a large organization or foundation. You could move on to working as the manager of a government department in the youth social services field."

49. Director

OF A FAMILY SHELTER

description: The responsibilities of a family shelter director, in a nutshell, entail overseeing the shelter or house of which they are in charge. Duties will range from keeping tabs on the day-to-day running of the shelter, to planning meals and activities, supervising the night and weekend managing, and coordinating the work of volunteers at the shelter.

The family shelter director might have to answer to a board of directors or some other supervisory agency. He or she has to deal with budgetary concerns and other fiscal matters. Representing the shelter to the public, in the form of speeches at public events, or via radio, television, or print media interviews, is another province of the shelter director. Fund-raising—applying for grants, going before funding committees, preparing reports for funding sources—might be handled by development staff, or it might be the director's responsibility.

salary: Salaries for shelter workers can range from $12,000 to $20,000 per year, depending on the type and size of the facility where they work, their responsibilities, and their experience. Shelter directors can command from $22,000 to $95,000 or more, again depending on their experience, and the size and type of the facility. For some workers, food and board will be included in their salary.

prospects: The need for facilities to house the homeless, AIDS patients, and other needy individuals is not going to go away. The question is whether there will be facilities available to meet those needs. Governmental cutbacks could slow the creation of new jobs in this area, but since these types of jobs don't appeal to everyone—the pay is on the lower end of the scale and the job can be emotionally draining—qualified applicants should not have difficulty finding employment.

qualifications: Some employers hire high school graduates, but most prefer those with some college courses, or even a four-year degree, in human services, social work, or a related field. The level of education you possess will typically dictate the responsibilities you will receive at the shelter for which you work. Familiarity with the house rules is something that workers will have to pick up.

For shelter directors, supervisory and management experience, as well as some experience in the human services field (whether on a paid or voluntary basis), are likely requirements.

characteristics: Shelter directors will need to be responsible (they will be charged with overseeing an entire residence, after all). They should be adept at handling people and instilling trust. Shelter directors will need to be good role models for their clients. They should also be caring, but firm when they need to be.

Donna Fortson *is the director of a family shelter located in Memphis, Tennessee.*

How did you get the job?

"I had been in investment banking ever since I got out of school," Donna says, "dealing with municipal bonds and other things that investment bankers deal with. That was what I did, up until last year. But 10 years ago, I got involved with a soup kitchen project through my church. Every Sunday I would help out, cooking meals and serving them. About four years ago, I began seeing the need for a shelter for women and children to stay at. So I started researching what it would take to open such a shelter. I started raising funds. And when a facility became available, I decided to try and get this place open.

"I found a lawyer who volunteered to do pro bono work. He helped us file for nonprofit organization status and helped us craft our bylaws. We then organized our board, and started to raise money and look for a site.

"Since we've been on-site, we've been here every Saturday, working on the facility, getting it ready to open."

What do you do all day?

"Right now, I am concentrating on writing grants and looking for night and weekend managers. We have one last renovation to go before we can get inspected to see if we can open the shelter.

"We plan on starting small, with four families drawn from homeless moms and kids. I anticipate families staying with us for around 90 days.

"We will have a kind of strict intake procedure, where we will ask prospective residents pertinent questions, trying to determine the reasons they are in the situations they are in, and what it will take to get them out of the situations. We'll set up short-term, realistic goals, train them in budgeting and parenting skills, help them get their G.E.D.s, help them write their resumes, whatever they need to nurture and stabilize their family situations. The children will have to be enrolled in school or some type of day care. If the mothers are on food stamps, they will have to buy their own food. We will use other agencies to provide the services to our clients. We will follow up on our cases, and try to get them in better housing situations. We have hopes to be a model program of this type.

"This project will only work with the help of a lot of volunteers. We'll have volunteers in the office, volunteers doing intake, volunteers helping with the children. Volunteers will provide tutoring, run errands, go shopping, plan social activities. Professional counselors will volunteer their time. I imagine it will take 25 to 35 volunteers to effectively run things.

"Once we start accepting clients, I will meet with them on a one-to-one basis. I'll conduct house meetings—there will be all kinds of meetings. I want to put together a newsletter. There will be a lot of record-keeping involved."

Where do you see this job leading you?

"I feel that this is what I was supposed to do," says Donna, "so I'm gonna stay with it. I want to see it through.

"I know a lot of people who have been in social service," she says. "They have had opportunities to move up and on. They've gone into teaching, into other agencies that have expanded, or have moved up in their current agency."

> ONE OF IVAN R. MISNER'S TEN COMMANDMENTS OF NETWORKING IS TO LEARN TO DESCRIBE YOUR PRODUCT OR SERVICE IN LESS THAN 60 SECONDS. THAT ADVICE IS EQUALLY APPLICABLE TO SOMEONE TRYING TO SELL THEMSELVES.

50. Director

OF DOMESTIC VIOLENCE HOUSING SERVICES

description: Domestic violence housing services programs are set up to help provide shelter for those people and their children who may be suffering in home situations marred by violence. Shelter is provided on an emergency, transitional, or permanent basis. Emergency housing programs usually house women and their children for three to six months, transitional programs for up to one year, and permanent programs for as long as is required.

These types of programs usually provide support groups and opportunities for psychotherapy for mothers and children. Parenting skills training, classes in independent living skills, and perhaps even job training, will be provided as part of most housing services programs.

Staffing for these programs includes site administrators, therapists, caseworkers, child care workers, and residential aides. All work under the direction of the site administrator.

salary: Though specific salaries vary from agency to agency, in general caseworkers can expect to earn from the low- to mid-$20,000s. Therapists and site administrators can earn around $30,000 a year. Child care workers should expect to earn in the low- to mid-$20,000s. At the administrative level, salaries can rise to between $30,000 and $60,000.

prospects: Though there is plenty of need for domestic violence housing services, they are social service programs that are more prone to the political budgetary ax than many other programs. Prospects in this field, therefore, will reflect the mood of this country toward social service.

And right now, the mood isn't all that favorable. However, the outlet for workers in the social service sector is expected to get better, as a 40 percent growth rate is predicted over the next 10 years.

qualifications: Qualifications for social service workers are usually very flexible—agency funding sources sometimes dictate requirements for different positions, as can directors of agencies. A high school diploma is a minimum requirement for entry-level positions, while therapists and housing directors will usually need a master's degree or equivalent experience. A bachelor's or master's degree will be held in high regard no matter what position you're looking for.

characteristics: One domestic violence housing services director says, "What I look for in applicants to my agency is raw intelligence—that's the first priority. I look for a good attitude; someone who is confident and humble. I look for people who are open-minded, and can consider the many different sides of an issue. I avoid extremes, people who can only see one side of an issue. Interpersonal skills are important—they're actually half the battle. One thing I also look for is a lack of defensiveness. If people don't give me a clear answer, make themselves seem more experienced than they are, or seem to try too hard to impress me, I tend to discount them."

Frances Anastasi *is a director of domestic violence housing services in New York City.*

- -

How did you get the job?

"I started as a child care worker, when I was 19, dealing with abused and neglected children," says Frances. "I think I was naturally drawn to the job—I was taking psychology courses and liked children—it just sort of all came together in that job. I got my degree—a bachelor's degree in psychology—then went on to get a master's of social work.

"I got a job here at Victim Services 10 years ago. I worked as a director, providing practical assistance and counseling to victims of violent crime. Then I took a short break from client services, and for three years served as the head of personnel at Victim Services, Inc.

"When I moved back to client services, I came back as director of housing programs."

What do you do all day?

"Victim Services has an overall staff of about 600," Frances says. "I supervise a staff of 50 at six different sites.

"My day typically involves a lot of administrative, program issues. I deal with billing and statistics—that's the way we collect data in our agency. I do program needs assessment, clinical supervision, administrative administration, and crisis intervention when that is needed.

"I think the common denominator to people's problems is the individual's inability to see their role and take responsibility for their situation. It's been a frustration, not being able to work one-on-one with people to help them address their problems. That frustration is what led me to the mental health field."

Where do you see this job leading you?

"For now, I enjoy the combination of mental health and administrative work," she says.

Frances says, "People tend to come into this industry and stay where they are, making lateral moves. You can move up from an advocate's position to that of a director, if that's what you want. If you have ambition, you can move up the ladder. Many things in the social service field are related," she says, "so this

FEDERAL JOB OPENINGS AND INFORMATION ON EMPLOYMENT WITH THE U.S. GOVERNMENT CAN BE ACQUIRED FROM THE FEDERAL JOB INFORMATION CENTER. (SEE RESOURCES, PAGE 211.)
- - - - - - - - -

work can be good preparation for other social service positions. You can learn fieldwork when you work as a caseworker, and you can learn how to supervise in that position as well. You can also learn how to be a therapist when you work in this field.

51. Human Services Director

FOR A NURSING HOME

description: Human services directors for facilities that care for the elderly could serve in an activities director capacity, in a social services director capacity, or as both.

Activities directors plan and direct the activity programs for the facility's residents, programs that should be designed to meet the physical, psychological, social, and mental needs of the residents. Those activities could range from reading groups, to bingo games, to trips out into the community.

Social services directors make sure that residents' needs are fulfilled—they help them get eyeglasses, hearing aids, dentures, clothing, and the like; if residents have no family to help take care of their legal and medical needs, the social services director finds someone who can do that; social services directors intervene in roommate disputes; they make sure residents' rights are protected, and prevent residents' families from taking advantage of them. Social services directors also help in the planning of funerals for residents.

If you enjoy history or genealogy, this is the job for you, as the residents with whom you will work will be living fonts of information in these areas. You will have to steel yourself, however, to the fact that the health of many of your residents will deteriorate over time, and you will lose some of them.

The nursing home industry is one of the most regulated industries in the nation, and a great deal of your time will be spent making your way through the tangled forest of these regulations.

salary: While entry-level workers (typically technicians or some other such designation) will earn only just over minimum wage, human services directors will earn from $15,000 to $25,000 a year. Your salary level will depend on your experience, your job duties, and the size and funding of the institution you're working for.

prospects: The population in this country is getting older—by the year 2030 more than 20 percent of the population will be 65 or older—and there will be an increasing need for facilities to serve this population. A growing trend will be toward home health care—serving the elderly in a home setting.

qualifications: You will need to be a national- or state-certified activities director to work in that position at a nursing home. Getting that national certification will require a bachelor's degree (in social services or a related field) plus attending a specified number of certification-course hours. You will also have to take continuing education courses each year to maintain your certification.

characteristics: Patience is the number one prerequisite for a nursing home human services director. You should be dedicated to what you're doing. Being outgoing and energetic will definitely help. You should be empathetic to different backgrounds, cultures, and religions, as you will be dealing with people from all walks of life, many of whom will be struggling with decisions they made in the past and the ramifications of those decisions as they near the end of their lives.

Karen Jones-Skaggs *is the human services director at a nursing home in Kentucky.*

How did you get the job?

As part of Karen's undergraduate work (she majored in rehabilitation and minored in social work), she participated in a 16-week internship, doing activity therapy for children in a psychiatric hospital.

"Once I got out of school, I worked for a physical therapy unit for six nursing homes," Karen says. "An activities director's job at one of those nursing homes came open. I applied for the job and took the position.

"At that time, a bachelor's degree qualified you to become a certified activities director. Now you need to take a 90-hour course. Each state will have its own certification program.

"I worked at that nursing home for one year," Karen says, "and then I got married and moved. At my first job, I looked at the Redbanks nursing home in awe—it is one of the largest nursing homes in the state, and it's not like a lot of nursing homes in that it is totally non-profit. Profit-making facilities typically don't provide powders or deodorants or things like that to their residents. We supply everything here—combs, deodorants, clothing.

> **MAKE USE OF FEDERAL AND STATE EMPLOYMENT OFFICES TO CHECK OUT POSTINGS OF JOB OPENINGS. YOU WILL USUALLY BE ABLE TO FIND APPLICATIONS FOR OPEN JOBS AT THOSE OFFICES. SOME EMPLOYMENT OFFICES WILL OFFER RECORDED INFORMATION AND JOB POSTINGS THAT YOU CAN ACCESS OVER THE TELEPHONE.**

"I got the job at Redbanks as the social services director in the month of February. In mid-October, our activities director left. I was qualified to do that job as well as the social services job, and the director of the home asked me if I would take on both responsibilities. I technically have two jobs, though I have assistants on both sides.

"The residents are what attracted me to this type of work. I relate better to geriatrics than to children. I enjoy sewing, cooking, arts and crafts, and a lot of activities that we do here at the nursing home. I enjoy making sure that nobody takes advantage of our residents."

What do you do all day?

"Redbanks Nursing Home has 255 residents and about 200-plus employees. I supervise seven employees—five activities technicians and two social service designees."

Karen describes a typical week's duties: "I plan and coordinate three activities or programs per day. Our activities are planned on a monthly basis; we put together a calendar we go by.

"We probably admit three or more residents per week. When we admit residents, my department goes over our facility policies with them; my department goes through all the federal regulations that pertain to their care; my department tells them the rights they have as residents.

"I deal with our residents and our nurse's aides. I act as our volunteer coordinator in the community, and do a lot of educational things—educating the community on the importance of our facility, and on the health and medical needs of their family members.

Karen says she generally works 40 hours a week, though she does bring a lot of work home with her. "There have been weeks where I've put in 60 to 70 hours, though," she says.

Where do you see this job leading you?

"I want to go on to the administrative level," Karen says. "With health care reform such a big issue, jobs like mine are becoming a voice in the debate." She hopes to make her voice heard in that debate.

"I wouldn't want to try to solve the financial problems inherent in a for-profit facility," she says. "I would go on to another nonprofit nursing home, but if that opportunity does not become available, I'll stay here.

"With experience like mine, you could go on to do licensing and regulation, investigating complaints and making sure that facilities are operated correctly, following federal and state requirements.

"Consulting is becoming a big thing—keeping companies and their employees up-to-date on federal and state regulations that pertain to them, troubleshooting for companies. This job is good experience for doing that type of work."

52. Job Developer

FOR DISABLED INDIVIDUALS

description: As a job developer for an agency that works with disabled individuals, your task will be to secure employment for your clients. That will entail discovering jobs that are available, going out into the community and convincing potential employers to hire your clients, training (or helping to train) your clients in the tasks they will have to perform in their job, and following up with visits to both your client and his or her employer, once your client is placed in a job.

This will involve a myriad of tasks. You might find yourself helping your clients learn how to get to work—you'll help arrange transportation for them to get to the job, help them learn bus routes, or walk with them to work.

You will probably find yourself following your clients to work when they first get started in their job, where you will help with any additional training, and monitor how they adjust to their job.

One of the advantages of this job is its flexibility; job developers typically meet with employers and work with clients on their own schedules, and then bill their agency for the hours they work.

salary: Salaries for job developers can vary widely, depending on the nature of the agency you work for, its sources of funding, the experience or training you bring to the job, and the exact nature of your duties. Starting salaries can range from $15,000 to $25,000 annually.

prospects: State mental health and mental retardation offices, state rehabilitation commissions, and organizations like United Cerebral Palsy all sponsor or house job development programs for mentally disabled clients. Overall, prospects are good in this field. Cutbacks in government agencies might result in the loss of some jobs in government agencies, but the corresponding push to move people away from dependence on government funds and programs will mean an increased need for job developers.

qualifications: Job developers will typically require—on paper at least—a degree in social work, criminal justice, education, or a related field. Experience will probably count for more than education, however. Indeed, people landing this job will more than likely have prior experience working with the disabled, and many will not possess college degrees. Sales and/or marketing experience will be extremely handy, since you will be marketing the skills and value of your clients to potential employers.

characteristics: Job developers should be confident in what they're doing. They should be able to sell themselves and help potential employers, who might be resistant to the idea of hiring the mentally handicapped, see the value of bringing such employees on board. And they must not be easily discouraged, since the success rate for finding employment for clients can be frustratingly low.

Jene Ebest *is a community employment consultant (CEC) at an employment services organization in Baltimore, Maryland.*

- -

How did you get the job?

Jene was reading the newspaper and came upon a job opening at Now Employment Services. "I noticed they needed someone with a degree in social work, criminal justice, or a related field. But I also noticed that you could substitute experience for those qualifications."

Jene had experience in education, having taught for five years at a high school special education department, and counting another two years of volunteer experience working with the mentally disabled. Her degree was in elementary education, with an emphasis in special education. She says her interest in special education stems from the fact that her parents "fostered my disabled brother and then adopted him. I grew up with the desire to work with the handicapped. No one took the time to vocationally train my brother, and I saw that as his downfall."

Part of her high school work entailed vocational training for the students she was working with. "I taught [students] job skills, survival skills, how to fit in in the work force. And now, my job is exactly that: I go into the work force and get jobs for my clients."

She had to go through a number of interviews—and endure long stretches of waiting—to land that job however.

"I think the fact that my brother is mentally retarded, and that I had worked with juvenile delinquents in the past (I taught a class of troubled kids when I was teaching high school) are what impressed them most," Jene says.

What do you do all day?

In order to place her clients, Jene says, "I look in the newspapers and see who needs help. Then I go to those people. Or I go into a job site, and watch the employees, to see what they might do that is 'unwanted work.' Then I go to management and submit to them the idea of hiring someone for minimum wage or a little bit over minimum wage, someone who will do the work that their other employees don't want to do. I attempt to show potential employers that hiring our clients will make their regular employees happier.

"Some companies are very receptive," she says, "while some say, 'Well, [your clients] can't run a register, so they can't work here.' But most restaurants, for instance, have jobs that my clients can do—sweeping up, cleaning tables, filling the condiment tray during a busy lunch.

"I spend a lot of my time on the phone, talking to employers and potential employers," Jene says. "I spend a lot of time meeting with managers, and a lot of time driving from job site to job site.

"I work one-on-one in training my clients, though some CECs do have group job-training sessions.

"Sometimes, I will take clients to the mall to see their interests, to see what foods they like, to see what stores they're interested in going into. That

> **THE JOB SEEKER'S GUIDE TO SOCIALLY RESPONSIBLE COMPANIES RANKS 1,000 DIFFERENT UNITED STATES COMPANIES ON 19 "INDICATORS OF SOCIAL RESPONSIBILITY," RANGING FROM THE COMPANY'S CHILD CARE AND COUNSELING PROGRAMS TO THEIR EMPLOYEE-MATCHING GIFTS PROGRAMS.**
> - - - - - - - - - -

gives me ideas of jobs to try for for those people. If I can place them somewhere they like, they will work longer.

"I am also the support system for my clients. That's a big part of my job. If there ever is a problem with a client, then the call comes to me. Which is how I would prefer it. I don't want us to lose any company that has taken the chance on hiring a disabled individual, because once a company has had one bad experience with a disabled worker, they aren't likely to hire another disabled worker ever again."

Where do you see this job leading you?

"In my agency, the entry-level position is what is called a community liaison," Jene says. "Community liaisons take people out to give them exposure to the community. They teach classes on survival and work skills.

"And from that position, or from my level, it is possible to move up in the agency. You could go on to become a vocational adjustment coordinator, working within a school system or school district to find jobs for people in high school. It is also possible to move on to different agencies that pay more."

53. Program Coordinator

**FOR A METROPOLITAN SOCIAL SERVICE
ORGANIZATION**

description: Each program is set up slightly differently, with different responsibilities and priorities, but in general, the responsibilities for program coordinators include planning, budgeting, overseeing volunteers, screening and dealing with clients, carrying out administrative duties, and more. Coordinators will find themselves doing publicity for the program they oversee. They could also find themselves doing community outreach and attempting to enlist clients in their program or programs. Program coordinators work with volunteer committee members, public employees, and their organization's advisory council or board of directors. They oversee the implementation and daily operations of their programs, and are on hand to handle any crises that arise. They take care of any paperwork that has to be filed in regards to their program. They oversee any other staff members working on their program.

salary: Program coordinators for social service organizations can expect to earn in the $20,000s.

prospects: Prospects for work at social service organizations can vary widely, depending on how much of their income is derived from governmental sources. Some organizations are primarily publicly funded, while others secure a large portion of their economic base through private donations. With the government in the mood to cut back on social service programs, and agencies and organizations consequently scaling back on their programs and staffing, work might be hard to come by in those organizations. However, as private sector and business donations increase to take up some of that slack, new opportunities and even entirely new organizations and agencies might arise.

qualifications: Social service organization program coordinators should hold a bachelor's degree and have some experience in the field of social or human services, whether that experience be paid or volunteer. They should be able to work with the type of client with which the organization deals (youths, the elderly, the handicapped, minority groups, etc.). Experience in other areas—computers, grant-writing, fund-raising, preparing budgets—will be highly regarded.

characteristics: Prospective coordinators of social service programs and prospective workers in social service organizations should be enthusiastic about the work they will be doing and, more importantly, they should believe in what the organization is doing or attempting to accomplish. They should be organized, but able to switch gears and take on new tasks and responsibilities at a moment's notice. Proficiency in public speaking will also come in handy.

D'Arcy Bryan-Wilson *is a program coordinator for a metropolitan social service organization based in Tennessee.*

How did you get the job?

D'Arcy attended Austin College in Sherman, Texas, majoring in communications.

"I moved to Memphis when my husband began pursuing his Ph.D. here," she says. "I did some day-care work, and applied at several nonprofit organizations in town."

The 100-employee-strong Metropolitan Interfaith Association is a Memphis social service organization that provides a number of services to people in need in the Memphis area.

"I like old people, and I like kids," D'Arcy says, "so I applied with the Metropolitan Interfaith Association, and got a job with the special-delivered meals program. I managed that program.

"Then, after working at that position for a while, I heard that the teen job services counselor/Christmas store coordinator position was open. I've been in this position since March. I've seen one summer program through, and have done the budgeting and buying for our Christmas program, which is another responsibility I have taken on."

> ONE OF THE "TEN COMMANDMENTS OF NETWORKING" IS "ACT LIKE A HOST, NOT A GUEST." WHEN YOU'RE ATTENDING A GATHERING OR PUBLIC EVENT, MAKE AN EFFORT TO MIX AND MINGLE. INTRODUCE YOURSELF TO AS MANY PEOPLE AS YOU CAN. REMEMBER NAMES. TALK ABOUT WHAT YOU ARE INTERESTED IN. DEVELOP JOB LEADS. EXCHANGE INFORMATION.

What do you do all day?

"Our Christmas store serves 14,000 children each year. We buy one toy and get the other donated. The parents bring us two cans of food for their toys. So the mother ends up leaving the store with two new toys. Participants call ahead of time and are screened.

"We send out letters to participants to let them know they have been accepted. We set up shop in a converted horticultural building, and run 28 shifts over the course of two weeks, two to three shifts per day, handing out toys. There are approximately 10 volunteers working per shift.

"I coordinate that whole program—the screening, volunteer orientation, buying the toys, getting in-kind donations, lining up the trucks to haul the toys to the site, checking in the toys, stocking and restocking the toys.

"Everything I do is so seasonal," D'Arcy says. "As the teen services job counselor, I have a director of youth services over me. One hundred teens are employed by us—we find them work with nonprofit organizations. They come to our organization and we teach them how to fill out job applications, how to put together a resume, decision-making skills, phone and communications skills.

"Then we do the same basic thing in an after-school program. We accept 40 teens into that program, taking into account evaluations from the work site, and the number of volunteer hours they put in.

"I organize the interviewing day, the certification day. I plan job skills training sessions. I travel to the various work sites.

We put together a career day. There is another teen job services counselor, and during the fall months, I am busy with the Christmas store project, but help out as much as I can.

"This is 40 hours a week minimum. During the planning stages of the teen program, and during the screening and running of the Christmas store, I put in a lot of overtime."

Where do you see this job leading you?

"I would like to go a little bit higher in the organization. I've been here awhile and I'm really, really happy with what I am doing, but I would like to expand this program. I would like to add a component where we help kids get into college or technical institutions, where we help them fill out the forms, study for the tests, and get information on programs they would like to attend. We did have a mentoring program, but we had a hard time getting mentors. I want to be part of the expansion of this program.

"With this job, though, I could go on to almost any nonprofit organization. I've done it all. I've done public speaking. I've done budgeting. I've done buying. I've had to solicit donations."

115

54. Social Service Researcher

FOR A PRIVATE CONSULTING FIRM

description: As a social service researcher, you'll be hired by outside entities to perform specific tasks; you may be evaluating one or more of their programs, or perhaps you'll be examining the entire structure of the organization that hired you. You might be doing client surveys, or you could be attempting to document whether or not there is a need for a specific service.

Researchers are responsible for determining research methodology, conducting research, preparing reports on the results of the research they've done, and then presenting those reports to their supervisors and co-workers in their firm, and to the clients that hired them.

You will conduct a lot of field research, canvassing the opinions of staff members, supervisors and clients—those affected by policy—in order to gauge their reactions to policies and proposed changes, to gather their suggestions, to get a feel for how the organization you're researching works, and to see what can be done to improve that organization's performance.

Depending on the structure of the organization you work for, you may have a great deal of say or next to none regarding which clients you work for and the types of projects you undertake. But you probably will be doing a wide variety of work—one month you could be working on a project to improve job opportunities for low income families, the next doing a staff evaluation for a nonprofit agency, and the next conducting a workshop on market research techniques.

salary: The biggest factor determining the salaries of social service researchers will be experience. Salaries start in the mid- to high-$20,000s per year, and can rise into the $50,000s.

prospects: Though, in these budget-conscious times, organizations and agencies are becoming increasingly cognizant of the need to determine the effectiveness of their programs and staffs, the number of private firms that research and evaluate these programs and organizations is still quite small, especially those that specialize in the social and human service sector. There are probably more research positions available in government, for example, then there are in the private sector. However, program evaluation is a growing field, so there should be more jobs opening up in the future.

qualifications: Positions will require a bachelor's degree in statistics or social services, and many will require a master's degree. Work experience, especially experience in research materials and methodology, and in conducting research or experience "in the field," will serve as a replacement for these prerequisites in many instances. Successful applicants will have strong writing skills, and an understanding of research tools and methods. If you have a working knowledge of policy issues and communication skills, this should be emphasized as well.

characteristics: A successful researcher will possess compassion and a dedication to producing quality work. One researcher adds that "integrity is essential to this job. It can be easy to go with what people want to hear, but you can't be an objective researcher if you go with what people want to hear. There are palatable ways of presenting your findings without hurting your integrity."

Sharon Ramirez *is a project associate at a research organization in Minnesota.*

How did you get the job?

"During college, I wanted to work with women's issues and with issues of social change," says Sharon, who earned a B.A. in philosophy, religion and women's studies at St. Olaf College in Northfield, Minnesota.

"I was eventually hired for a child advocacy position. I started working with battered women's groups, doing crisis counseling there, working with women as they went through the legal system, and helping them find housing. I became the volunteer coordinator for an intervention project, where volunteers would go to women immediately after a domestic violence assault."

Sharon went on to become an organizer with a group called Women Work in Welfare. She was the housing management specialist for West Bank Community Development, a residentially run development project, working with the tenants there to build a movement around their issues and concerns. "I worked a couple of short-term positions through the Center for Urban and Regional Affairs and worked on the development fund for the

> THE JOB SEEKER'S GUIDE TO SOCIALLY RESPONSIBLE COMPANIES RANKS 1000 COMPANIES USING 19 INDICATORS OF SOCIAL RESPONSIBILITY, RANGING FROM ON-SITE CHILD CARE, TO COUNSELING PROGRAMS, TO EMPLOYEE MATCHING GIFTS PROGRAMS. THE GUIDE ALSO RANKS SOCIALLY RESPONSIBLE COMPANIES BY INDUSTRY AND GEOGRAPHIC LOCATION.

United Negro College Fund, connecting with donors," she says.

During this time, she earned a master's degree and studied community development and women and policy. A professor at the institute knew that Rainbow Research was looking for someone with broad nonprofit experience to work there as a project associate, and told Sharon about it. Rainbow Research describes itself as "a nonprofit organization specializing in evaluation services that assist socially concerned organizations in responding more effectively to social problems."

What do you do all day?

"I'm an evaluator," Sharon says. "I go out and interview people and make sure that people's voices are heard. I do face-to-face, one-on-one interviewing, overseeing focus groups, conducting workshops. I do site visits, spending a number of days at the site of a project to see how that project is progressing. I also make sure that the information I gather is presented in a format that people can use.

"After the research is done, you debrief your notes. You put your research together into a framework for analysis. I develop reports and assessment tools. I do a lot of writing in this job.

"The organization is run almost like a law firm in the sense that funders or grants allocate a certain amount of money towards the research, and project associates and senior project associates here count up our billable hours.

"I spend a small portion of my time looking for clients and reading books—urban history, local development policy,

school reform, all sorts of things—learning about new issues, trying to stay on top of things.

"Deadline time—when our reports are due—that's when we're the busiest. And when we're traveling." She adds that she typically works more than eight hours a day.

Where do you see this job leading you?

"You can make this position what you want," Sharon says. "Someone from Rainbow Research went on to do international consulting. There are people who want to be involved in more direct service, and you can go from a position like this into something like that. From here you could go out on your own. You could become a program officer for a philanthropic organization. You could become the director of an organization; we have people here who used to be organization directors."

Sharon says that she plans on making a career switch of her own. "I have decided that I need to focus my skills and talents on issues that move me the most—women's issues and issues of persons of color."

55. Teen Center Director

description: Directors of teen centers have a multitude of responsibilities and have to wear a variety of hats. One of your main responsibilities will be coordinating and overseeing the different activities of the center. You might be in charge of matching up volunteers (tutors and so forth) with people that need to be served. Coming up with new programs that keep your clients—children, youths, and teens in the community that you serve—coming to the center and taking part in those programs will also be one of your responsibilities. In a large part, you'll be a liaison to the community—you will serve as the voice of your center, and your words and actions will reflect on how the center is perceived.

One advantage of the job is that you will most likely have direct contact with the clients you're serving. Unlike many jobs in the nonprofit sphere, you'll be "in the field," on the front lines. That being the case, sometimes you'll be face-to-face with failure—before your very eyes the people you're trying to reach will slip through your fingers. This can be one of the disheartening things about the job, and one of its disadvantages.

salary: Speaking of disadvantages to the job . . . the maximum salary you can expect to make as the director of a teen or youth center is $25,000 a year. Without any niche skills, such as computer experience or fluency in a second language, you probably would not start at more than $20,000 a year. The type of organization funding the teen center, how that organization comes by its funding, and the area of the country in which you are working could serve to modify those salaries.

prospects: Most urban areas have some sort of teen center, so these types of jobs are out there. City recreation departments often operate a number of recreational centers. Some cities will have more of these types of programs than others, in both the private and the public sector. Inquire into the funding sources of the organization you might be serving, and be wary of those organizations where more than 15 percent of the budget comes from the government. (Government-funded activity centers are more prone to the budgetary ax than those whose funding comes from other sources.) Oddly enough, in a recession, funding is sometimes easier to come by for these programs. When everyone is feeling the pinch, they are perhaps more aware of the need for recreation centers and similar programs.

qualifications: City-funded centers or programs will more than likely require a college degree in education or a related field. The more volunteer experience you have to your credit, the better. Highlight skills that make you stand out from the crowd, such as a background in outdoor education, a facility with a foreign language, or computer knowledge. Experience as a summer camp counselor is excellent training for this type of work.

characteristics: Most importantly, you should be able to relate to kids. You should get along with them as a peer, but you should also be able to exercise authority when the need arises. If you're patient, nonjudgmental, and open-minded, you've got the stuff that you'll need to succeed at this job.

Ronald Del Sesto *is codirector of the Good Shepherd Ministries Teen Center in Washington, D.C.*

How did you get the job?

Ron began doing volunteer work when he was in college, majoring in philosophy and history at Georgetown University in Washington, D.C. "Volunteering was a real eye-opener for me," he says. "I had never met children in poverty before, and when I started this job, that was a real problem. I didn't have any background at all in poverty—I come from an upper-middle-class background—and so in order for me to relate we needed a neutral space in which to meet, where it wasn't like, well, 'I'm going to show you what to do, and you're going to follow.' Computers allowed for that. I wanted to create an electronic space where kids and someone like me could meet on an equal footing." It was his volunteer experience and his knowledge of computers that proved most beneficial in landing the job with Good Shepherd.

Good Shepherd Ministries is a Washington, D.C.-based organization that works with children ages 5 through 19. When Ron joined the organization, their teen center, located in the basement of an inner-city D.C. apartment building, had been closed for half a year. He saw an opportunity at that center, and took it.

Bringing in some Macintosh computers, Ron set up a computer lab in the teen center and began teaching the 15 or so kids that showed up at the center Hypercard and some other basic programs. It was tough going at first, he says, though about 60 kids are now members of the center. Ron and some of the kids working in the computer lab put together a multimedia presentation that caught the notice of the comedian Sinbad, who flew the kids out to Los Angeles for an awards presentation honoring their work.

He cautions anyone thinking about entering his field to be willing to make a commitment to the people you'll be working with. "These kids really have some heavy stuff to deal with; since I've been at the center, seven kids have been killed. A lot of them come from single-

> **A COMMITMENT TO A PROGRAM LIKE THIS NEEDS TO BE FOR A MINIMUM OF TWO YEARS.**

parent homes and are already dealing with feelings of abandonment. If you come into a situation and begin to establish a relationship with someone, then leave a year or six months later, perhaps you'll be doing more harm than good."

Still, Ron says, "There's a lot of hope in this community. Every kid who makes it becomes an inspiration to others. Last year, four of our kids went on to college."

What do you do all day?

Ron's primary responsibilities lie with the computer lab he set up. "I'd say 25 of our kids use computers on a regular basis. I show them the basics and help them work through the programs, but I have no say over the content of what the kids produce." Using programs such as PageMaker, Photoshop, and video- and sound-editing programs on the lab's four computers, the teen center's clients create their own programs— producing computer animations, and fliers for their band, or synchronizing their own voice with video images of the Power Rangers.

Ron works at the center three days a week. If he's not in the computer lab, he says, he'll most likely be tutoring, helping teens with schoolwork or school and job applications, or working on grants and paperwork. He also coaches the center's basketball team.

Ron has a second job as well. He helps manage the computer system and network of a group of nonprofit organizations in the Washington, D.C., area.

Where do you see this job leading you?

Ron says he has applied to law school. He hopes to get into child advocacy work. "I feel a need to have a higher impact on the community," he says, "perhaps by getting into legislative work.

"I see a blind-sightedness in terms of what programs are offered here. I would love to see job-training programs established here in the inner city. My own desire is to serve as a bridge between two worlds—the worlds of power, and those of the inner city. In a larger sense, I see my role as helping people who are highly educated see that they have community responsibility, responsibility that perhaps they never knew they had."

56. Assistant Program Coordinator

AT THE NATIONAL LEVEL

description: As the assistant coordinator of a national-level program, you'll be working under the direction of your supervisor—the program's director or coordinator. As most nonprofit organizations are understaffed, however, you can expect to operate with a great deal of autonomy. Your boss will probably lay out some general program goals, projects, or priorities and then let you see those programs through to completion.

You might be called on to develop materials for member use for specific programs. This could involve researching, writing, and developing materials. Perhaps you'll be called on to produce a brochure or program guide.

You might find yourself working on (or even spearheading) campaigns that your organization involves itself in. You might help develop future campaigns. You could be called to serve on task forces regarding certain issues or directions the organization is considering pursuing.

And, of course, you will find yourself dealing with member requests and questions.

salary: An entry-level job in many cases, assistant program coordinators can expect to make anywhere from $10,000 to $23,000 per year. Salary is dependent far more on the size of the organization and its funding structure than it is on experience.

prospects: These jobs are going to be concentrated near the national headquarters of nonprofit organizations—Washington, D.C., New York City, and California. Atlanta and Chicago could be considered secondary centers of nonprofit activity. In these places, jobs tend to become available on a regular basis, as assistant coordinators and program assistants move onward and upward at a regular rate.

qualifications: A grassroots background will prove helpful in securing a job of this type, since it will show that you have experience working with people on that level. Organizing experience will also look good on your resume. Communications and research skills, and experience in graphic design and layout are some of the other talents organizations look for.

characteristics: A demonstrated commitment to the cause you will be working for will serve you in good stead. You should possess or develop the ability to take direction, and then to pursue a task without much supervision.

Nick Crosson *is a national youth program assistant coordinator for a human-rights organization based in Washington, D.C.*

How did you get the job?

Nick Crosson got his first taste of what Amnesty International is all about when he was in high school and attended a U2 concert. "They had a table set up at the show," he says, "and were having a big push to start Amnesty chapters in high school and college. I helped start a chapter at my high school, and then got progressively more and more involved in Amnesty on a volunteer level.

"When I went to college, I became the Amnesty International college coordinator, which was a voluntary leadership position. Then I became the student area coordinator, and helped provide basic contact information to college chapters in the area. At that point, as I became responsible for things beyond my own campus and was going out and speaking at other campuses, Amnesty started providing me with a small budget to work with. That was my bridge between volunteer work and full-time serious activism.

"I was in my school's career center and saw in a newsletter there that there was a fellowship that would pay for a year's salary so that you could involve yourself in activist work. I checked with Amnesty International to see about ground-level positions they might have available. Then I applied for the fellowship I was eligible for—unfortunately it's no longer in existence—and got it.

"I worked for a year in the regional office as the student program coordinator. I worked with 200 groups in our region. From there, once the fellowship ran out, I came to my current position."

> CONCENTRATE YOUR JOB SEARCH ON GEOGRAPHIC AREAS YOU'RE INTERESTED IN AND WILLING TO MOVE TO. CHECK OUT NEWSPAPERS AND ONLINE FORUMS FROM THOSE AREAS. GET IN TOUCH WITH ORGANIZATIONS AND INDIVIDUALS WORKING THERE TO FIND OUT ABOUT POSSIBLE JOB OPENINGS AND CONTACTS.

What do you do all day?

"I develop materials that student groups use to start their own Amnesty International groups," Nick says.

"We work on campaigns that change each year, campaigns focusing on specific issues and countries.

"I develop stickers and documents—I filter all the information we gather on these countries and issues down into a 20-page report. Ten pages concern what's going on and Amnesty International's position on what's going on. Ten pages are on what you can do about the situation. I'd say I spend 60 to 70 percent of my time developing materials," Nick says, "putting together these types of documents, and answering questions from Amnesty International student members.

"The other 30 to 40 percent of my time is spent doing no one thing. Part of my time is dedicated to projects I created when I started here. Every year there is an Amnesty International plenary, where 100 to 200 people get together to determine policy. And student members can get real lost when they attend plenary for the first time. I created a document that explains what goes on at plenary.

"The rest of my time is spent doing other day-to-day tasks. And I spend some time dealing with future campaigns and organizational projects.

"The work here goes in cycles. The beginning and end of the school year are both very busy. We usually work about 35 hours a week, but as projects near completion, we're all putting in 12-hour days."

Where do you see this job leading you?

"We don't have a large staff here, so I've gotten the chance to do a lot of stuff. I've been given a lot of responsibility in a short time because, well, basically, they don't have a choice. They don't have the staff.

"I consider this a stepping-stone to work with a civil rights organization," Nick says. "I've seen people go on from work like this to reasonable positions in other organizations. I've seen people go on to law school, to work at a radio station. One person got a journalism master's degree and is going on to Sweden. Some people have founded their own organizations."

57. Child Support Case Officer

description: Child support case officers work to ensure that child support awarded by the court is paid. They investigate those cases and prepare documentation on cases to be taken to court. However, the specifics of this work can take many forms.

Some case officers are responsible for locating absent parents who have been ordered to pay child support. Once an absent parent has been found, some officers prepare the documents necessary to establish responsibility. Others are responsible for enforcing payment.

One disadvantage of this work is the sheer number of cases to oversee. Child support offices are chronically understaffed, and the heavy workload can lead to burn out. On the plus side, you will achieve satisfaction as you work to ensure that the needs of children are being met.

salary: Child support officers can expect to make from $16,000 to $32,000 per year, depending upon experience, education, and the agency's requirements.

prospects: Though social service programs often are the first to fall under the budgetary ax, the simple fact is that because people are still getting divorced and child support payments are still required, child support enforcement jobs aren't going away. Jobs are likely to be more plentiful in state capitals, where state child support enforcement offices are located.

qualifications: Candidates for child support officer positions should possess a college degree and one or two years of experience in the child support system or in a related field. Demonstrated analytical abilities and oral and written communications skills will also be highly valued.

characteristics: This job has a definite customer service component, as officers have to deal with estranged ex-spouses in a civil and competent manner.

Chris Gola *is a program specialist/policy analyst in the Office of Texas Attorney General Child Support Division, Austin, Texas.*

How did you get the job?

"I had a friend at the Attorney General's office working in the child support division who told me about an opening there," says Chris Gola. "I had worked for a law firm for two and a half years; I already had the clerical experience the job required. And I had the inside track because of my friend working in the A.G.'s office.

"I got the job and spent six months working in the file room. I came in at the very bottom rung, but when I was hired, I told my boss that I didn't want to just get by; my ambitions were higher than the file room.

"About six months after I started, I began work as an intake clerk. My duties included processing child support cases, opening up cases for people who apply to receive child support, and getting support levels set. We would verify the information on our cases by calling the custodial parent to see if they had any information on the absent parent, for instance.

"A few months later, a child support officer position came open. The job description called for a college degree, which I didn't have. But the description also said you could substitute experience for

> HONING ORGANIZATIONAL SKILLS AT WORK AND AT HOME CAN BETTER PREPARE YOU TO DEAL WITH THE HEAVY CASE LOAD YOU WILL MOST LIKELY ENCOUNTER AS A CASE OFFICER.

schooling on a year-for-year basis. I had about 100 hours of college credit by that time, and with my time on the job, I was able to meet the qualifications for the position.

"In that position, the cases I had been opening were the cases I was now working on. I was responsible for enforcement of child support orders," Chris says. "My job was basically to get guys to pay.

"After two years of doing that, I was so burned out that I was close to quitting. Then a friend of mine told me about a position opening up at the state level, the position of policy analyst. I met the qualifications for that job, which were one to two years of child support experience and a college degree with, again, work experience

substituted for college credit on a year-for-year basis. I had to submit a writing sample, showing that I could write documentation. I had a great rapport with my boss, and she passed along the good word. I went in and had a good interview, and I got the job.

"In this job, I work to change and edit our department's policy and operations manuals to meet changing legislation. I write and revise policy, review state and federal statutes, and make sure our department's policies match those statutes."

What do you do all day?

"As a child support officer, I would arrive at work by 8 a.m.," Chris says. "You have to be ready to deal with the public on a regular basis. People walk through the door, call and ask you what they need to do to come into compliance, or call you to tell you that their job situation has changed and that they need to change their payment requirements.

"On all cases, you're filling out paperwork and prepping the case. By the time the case gets to you, there has already been an order filed for support.

"If they didn't pay, I would get in touch with them either by sending a letter or by calling

them. We have some absentee parents that would simply refuse to pay. We would do the paperwork on those cases, make sure we had the parent's location, and turn the file over to an attorney."

Where do you see this job leading you?

"I'll stay at this job a minimum of two years," Chris says, "which is about how long it will take me to finish my college degree. I'm majoring in computer science and, if I stay with the agency, I would want to move into the Management-Information Systems or Data Services divisions of the A.G.'s office. Within the Attorney General's office, I can see myself working as a systems analyst or a project manager.

"Some people will move from being child support officers in a field office to field supervisors, or they go on to other field offices or to other branches of the Attorney General's office. People tend to stay within the A.G.'s office, but move on to different sections."

But, he adds, the experience acquired working in child support can be applicable to many jobs in the fields of both government and law.

58. Direct Marketer

description: Nonprofit direct marketers will use marketing techniques, particularly direct mail and tele-marketing, to find new donors for their organizations. Once those new donors are found, direct marketers will cultivate them, working to convince them to increase their funding levels, and to establish a long-term relationship with the organization.

A nonprofit organization will typically use four main techniques to solicit donors: television advertising, print advertising, direct mail, and telemarketing.

Direct marketers will begin their job tasks by developing the organization's long- and short-term strategic and revenue plans, looking for ways to develop new products to cultivate donors. These efforts will be coordinated with the television and print advertising efforts, and with the overall plans and goals of the organization. Once those plans have been formulated, direct marketers work to implement those schemes, developing direct marketing mail-outs, supervising or participating in telemarketing efforts, and coordinating work with an advertising agency, should the organization be using one.

Part of your duties might also entail staff development and training, and keeping abreast of developments in both the nonprofit and advertising/marketing worlds.

salary: You can expect salaries for direct marketers to be lower for nonprofit work than they are in for-profit work. Beginning marketing salaries can start in the low $20,000s. Salaries can rise significantly higher with greater experience, from the $50,000 to the $100,000 or higher range, depending on the size of the organization.

prospects: The prospects for finding marketing work with nonprofit organizations are perhaps better than for those of any other nonprofit position. Even in times of slow or suspended growth, nonprofits still need to raise money. With the proper experience and level of energy, enthusiasm, and creativity, prospective marketers should enjoy success in procuring a job with a nonprofit organization.

qualifications: Karen Childers, director of direct marketing and merchandising for the Save the Children Foundation, says, "For an entry-level position—if I'm hiring an assistant marketing manager—I will look for marketing experience, three years minimum. It doesn't matter to me if the experience is in fund-raising or in consumer marketing. What matters is that the experience was in some form of mass-marketing—print, television, direct mail. I don't give bonus points for fund-raising experience, though other managers might feel differently."

Karen says that another important qualification is demonstrated experience in executing a marketing campaign, or in using the techniques of direct marketing.

For a managerial position, five to 10 years of direct marketing experience will likely be required, along with some management or supervisory experience.

characteristics: First, direct marketers should have an intrinsic love of marketing. People working in nonprofit direct marketing should also be extremely organized, as they will have to work on several campaigns and projects simultaneously. Good interpersonal and management skills are definitely a plus.

Karen Childers *is the director of direct marketing and merchandising for a child welfare organization in Westport, Connecticut.*

- -

How did you get the job?

"I came to Save the Children out of a consumer products company, running a catalog company," reports Karen. "I had 10 years experience with consumer products, and came out of a for-profit company. I came to Save the Children to run the consumer products part of our operations, the Save the Children catalog business and retail stores. That was six years ago.

"I knew nothing about the fund-raising side of things when I came here, but through downsizing, upsizing, and reorganization of the foundation, I added on doing direct marketing, which is pure fund-raising.

"Fund-raising marketing, though, is conceptually no different than consumer marketing. What you're doing is putting together a buyer and a seller. With fund-raising, the product you're selling is not tangible, and the buyer is called a donor. What a nonprofit needs to do is prove that the buyer's donation is accomplishing something. A nonprofit needs to create a reason to give."

What do you do all day?

"I put in 50 hours a week minimally," Karen says. "But really, this is a job where you should never stop looking for new ideas. You come up with a creative idea, and then you project the revenue it will bring in, and the expenditures of doing it.

"An example of a campaign we conducted that crossed all of our mass-marketing areas was a campaign that focused on starvation in Somalia. We developed a campaign theme—'Phone Lift'—with an 800 number. We thought it was a good theme—simple and direct. We asked ourselves, 'Which medium would be best served to do this?' and we tested the campaign in various media—telemarketing, direct mail, television, and print advertising. Based on the results of those tests, we pursued some media more aggressively. We took that theme and decided where to use it, what would be the best way to reach our audience given the projected revenue, and the projected cost of conducting the campaign in a variety of different media."

"Telemarketing can be effective in two ways," Karen says. "We can let you call our 800 number to make a donation. On the other side, I can call you at dinnertime and see if you would be interested in making a donation. Both can be very effective if used at the correct time.

"Someone who has been regularly giving, you might want to send them a direct-mail package to encourage them to continue contributing. Someone who has stopped giving, who hasn't donated to you for a year or two, you might find it more cost-effective to call them. Part of the job of the direct marketing director is deciding where to best allocate those resources."

Where do you see this job leading you?

"My compatriot at Save the Children handles television and print advertising," Karen says. "I could go on to head up all of this or another organization's mass-marketing fund-raising. I could move into development work, or into the corporate arena.

"People can move up from a small nonprofit to a larger one, or they can go out into the corporate world."

> ONE OF IVAN R. MISNER'S "TEN COMMANDMENTS OF NETWORKING": WRITE COMMENTS ON THE BACK OF BUSINESS CARDS YOU COLLECT. THE COMMENTS YOU WRITE WILL GIVE YOU INFORMATION TO USE WHEN PURSUING FURTHER CONTACT WITH THE INDIVIDUALS YOU MEET AT NETWORKING OPPORTUNITIES, AND WILL HELP YOU REMEMBER WHO IT IS YOU HAVE JUST MET.

59. Director of Development

description: Organizations typically rely on a combination of corporate, foundation, and individual support, and the kind of fund-raising efforts the development director will be involved in depend on where his or her particular organization's funding comes from. As a development director, you will be spearheading your group's fund-raising efforts, whether that is organizing a public fund-raising event, writing proposals for foundations, or appealing to the corporate community. A development director will probably have a close working relationship with the organization's board of directors—tapping them for their possible fund-raising connections, or enlisting their aid in projects and fund-raising efforts. Part of the job will more than likely involve putting together the organization's newsletter and other public relations materials. In this type of job you'll be dealing with a lot of people—from the individuals and corporate heads you'll be attempting to raise funds from, to the members of the board of directors you'll be working with.

salary: Starting development directors can bring in $30,000 to $35,000 a year, depending on experience. That figure can vary, depending on geographical location and the type of association for which you work. The starting salary for development assistants is $22,000 to $25,000 a year.

prospects: Though most nonprofit organizations have someone who does the development director's work, not all organizations have a specific position dedicated to this task. Many organizations combine the positions of program manager and development director, for example. The best bet for rising to the level of development director is from the development assistant position—an entry-level job in many cases.

qualifications: A college degree is mandatory for most development director positions. Showing interest in the field, however, can be just as important as a piece of paper from a university; the more volunteer work you have behind you, the more able you are to demonstrate your commitment to this kind of work.

characteristics: The ability to work with different types of people—people of different socioeconomic levels than your own—is of paramount importance, since as development director, you will be working with people from the community you serve, the corporate community, and government types, all on a daily basis. Newsletter writing skills and basic knowledge of how a newsletter is put together are important assets for workers in any nonprofit organization.

Rachel Tillman *is the director of development for a Washington, D.C.-based nonprofit organization.*

How did you get the job?

When Rachel first graduated from college, she worked as the crime reporter for a small newspaper in the Baltimore, Maryland area. "But there wasn't a whole lot of crime there," she says, "and as a consequence, I did a lot of other writing. I ended up writing a lot of features—and I wrote features on nonprofit organizations—that's what first piqued my interest in nonprofits."

She moved to Washington, D.C., and got work with Jubilee Support Alliance, an organization that raises money for Jubilee Housing, a low-income housing project in the nation's capital. Rachel worked for Jubilee for three years, organizing special events and coordinating meetings for the board of directors.

"The reason I decided to move on is that I was really interested in bridging what people do in nonprofits with the business community. I think that's a very important link."

> "THE CHRONICLE OF PHILANTHROPY IS A NEWSPAPER FOR NONPROFITS," RACHEL SAYS. "IT'S ABOUT FUND-RAISING AND FOUNDATIONS. IT'S JUST AN EXCELLENT RESOURCE. AT THE BACK OF EACH ISSUE, THEY HAVE AN INCREDIBLE HELP WANTED CLASSIFIED SECTION. IT'S VERY EXTENSIVE AND LOTS OF NONPROFITS ALL OVER THE COUNTRY USE IT."

These sentiments made Leadership Washington an ideal place for her to move on to. This 10-year-old nonprofit puts on a yearlong educational program for business, community, and government leaders, introducing them to the problems in the D.C. area, and providing them with a place to network and develop solutions to those problems. (There are typically 150 applicants for the 50 slots available each year.)

"I had a really good reputation at Jubilee," Rachel says. "I made sure all of the details were taken care of, and made a good impression on the people on the board. So, when it came time for me to move on, I had really good references."

What do you do all day?

Rachel says that a typical week will see her put together a mailing that will be sent out to Leadership Washington's membership, to its board of directors, or to the general community to let them know what the organization is doing. She also spends part of her time writing thank-you letters.

"I probably spend a tenth of my time following up on leads for sponsorship," she says.

Though she works a 9-to-5 schedule, Rachel says there is some overtime she devotes to the job. "The board and special committees will typically meet at night, since those bodies are made up of people from the business community, and I have to make sure I'm at those meetings."

Where do you see this job leading you?

Rachel says, "Across the board, what I've seen is that people start out as administrative assistants, then move on to program assistant or development assistant positions. The next step would be to program manager, program director or development director, and from there to executive director." The woman who had her position at Jubilee before she did is now the director of Denver's YMCA program, for instance.

"I think I have a good sense of how to help an organization be financially stable," she says. "A corporate attitude, I think, is important. Too many nonprofits aren't run on a very fiscally-sound basis, and I think it's important that a nonprofit business is run like a business.

"I do want to stay in nonprofits. My dream job would be as a program officer in a foundation—deciding who gets the money instead of always asking for money, that would be nice."

60. Human Resources Department Worker

description: The term "human resources" conjures up in many people's minds the image of that place where you send your resume, where it is then tossed in the trash. While it is true that the human resources department is that department prospective job-seekers interact with most often in their quest for information about a company and employment prospects within it, the work of a human resources department entails more than mere resume shuffling and interview scheduling.

People in the human resources department spearhead their employer's recruitment efforts as well. They ensure adherence to all state and federal hiring regulations, as well as to internal company policies regarding employee interviews and orientation.

Human resources departments also handle most of their company's internal promotional efforts and employee training. They work at resolving inter-staff conflicts and employee grievances. When an employee is hired, human resources personnel plan and execute employee orientation sessions. Workers in this department handle the explanation and implementation of employee benefits and retirement savings programs. They deal with workplace safety issues, and enforce compliance of safety regulations.

salary: Salary levels for human resources workers vary depending on the size and nature of the company that employs them. Nonprofit organizations will pay on the lower end of the wage scale; working for nonprofits might net you in the low to mid-$20,000s, while workers at for-profit organizations can earn into the upper $30,000s. Management salaries can rise into the $50,000s for nonprofit work, and into the $60,000 to $70,000 range for for-profit managers.

prospects: Oddly enough, in the current era of corporate downsizing and trimming of staffs, the prospects for human resources work look to be on the upswing. Employers are attempting to do more with fewer resources, and they need good people in place to help them do that. It is the human resources department that helps them find and retain qualified applicants.

qualifications: Candidates for human resources positions will usually be required to possess a college degree. Though much of the particulars of human resources work can be learned on the job, an advanced degree will probably be required of candidates for mid- and upper-level management positions. Human resources workers should have a basic understanding of OSHA and EEOC guidelines, and of employer benefit packages.

characteristics: Prospective human resources department workers should be analytic thinkers. They should be shrewd judges of character, but must be fair-minded—especially relating to labor law. Human resources workers should be excellent "people people" as well, able to de-escalate the problems of a frustrated worker, and to relate to people from a variety of backgrounds and social situations.

Scott Squeglia *works as a human resources manager of an international nonprofit organization in Americus, Georgia.*

How did you get the job?

"My wife and I decided to do volunteer work. We chose Habitat for Humanity because their international headquarters provided housing, a stipend, and minimal health insurance.

"It was an exceedingly upwardly mobile position for me. I worked the Habitat for Humanity helpline for one month, then moved on to being the human resources department's data-entry clerk. I then became the employee compensation allowance person, the re-entry coordinator, and then the interim recruitment manager. I was soon hired as the manager for international recruiting. A few months later, I became the grant manager for Americorps."

What do you do all day?

"I handle recruitment of people for our international programs," Scott says. "I place advertisements in magazines, newsletters, and with the Peace Corps hotline (a service for returned Peace Corps volunteers).

"We send out applications to people who request them. Then we do a screening of the application. We also ask specific questions of applicants—do they have management, project development, or volunteer experiences. If they don't have those qualifications, we make the cut. About 10 to 20 percent of our applicants each year are accepted.

"After the initial screening, we take a second, harder look at the applicants. Area directors supervise our programs overseas, and we try to match our applicants with area directors, in terms of personalities and job skills. Area directors review the applications, and then we have a phone interview, conducted by the area director. We invite people for face-to-face interviews on the basis of those 'phoners.'

"After applicants are chosen, we have the orientation phase of our program. Then we do six-week training sessions twice a year.

"Once the training starts, we start gearing up for the next recruitment phase.

"We're currently involved in projects in more than 46 countries, and have about 110 people in the field. I deal with issues those workers have. I have a budget to provide educational supplies for couples in the field, since almost all of them home school their children. I do a compensation analysis.

"Managing the Americorps grant mostly deals with supervision of staff. I make sure people do proper follow-through on interviews, make sure we are following EEOC recruitment policies, that we are looking for possible avenues of minority and disability recruitment.

"I talk with the volunteer managers of our eight Americorps sites, and handle personnel problems, conflict resolution, and other problems that come up.

"I also do exit interviews with both international program and Americorps staff.

"I supervise five people, spread over the international and the Americorps programs. I have a counterpart who deals with local volunteers who come to Americus—he deals with

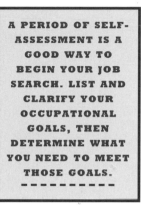

A PERIOD OF SELF-ASSESSMENT IS A GOOD WAY TO BEGIN YOUR JOB SEARCH. LIST AND CLARIFY YOUR OCCUPATIONAL GOALS, THEN DETERMINE WHAT YOU NEED TO MEET THOSE GOALS.

housing for those people. We have another personnel member that handles the organization's paid staff.

"The core staff members here are paid staff members, but the rest are volunteers."

Where do you see this job leading you?

"I would eventually like to be a director of a human resources department for a college or a nonprofit organization," Scott says. "Right now, I'm looking at an MBA program dealing with nonprofit human resources work. My wife is finishing college, and we're waiting for her to do that first. Right now, I'm concentrating on getting more real-life experience."

61. Meetings Director

FOR A NATIONAL ORGANIZATION

description: A meetings director for a national-level organization plans the major meetings and conferences for his or her organization. The organization might hold one annual convention for which the meeting director is primarily responsible, or it could hold a number of regional conferences that fall under his or her jurisdiction.

Meetings directors line up facilities in which to hold these events, find and solicit speakers and people to put on workshops, and are responsible for getting out the word about these conferences and meetings, procuring and registering attendants. They find themselves making hotel and plane reservations, raising funds to support their efforts, planning and keeping a budget, and performing many other miscellaneous tasks.

They network continuously, to keep abreast of developments in their field that should be addressed at events they put together, and to have a list of names and phone numbers of potential speakers to call on when the need arises.

salary: Meetings directors of national-level organizations can expect to start at between $22,000 and $28,000 per year, depending on the size and location of the organization, and the importance the organization places on its conferences and meetings. Salaries at some of the larger organizations can rise to $40,000 per year or more.

prospects: Conferences and annual meetings are some of the best ways for organizations at all levels to reach out to their members, so most nonprofit and advocacy organizations will have a meetings director or someone who fills a similar role. Those duties might be combined with those of a membership or outreach director, but these types of positions are out there.

qualifications: Meetings directors will need to be good relationship-builders. They need to have experience and proficiency in developing, managing, and making presentations to a wide range of people. Good communications skills, both in speaking and writing, are essential. They should have, or should develop, fundraising experience as well. Public relations experience will also come in very handy.

characteristics: Meetings directors should enjoy working with and meeting all types of people. They should be interested in learning—learning new things about their field, and learning of people doing interesting work in their field—and should greet every new person they meet as an opportunity to learn something. They should be open-minded and flexible, adaptable to new circumstances. They should be willing to work with other people, and not feel the need to shoulder the entire burden of a given project by themselves—but they should not have to be told every step how to get a job done.

Dawn M. Hutchison *is a national meetings director for an outreach organization in Washington, D.C.*

- -

How did you get the job?

"When I graduated from college, I worked as an administrative assistant at the Wisconsin Humanities Council, which is the state branch of the National Endowment for the Humanities. I spent two years there, working as an administrative assistant.

"I then realized I needed something more. I wanted to work with people, and was interested in how people come together around an issue. So I packed my bags and moved to Minneapolis.

"Which is where I found out about the Campus Outreach Opportunity League (COOL), a project that focused on the coalition-building model, attempting to get everyone on campus involved in community issues. The goal of the organization is to educate and empower college students to get involved in community service."

At COOL, Dawn first served as a technical assistant, and then took a job in the meetings department.

"And then I became COOL's meetings director, going to Tempe, Arizona, and putting together COOL's next national conference. I was responsible for overseeing the development of the whole conference, doing logistics and public relations with the help of two interns.

"And now I'm in D.C., organizing this year's conference."

What do you do all day?

COOL has four full-time employees, Dawn says, and usually works with four to five interns at any one time as well. The organization's headquarters are in Washington, D.C.

"Sometimes I describe my role as that I am here to help students in organizing students," she says. "And for our annual national conference, I manage the process of doing fund-raising, picking the workshops that we will feature at the conference, getting speakers, setting up workshops, networking, informing the 2,200 students that will participate in this conference about the conference, and getting them registered.

"I move about every eight months to the site of our next conference. We put on a leadership summit in the summer, and I will either go to the site of that summit or to D.C. for the other four months of the year.

"My timeline runs something like this: In the summer, I'm doing the initial set-up work, figuring out the logistics of the conference, picking someplace that is big enough,

> **MEETINGS DIRECTORS SHOULD BE INDEPENDENT WORKERS.**
>
> - - - - - - - - - -

and has enough classrooms for 150 classes over the course of the conference, someplace where I can line up free housing for the approximately 500 people we will bring in to the conference. I'll set up the major agenda for the conference and begin identifying and inviting speakers, beginning with our keynote.

"In the fall, we start our recruitment phase. We put together and send out 30,000 brochures. We develop student committees and subcommittees, and elect chairs for those committees. We start sending out requests for in-kind donations.

"In the spring, we focus on external recruitment, the gathering of participants for the conference.

"January is when things get much more intense. Student volunteers are constantly running in and out of the office. Someone is at the computer 18 hours a day. We're making travel arrangements for our board of directors; we're working on scholarships for students. We're identifying new recruits—volunteers to work at the conference; we're making up schedules

with 300 slots for volunteer times. We're planning the layout of the Opportunity Fair—the conference's national exhibit of organizations. We're planning receptions and lunches.

"And then the conference happens in March. When the conference happens, it's great. You see all these people getting motivated. And you see how this conference really changes people's lives."

Where do you see this job leading you?

"I have been thinking about what I want to do next, and how I can transfer my skills to what I do next," Dawn says. "Hotels have meeting trainers for instance, and grassroots organizations hire people to organize other people around particular issues. I could move on to a more national mainstream organization such as the United Way or the Girl Scouts—they put on huge conferences, and that would be taking this job onto another level. I could work for political campaigns or do marketing in the for-profit sector.

"I eventually want to get into museum education, using the idea of the museum as a community center to provide cultural and educational programming."

62. Policy Analyst

description: A policy analyst will, first of all, monitor legislation on the state or national level, looking for pending legislation or issues that may affect her or his organization's constituency or interests. Policy analysts will examine such policies and legislative agendas to see what the possible affects will be on their constituencies. They draft and perhaps present testimony to legislative committees and bodies, explaining their organization's position on the legislation.

A good portion of their effort goes toward maintaining relationships with legislative members and their staffs.

Policy analysts also maintain relationships with media representatives, preparing press releases to send out to them, writing editorials for their newspapers, and talking with reporters and editors to keep abreast of local developments.

They also engage in a little grassroots lobbying—speaking to interested civic groups and telling them how pending legislation could affect them, as well as what they could do to affect the outcome of that legislation.

salary: Policy analysts can expect to make between $20,000 and $40,000 per year. Salary level will depend on the sources of income and income level of the organization for which they work, as well as the part of the country they live in and their experience.

prospects: People with the prerequisite experience should be able to find work in this field. Issues—and the attention paid to them—seem to operate in cycles, and as certain issues become thrust (or thrust themselves) into the limelight of public attention, groups will arise—and positions will become available—to work on those issues.

Established working relationships with legislators and organization staffers will aid analysts in their work, and will better their chances of hearing about openings in the field—and their chances of being offered those jobs.

It is, perhaps, tougher to stay in this profession than it is to get involved. This sort of work is draining and can sap every last waking hour from people involved in it.

qualifications: Prospective policy analysts should possess a basic understanding of the political process and of the issues affecting the constituency of the organization with which they hope to work. Most often, that understanding will come through experience—whether it be in legislative, organizing, or policy research.

Internships are a good way to get your foot in the door.

characteristics: Policy analysts need to be detail-minded activists. They must possess the persistence to stay on top of pending legislative efforts, and be drawn to the agenda of the organization for which they work. They must be self-motivated, and willing to fight when their organization and its constituency's interests are challenged.

Jesse Romero *is a state policy analyst for the San Antonio regional office of the Mexican-American Legal Defense and Educational Fund in San Antonio, Texas.*

How did you get the job?

"I first started organizational work in college," Jesse says. "I was a history and political science major at Southwest Texas State University, and managed to get an internship with the Mexican-American Legislative Caucus in the Texas House of Representatives.

"Through interning with the caucus, I became friends with the caucus director," Jesse says.

"He submitted my name to [a group called] Neighbor-to-Neighbor, and I went to work for them. I went to work in Chicago on their lobbying campaign.

"That drive finished up; the caucus director also had connections with a group called Southwest Voter Registration, and he put them in touch with me. I was recruited to work the Coastal Bend area of Texas.

"I was based out of San Antonio, but I lived in my car and went from city to city organizing voter registration drives. I eventually became the organization's Texas-New Mexico field organizer.

"I continued my connection with the Mexican-American Legislative Caucus, however, and when a new chair took

A BOOK CALLED <u>NONPROFITS' JOB FINDER</u> DESCRIBES ITSELF AS "THE QUICK AND EASY ROUTE TO JOBS, INTERNSHIPS AND GRANTS IN EDUCATION, AND ALL OF THE NONPROFIT SECTOR." WITH JOBS BROKEN DOWN INTO DIVERSE CATEGORIES, AND A STATE-BY-STATE LISTING OF JOB AND GRANT SOURCES, AS WELL AS GENERAL JOB SEARCH TIPS, THE BOOK CAN BE A VALUABLE TOOL FOR SOMEONE LOOKING FOR WORK IN THE NONPROFIT SECTOR.

over, I was hired to be the staff director of the Caucus. I researched issues. I helped draft legislation. I monitored legislation. I helped members and their staffs. I compiled voting records. I did media work and wrote articles for newsletters. I was a liaison to other members of the legislature and to civil rights groups like the Mexican-American Legal Defense and Educational Fund (MALDEF).

"I was friends with Velma Luna from Corpus Christi, and when she was elected to the state legislature, she asked me to come over and help set up her office in Corpus Christi. So I worked for her for about a year, and then I moved up to the state senate, to the office of Rodney Ellis.

"I had known MALDEF and its staff members, and had

worked with them on various issues. They were looking for a state policy director, and they approached me about the job."

What do you do all day?

"As I come in, I try to plan out my workweek," Jesse says. "I might plan a speaking engagement, or work on ongoing issues. I'll take care of phone calls, or complete assignments, or handle emergencies that arise.

"The thing about this job is that you never know what could come up. Our Washington, D.C., office could call and tell us that tomorrow there's a vote due on legislation affecting affirmative action regulations or some other measure, which means our office will need to

put out a legislative alert—we'll pass the word on to 25 civil rights organizations who work together in a coalition on these issues, so they can get the word out to their constituency.

"I work typical business hours during the week, but always end up working more than 40 hours. That's because, on Saturday, I'm always either in Houston or Austin, San Antonio or Laredo, on speaking assignments.

"During the legislative session, I'm typically working 12-hour days, seven-day weeks. During the last legislative session, I lived in the state capital."

Where do you see this job leading you?

Work as a policy analyst can lead people in many directions. Analysts could go on to do legislative research for another organization or within the legislative branch itself. They could go on to other positions in their organization or in like-minded organizations. They could move into the legislative arena, working for a legislator or committee. Lobbying work, or work in a governmental think-tank, might beckon them as well.

63. Program Evaluator

description: People in these positions, which may also be called "administrative support," provide evaluations of the performance of organizations, or of organizations' specific programs, setting goals for those organizations and programs, and establishing methods for determining whether or not those goals are met. Program evaluators do this by meeting with workers in all areas of the organization to determine those goals, creating and administering surveys and other data-collection devices, collecting data, and then organizing that data into forms that can be used by members of the organization and the general public, and that can also be manipulated to influence government agencies and potential fund-raisers. Because evaluators deal with all members of the organization—from the people working in the field to the administrative heads of the organization—and because they deal with all facets of social services, the job is a varied one. Because these sorts of jobs are fairly new, a program evaluator can have the opportunity to be his or her own boss, which can be both a good and a bad thing.

salary: Beginning salaries for program evaluators can range from $20,000 to $26,000 per year. With experience, that salary can rise to $35,000 to $40,000 or more per year. Salaries can vary depending on geographic location and the funding sources of the agency.

prospects: "Outcome-based funding" is the buzzword among nonprofit and government-funded organizations at the moment, so prospects for these types of jobs are quite good. Federal and state governments, as well as private donors, are looking for evidence that the money they're providing to organizations is having concrete results, so the job of the program evaluator is becoming ever more important.

qualifications: Most positions will require either a bachelor's degree in statistics or social services, or a master's degree. Training in quantitative analysis, policy analysis, management, and statistics is necessary for this job. Basic computer skills are also a plus.

characteristics: Since your job, in large part, is teaching people to recognize whether or not they're doing their job effectively, a sense of tact and an ability to communicate effectively with other people are essential. Because you will function independently much of the time, self-motivation is important. This is the type of job where the rewards are more intangible than concrete, so program evaluators must be satisfied with results that will not be immediately apparent.

Tara Singh *is the program evaluator for the United Cambodian Association of Minnesota and the Association for the Advancement of Hmong Women.*

How did you get the job?

Tara was an international studies major in college, with an interest in Asian culture. She landed a summer job coordinating the national convention for the United Cambodian Association of Minnesota. "I found organizations that I wanted to work with and called them up about possible internships," Tara says. "This Cambodian Association said, 'We don't have any internships, but we've got this big project coming up, the national convention.'"

She made a good impression organizing a successful convention. "I was very honest with the people about the skills I had," she says. "I didn't promise more than I could deliver, and I delivered more than I promised." When the need for a program evaluator became apparent after that convention was complete, Tara was able to step into the role. The Cambodian Associa-

tion was about to lose all of its federal funding, which comprises about 10 percent of its income, so the pressure is on Tara to detail the effectiveness of the organization so it can solicit other sources of funding.

What do you do all day?

Much of Tara's day is taken up working on the computer, designing survey tools for use by the agencies' workers, or creating ways to present that survey information to potential donors. "I spend about an hour-and-a-half per day preparing for meetings," Tara says. "I spend a lot of time talking with people and getting information from them. For instance, I helped put together a one-page questionnaire that was a survey on the youth

camps the Cambodian Association sponsors in the summer. That survey had three goals: to generate a basic evaluation of the camps, the activities that worked and the activities that didn't; to gather demographic information on the camp participants—how many came from single-parent households, how many live in public housing, etc.; and to get an emotional/psychological handle on the kids, how they're fitting into the mainstream American culture. I met with the camp staff, and it was the first time that many of them had really articulated the goals they had for their program." For this particular project, she had one week to do the survey analysis, write a report on that analysis, and present it to the camp leaders so they could

implement any changes in time for the next camp session.

"In a nutshell, the organization's workers teach me what they do, and I teach them how they can communicate that to other people."

Where do you see this job leading you?

For the next five to 10 years, Tara anticipates working "in the realm of social services." She can see herself working with child pregnancy and poverty prevention organizations, or as a planning specialist for city or county government.

Tara is currently working on a master's degree in planning and policy analysis. She also does contract consulting, for which she charges about $18 an hour. (Experienced consultants charge up to $80 an hour.) Tara says that once she gets her master's degree, she will charge $25 to $30 an hour. She would like to eventually go back to school to get a Ph.D., and to teach at the undergraduate level.

> **KEEP A JOB SEARCH FILE OF INFORMATION—BROCHURES, NEWSPAPER AND MAGAZINE ARTICLES, BUSINESS CARDS, NOTES FROM CLASSES OR MEETINGS—ANYTHING THAT MIGHT PROVIDE YOU WITH INFORMATION ON A JOB YOU MIGHT BE INTERESTED IN OR ON AN ORGANIZATION YOU MIGHT BE INTERESTED IN WORKING FOR.**

64. Recruitment Coordinator

description: A recruitment coordinator for any volunteer-driven organization is responsible for enlisting volunteers to work with the organization, and perhaps for enlisting clients for those volunteers to serve.

Much of the work that recruitment coordinators do is public relations work—attempting to draw attention to their organization, its mission, and the work that it does. Recruitment directors plan, oversee, and implement whatever sorts of recruitment drives the organization undertakes. Recruitment coordinators work closely with their manager, as well as with their organization's board of directors, and perhaps with a recruitment committee. They represent the organization at community fairs and other public events; they appear on public affairs programs representing the organization; they write letters and editorials for newspapers, magazines, and newsletters.

They are one of the first representatives of their organization whom volunteers meet.

Depending on the size of the organization and its structure, the recruitment coordinator might also be responsible for training and placing volunteers.

salary: Salary level can vary widely, depending on the size of the organization and the scope of the recruitment coordinator's duties, but most salaries will range from $17,000 to $25,000 a year.

prospects: For those nonprofit organizations that are volunteer-driven, recruitment coordinators are among the most vital of positions (second, perhaps, to those in the fund-raising department). Positions tend to turn over quickly, and prospects for qualified applicants are quite good, depending on the part of the country in which they are looking for the job.

qualifications: John DeMuro, former recruitment coordinator for Big Brothers-Big Sisters in San Antonio, says, "The San Antonio chapter was looking for someone with a B.A. in marketing or public relations, plus two years experience. I didn't have that—my undergraduate degree is in English. But I could write press releases. I could give speeches. I could understand the concepts of target marketing and recruiting. I did have the computer skills needed to put out the organization's bimonthly newsletter. I did have to teach myself Pagemaker for this job. But even if I didn't have the qualifications they were looking for on paper, I was able to show them that I had the skills that this job required."

characteristics: Recruitment coordinators need to be friendly; they need to be willing to talk to anyone and everyone about the program they're involved with. Organization and time-management skills are necessary as well, because, as in so much of nonprofit work, recruitment coordinators will be called on to handle many projects at once.

John DeMuro *works in the recruitment center of the Big Brothers-Big Sisters program in Chicago, Illinois.*

How did you get the job?

"I ran into some VISTA (Volunteers In Service To America) workers here. The first person in the organization that I met told me that it was cool, that they were getting a lot out of it.

"So I joined VISTA, and was placed with the local Habitat for Humanity branch. For one year, I worked as the fund-raiser for the Habitat for Humanity office. In that year, I was able to raise $100,000, through grants, through phone solicitation, and through organizing corporate projects.

"Once that year was over, they didn't want me to leave. They hired me as their office manager at Habitat; that happens a lot with VISTA volunteers who show initiative and decide to stay—the agencies will find a way to keep you.

"I was making $17,000 a year, and I was answering phones and ordering paper clips. So I quit that position.

"I moved to Albuquerque (I had a brother there). And I was hired by a nonprofit agency as their resource development coordinator, in charge of fundraising and volunteer recruitment.

"I realized that I wanted to return here, and so I did. I started looking for jobs, and ended up finding two jobs in one day. One was with a program called City Year, a volunteer corps tied in with Americorps and working with 17- to 23-year-old kids. They needed a supervisor for the kids, a fund-raiser, and someone to find projects for them to do." The other was with Big Brothers-Big Sisters, where John is now employed.

What do you do all day?

"This chapter of Big Brothers-Big Sisters has 270 active matches," John says. "We've got another 270 kids on a waiting list; 250 of those kids are boys. So our problem is how to get men to volunteer. It is incumbent upon us to find out how we can get more male and minority volunteers. Nobody has really had much success in that area, so whatever I do will be noticed.

"I coordinate our annual recruitment drive, which includes a celebrity softball event and other details. Our six-week-long recruitment drive starts at the end of August, and the fall is really the busiest time of the year for someone in this position.

"For instance, right now, about 60 percent of my time is spent organizing a celebrity softball game," John says. "I've been contacting celebrities to get players for the softball game. I've been calling to get donations for the game.

"About 10 percent of my time is spent talking to anyone who calls to inquire about the program.

"The job is supposed to be 40 hours a week, but I put in a lot of night and weekend hours. I coordinate our presence at community volunteer fairs and at community events; I hit pretty much all the community fairs that come down the pike.

"At least two times a week, I go out to speak—to a group of employees or to a civic club. Or I do a radio interview. I do two volunteer introductions a month. I coordinate our volunteers, and do a lot of mindless work—finding directions to a fair, getting maps for people, getting volunteers to man a booth at a fair, putting together materials for a booth.

"The rest of my time is spent in committee or staff meetings, or in doing back-burner projects, like writing the copy for radio ads for our recruitment campaign, or developing other projects."

Where do you see this job leading you?

"At this point in my career, I need to put in one year at the very least. I need to prove that I don't move every six months," John says.

"I'm going to try and get a public-access television show together. What I want to do eventually is to make movies and to produce television shows—to work in something less serious and more creative."

> **THE JOB ENTAILS A LOT OF SOCIALIZING WITH VOLUNTEERS.**

65. Volunteer Coordinator

description: The "labor force" of many nonprofit organizations is made up of volunteers. As a volunteer coordinator, you'll be responsible for overseeing the work the volunteers do. You will make sure that those volunteers make the best use of their talents and time, and see that the volunteers feel satisfied in their work. If the organization has a training program for its volunteers, the coordinator is in charge of administering it. Perhaps the most daunting task is finding people willing to donate their time for your cause.

One of the most rewarding aspects of this job will be the people you meet. The level of commitment exhibited by volunteer workers can serve to refuel your own commitment to your cause.

The biggest downside to this job could be—as in most jobs in the nonprofit sphere—the amount of hours you'll be putting in. Frustration, due to the lack of funds needed to implement the projects you envision, can also be a problem.

salary: As a volunteer coordinator, your salary should range from $20,000 to $25,000 a year. At smaller agencies, the salary will be a bit lower, perhaps starting at $18,000.

prospects: As federal and state governments relinquish many of the social service roles they have long assumed—as seems the current trend—there will be an ever increasing need for other organizations to assume those duties. Nonprofits are perhaps the foremost of these organizations. And as the need for nonprofit aid increases, the need for volunteer coordinators will increase as well.

Corporations, too, often have an employee (usually in the human resources department) in charge of volunteer projects for the company as a whole, so you should consider exploring volunteer coordinator positions outside the nonprofit realm.

qualifications: Although many organizations will state that they prefer candidates with a master's degree, just as often a paid position is filled from within the pool of that agency's volunteers. Especially in volunteer-driven organizations—the very ones that are going to need volunteer coordinators—volunteering your time can lead to a paid, permanent position in the long run.

characteristics: Volunteer coordinators need to be personable and to have good listening and organizational skills. This is a job that will hone your motivational abilities—but it's good to have a base upon which to build.

Judith Manriquez *is the volunteer coordinator for an adult literacy council in Cleveland, Ohio.*

How did you get the job?

After graduating from college, Judith first worked for a small nonprofit agency and then spent a year working as an assistant to the board of directors at her state's Department of Human Services, while she was getting a master's degree in public policy. Following a stint as a mayor's aide and the completion of her degree, she was hired by the Travis County Adult Literacy Council.

"I came into this job at a time when they needed a lot of organization. Coming out of graduate school, I think I was prepared to pretty much handle anything. We had changed from being administrative offices to being direct service—a very direct role. I've kind of fulfilled a different role in that I have maintained a lot of the administrative part of this job. I keep my hands out of the direct service."

Judith's fluency in Spanish proved to be an asset in an environment where people are being taught English as a second language.

What do you do all day?

Volunteers undergo 21 hours of tutoring training in both literacy and ESL. Though another employee does the actual volunteer training, it's after this that Judith steps in. It's her job to match students up with

> VOLUNTEERING CAN NOT ONLY BE A WAY TO GAIN EXPERIENCE OR LEARN MORE ABOUT A FIELD YOU MIGHT BE INTERESTED IN, BUT CAN ALSO BE A WAY TO BUILD CONTACTS.

prospective tutors. "I spend time with everyone, determining who has been an active student and who has not, who should be matched." (The agency has a waiting list of students, so tutors are reassigned to new students if their old ones don't pursue their training on a regular basis.)

"I do assessments [of students to see which volunteers they should be matched up with]. I also train assessors. Our volunteers also do assessment—they do that first interview with students, and I train them. Part of that training requires observation, so I will spend quite a bit of my time doing that. So that means I'm sometimes here until 8:30 or 9 at night, because that's when our volunteers and our students are free.

"I've been very gifted in matching [students with volunteer literacy or ESL tutors]," Judith says. "I've been very lucky with that. The thing that's great about working here

is that students come here of their own free will. Volunteers come here because they want to help somebody. When you put those two elements together, there are very rarely any problems."

"I will spend a good portion of my day talking to volunteers who either drop by or call in. I could also spend my time doing solicitations to corporations for funds," she says. And she works on the organization's newsletter.

Where do you see this job leading you?

Though Judith has a dream of someday opening her own restaurant, she says she hasn't really thought about what comes after this job. "There's a lot of opportunity here, and this is a very positive atmosphere to work in.

"I tell everyone I talk to that they should not expect to be in social work forever. Leave and come back if you want to, but if you don't leave, you can easily burn out. The hours are so long and the pay is so minimal that it is easy to burn out."

66. Communications Director

FOR A TRADE ASSOCIATION

description: A communications director at a trade association is responsible for keeping the members of the association informed on what their association is doing for them. Communications directors usually accomplish this through newsletters, direct mailings, and one-on-one conversations with association members. As a communications director, you will be responsible for implementing outreach programs directed at the association membership—annual conventions, training seminars, special programs, speakers, etc. Communications directors may also be responsible for relaying the needs and wants of the association membership—determined through surveys, polls, phone calls, and other techniques—back to the association administration. Association staff members are ultimately responsible to their association's membership, which makes the nature of this job more focused, perhaps, than that of a communications director for an activist or nonprofit organization. Less of your effort will be spent in membership recruitment-type activities, for instance.

salary: Communications director salaries will vary according to the size of the association and the region of the country that the association is based in, but starting salaries should range from $25,000 to $35,000 per year.

prospects: Every state has a city (usually the state capitol) that is its center for association activity, and some states have multiple cities that serve as hubs. There are also possibilities with national association headquarters, located in Washington, D.C., and throughout the country. Since there are associations for every interest, the job prospects for association communications directors nationally are quite good. Not all associations or association chapters will have communications directors, however. And since associations will be congregated in certain locations, the competition for jobs at them can be quite fierce. Though associations can wither and die due to lack of membership interest or changes in the industry or industries the association serves, the death of an association is an uncommon occurrence; most associations are around for the long haul.

qualifications: Most communications director positions require a bachelor's degree in journalism, communications, or some other related field. Some previous experience will likely be required, though getting a communications director job straight out of college is not unheard of.

characteristics: Most communications directors will be functioning with a staff of one—themselves—so the ability to work independently is crucial to success in this field. Having an attention to detail, time-management skills, the ability to prioritize tasks, and proofreading skills are also assets when it comes to this job. Since you will be dealing with a wide range of people, a pleasant demeanor is also a helpful characteristic.

Pam Moen-Thieding *is a communications and seminar director with a homecare association in Madison, Wisconsin.*

How did you get the job?

After graduating with a broadcast journalism degree from the University of Wisconsin-Platteville, Pam worked as a reporter for an Iowa television station. When her husband secured a position in Washington, D.C., Pam followed and became press assistant to the Dick Gephardt presidential campaign. "As campaigns are, that one was fairly short-lived," Pam says, but that position led to her becoming press secretary for a Wisconsin senatorial candidate. Once that campaign was complete, she served as press secretary for another Wisconsin senator, a post she held for three years.

After four years in Washington, Pam and her husband moved back to Wisconsin. She saw an ad in the newspaper for the communications and seminars director with the Wisconsin Homecare Association, applied for the job, and got it. The association serves home health care providers in the state, monitoring the industry and government regulations that affect it, and providing continuing education for home health care providers.

"My journalism degree and (reporting) experience were attractive from the communications end of things," Pam says. "I found that my political experience in Washington was valued pretty highly at the state level."

What do you do all day?

Pam says her time is split pretty evenly between her communications and seminar-planning duties.

"The seminars part of my job involves planning, coordinating, and staffing our educational seminars for the home health professionals." Pam says the association typically offers 10 to 12 meetings plus two conventions per year for home health aides, nurses, and administrative personnel. "We have an organization planning committee for these types of programs,"

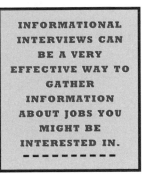

INFORMATIONAL INTERVIEWS CAN BE A VERY EFFECTIVE WAY TO GATHER INFORMATION ABOUT JOBS YOU MIGHT BE INTERESTED IN.

she says. "So I meet with them and work to develop the seminars we intend to offer throughout the year. I coordinate with the facilities, the different locations, and the speakers. Then I will be there to staff these conferences as they go on."

Her work on the communications side of things involves talking both with the public about what the association's members do, and with the association's membership, addressing their concerns. She consults with the association's contract lobbyist, who promotes the association's agenda before the state legislature. She also edits a monthly 12-page newsletter for the association, writes and produces some of the association's membership and public relations materials, and works on the association's media relations.

Where do you see this job leading you?

"I have considered staying in the association profession," Pam says, "and possibly advancing the level of my employment, perhaps to the association management level. I don't think I ever see myself going back to journalism proper.

"So much of my career was spent in transition—the longest job I've ever had is the three-year term as a press secretary in Washington. When I came back to Wisconsin, I was really looking for a job with some stability. I wanted a job that was well suited to my talents, and where I could stay for a while. I hope I've found that. I see our association as one that is growing—I'm content here, at least for the short term."

67. Governmental Affairs Officer

FOR A TRADE ORGANIZATION OR LOBBYING ASSOCIATION

description: A worker in charge of governmental affairs for a trade or lobbying organization works to monitor and track government issues—on both the federal and the state level—that affect their member's interests. They attend meetings of governmental committees and subcommittees, and keep abreast of the movement of bills through the legislative process. They pore over mailings, too. A governmental affairs officer's job can be summed up as staying on top of, and reporting back on, issues of concern to his or her members.

Governmental affairs officers might be called on to lobby on behalf of the organization's interests as well. Their job might focus more on promotion or more on research, depending on the nature of the agency or association for which they are working.

salary: Governmental affairs officers can expect to command salaries anywhere from $40,000 to $100,000 per year, depending on their skills, experience, and how closely their talents match up with the association's or lobby's goals and expectations. Officers in state-level associations or lobbies should expect lower salaries.

prospects: There will always be associations interested in tracking the government's activities, and lobbying organizations interested in affecting governmental policy. As new issues arise, new associations and lobbying organizations will spring up around them. Association headquarters are likely to be located in state capitals or in Washington, D.C., so if you're not willing to relocate to these areas, your chances of finding work will be considerably slimmer.

qualifications: Perhaps the most important prerequisite for this job is prior legislative or governmental experience. This experience will show that you know your way around the corridors of state or national power, will prove that you have experience dealing with government types, and will give evidence that you can maneuver your way through the bureaucratic labyrinth and ferret out the information in which your association members will be interested. Another important skill set is demonstrated written and oral communication skills.

characteristics: Someone who is interested in work as a governmental affairs officer should be confident, diplomatic, and a good tactician. A thorough understanding of the issues your organization is involved in is also crucial to your success.

Leslie Cahill *is the vice president of governmental affairs for a trade association based in Washington, D.C.*

How did you get the job?

Leslie grew up in Missouri, and after graduating from college, she worked in Washington, D.C., as a legislative aide for a congressman from her home state.

After four and a half years working on the Hill, she went to work with the United States Department of Agriculture as an assistant secretary for natural resources and the environment. She worked as a researcher and writer, covering soil and natural resource conservation, doing testimony- and speech-writing. From there, she moved on to the Office of International Cooperation and Development within the USDA, doing the same sort of thing that she had been doing in her previous job, but this time working with co-op programs with foreign countries. Leslie then moved on to

THE ENCYCLOPEDIA OF ASSOCIATIONS IS PUBLISHED BY GALE RESEARCH COMPANY, AND PROVIDES DETAILED INFORMATION ON TRADE AND OTHER ASSOCIATIONS ACROSS THE UNITED STATES.

the USDA's Undersecretary's Office for Small Community and Rural Development, writing speeches concerning crop insurance and the Rural Electrification Administration.

Five years ago, she came to the American Seed Trade Association, an association made up of seed and related-industry companies in the United States, Canada, and Mexico. Leslie is now their vice president of governmental affairs.

What do you do all day?

"I deal with the Food and Drug Administration, the Environmental Protection Agency, the United States Department of Agriculture, the Federal Highway Administration, and a host of other offices and agencies," Leslie says. She attends meetings of these and other agencies, to get a sense of where the focus of government is going as it pertains to the association's members' interests. "The issues are constantly changing, and my job is keeping our members informed about those changes." She travels to attend local chapter meetings, to meet with commodities groups, commissioners of state-level organizations, and representatives of state seed control groups.

Leslie develops programs to keep the association's members abreast of the latest regulatory changes. The hot issues her association is currently dealing with involve biotechnology, intellectual property rights, and legal issues, Leslie says. She fields questions from, and gives advice to, members who call in or visit her in the association's D.C. offices. She puts together the association's monthly newsletter to let members know what Congress and the association are up to. She also helps organize the association's annual conventions.

Where do you see this job leading you?

Leslie says, "It's taken me every bit of this five years to learn the industry I'm working in. I think I'm here as long as I can be useful."

She says it would be fairly easy to transfer the skills she has mastered to another agency, one that deals with different issues. She could also see moving on to a bigger agency.

68. Educational Worker

WITH A NATIONAL-LEVEL YOUTH ORGANIZATION

description: Many national-level activist and labor organizations will have youth-oriented programs or departments aimed at getting their message out to a college- and high school-age audience. Much of this work is aimed at creating the activists of tomorrow, giving young people the skills and exposure to ideas they need to prepare them for involvement with these types of activist movements throughout their lives.

The duties of someone working in this position range from program development to fund-raising, to directing and developing field staff, and to the planning of conferences and workshops. You'll end up speaking about the organization, and traveling to different campuses to participate in various events or direct actions. You'll work with students on their campuses, and you'll give them tours of your offices and the community in which you work. You will be a liaison and a resource for young organizers, helping them out in whatever way you can.

salary: Working for youth groups or educational organizations on a national level, you can expect to make from $19,000 to $26,000 a year. If you're working out in the field, the pay will probably be a bit less—from the upper teens to the mid-$20,000s. Within the labor movement, those salaries can rise into the lower $30,000s.

prospects: The labor movement was dealt a tough blow in the early 1980s when union-breaking legislation was the order of the day. It is now recovering from those setbacks, and the outlook for work is expected to increase slightly. The nice thing about youth-oriented organizations is that they tend to be staffed by younger workers, and are perhaps more receptive to prospective employees who make up for lack of experience with their enthusiasm for working hard and their eagerness to learn. The labor movement as a whole always seems to be on the lookout for young workers with talent.

qualifications: If you want to work in an organization whose educational efforts are aimed at college and high school students, you should possess a college degree. But you should have more than a degree going for you— prospective employers will look closely for evidence of previous organizing experience or campus or community involvement while in college. Written and verbal communications skills are also important.

characteristics: Applicants should be passionate about the cause they want to work for, and should be able to convey that passion to others. They should possess—and constantly work on improving—leadership skills. They should be able to develop a plan of action, and then have the tenacity to follow through on that plan. A willingness to take risks will also come in handy.

Cheryl Graeve *is the executive director of a Washington, D.C.-based grassroots union organization that targets leadership development among young people.*

How did you get the job?

While in college in Minnesota, Cheryl was active in campus politics, and was a member of her university's student senate. Once she graduated, she went to work for the Minneapolis Public Interest Research Group (MPIRG).

"The Public Interest Research Groups are one of the best social-change organizations I am aware of," Cheryl says. "They're involved in youth issues, the environment, women's issues, consumer issues. I started doing canvassing door-to-door with them, doing fund-raising, getting people to sign petitions, doing public education work."

She was hired by Minnesota's Nuclear Freeze Campaign as that organization's canvassing director. Then Congressman Jerry Sikorski came calling. "There I worked with a variety of constituent groups, and represented the congressman at different meetings in Minnesota— I was sort of his field representative in Minnesota."

After two years with the congressman, Cheryl says, she felt the desire "to get back into social-change work." So she went back to the Minnesota PIRG, this time as its legislative director. "In that position, I helped train students as grassroots organizers, I attended hearings, I wrote and gave testimony, and I monitored legislation for our group."

Cheryl soon left for the nation's capital with the intent of going to grad school there, but soon ended up working with the Sea Farers Union for a year, helping them with their political action committee.

"I liked this form of grassroots organizing, and learned that there was an opening at Frontlash, an AFL-CIO grassroots mobilization effort that deals with leadership development among young people, with an eye to teaching them about the labor movement."

She was hired as a Frontlash campus organizer. She served in this position for two years, then moved up to assistant director of Frontlash, where she stayed for a year and a half, before moving on to her current position as executive director.

What do you do all day?

"We take on basic programs that teach and train students about democracy, the electoral process, and the labor movement, and that develop those interested in becoming involved with the labor union movement," Cheryl says. "On the issues end of things, we work to improve the relationship between unions and college students, and work together with them on issues of importance to both of us.

"The work I do varies each day," she says, "from program development to fund-raising, to directing our staff in the field, to development work, to doing conferences. We have a small staff—five people plus our interns—and my primary responsibilities are the financial end of things, the development of our training programs, speaking about our organization, and organizing in general and networking.

"As the director of Frontlash, a typical week for me involves a lot of work on the phone and a lot of travel. I conduct conferences around the D.C. area, and put on national student events. Last week I was in Mexico for a meeting of the Continental Young Unionists, to talk about youth and unemployment, and how different countries address that problem."

Where do you see this job leading you?

"Frontlash is a great beginning opportunity in the labor movement. You could go on from here to the political affairs arena of the labor movement, or to field staff for the AFL-CIO, or to positions in the local, state, or national level of unions.

"As for me, I believe that the labor movement is my home. Will I go on to political work? Probably. The international affairs side of this movement also attracts me," she says.

> COLLEGE CAMPUSES PROVIDE MANY OPPORTUNITIES TO BONE UP ON YOUR COMMUNICATION SKILLS. TAKE ADVANTAGE OF THOSE OPPORTUNITIES. SPEND SOME EXTRA TIME IN YOUR SCHOOL'S COMPUTER LAB. LEARN SOME USEFUL PROGRAMS. PICK UP SOME COLLEGE RADIO OR TELEVISION EXPERIENCE. TAKE A CLASS IN PUBLIC SPEAKING.

69. Labor Union Organizer

description: Labor union organizers work to assist workers in their efforts to organize their work site, and achieve some collective bargaining clout. Organizers typically go into a work site and help develop an organizational committee; they identify leaders or potential leaders at the work site, and then recruit and train those individuals. Organizers work with those leaders to identify issues and concerns at the work site. They help those leaders strategize a campaign for building a union. They participate in house meetings and site visits, working to drum up support for a union. They work to get 50 percent or more of the workers at the site to sign a petition saying that they request a union election. The goal of a union organizer at this point is to win that election.

Many employers will run anti-unionizing campaigns, and organizers have to work to counter those campaigns.

Since many places where organizers work run in shifts, workers in this field have to be willing to put in not just long, but also unusual, hours.

salary: What you get paid as a union organizer can vary greatly, depending on which union you are working for. Union organizers, in many instances an entry-level job, can expect to earn anywhere from $18,000 up to $40,000 per year.

prospects: There is an almost constant demand for good organizers in the labor union movement. Turnover is high, since organizing is a high-stress job that puts tremendous demands on people's time and energy. The AFL-CIO recruits people through its Organizing Institute. Other unions recruit new organizers as well. If this is the kind of work you want to do, chances are excellent that someone will need you to do it for them.

qualifications: Unions are always on the lookout for people committed to their movement. And that is probably the most important characteristic for union work—a commitment to that work. Unions recruit through their membership. They also work with college graduates. But a college degree is not necessarily a prerequisite for doing union work.

characteristics: One thing you will need to possess if you hope to become a union organizer is energy—energy enough to thrive on work days that last 12 or more hours. An ability to sympathize and empathize with workers is another essential ingredient. A cheery disposition or an optimistic outlook is also desirable, as you will lose more battles in this work than you will win, and it's important to keep the bigger picture in mind when you encounter setbacks.

Raahi Reddy *is a union organizer in New York City.*

How did you get the job?

"I was active with progressive unions in college, worked with an Asian student coalition, and served in the governing association of Rutgers University as a senator.

"I also worked at the Center for Women's Global Leadership at Rutgers for two years while I was in college, an institution that works for women's rights and human rights.

"I was recruited at school by the Asian Pacific American Labor Alliance, a group within the AFL-CIO. The Asian Pacific American Labor Alliance sponsored a joint three-day training session with the AFL-CIO Organizing Institute. I attended that and I loved it.

"After the Organizing Institute, I spent a three-week internship with the Teamsters in Rhode Island, where I was involved in a campaign to organize a hospital there, the second-largest employer in the state. Those internships the Organizing Institute sends you on are good reality checks. That's where you find out whether or not the reason you wanted to get into organizing work is a good reason. It lets you understand what the movement needs from you.

"After that, I went straight to an internship with the Service Employees International Union. Once I completed my internship, I called them and said, 'Hey, I'm on the market.' And I've been working here ever since."

What do you do all day?

"In a typical campaign, I will go out to the work site at 6:30 or 7 A.M., whenever the workers enter and leave the work site. I'll talk to people as they're coming and going, tell them what we're trying to do, find out what their concerns are. And then I will head back to the office. I'll do some leaflet or other organizational work. Then I'll do house visits of different workers, especially those who are undecided. At about 3:30 P.M., we'll head back out to the site for the shift change. In the evening, we do more house visits until 8 or 9 P.M. During the late afternoon, we typically have a little downtime where we'll have lunch or debrief each other on who we have talked to. It is never a 9-to-5 schedule. You basically work 12 to 14 hours a day. As you get closer to an election, you get up to 16 hours a day, when we enter what we call 'war mode.'

"A typical campaign is three to five months long," Raahi says. "The first year I worked here, I went from live campaign to live campaign to live campaign. Now I'm based in New York City, where I'm helping to strategize our campaigns, making sure we stick to the plans we have developed. I coordinate other people as well.

"I've been working in New York City for the past four or five months, working in the private sector on a nursing home campaign. Once you file for an election, you're supposed to have one within 50 days. But in some instances, the wait for an election is horrible. Employers will make their employees wait six months for an election. Which of course gives them more time to run an anti-union campaign. Unions only win about 40 percent of their campaigns."

Where do you see this job leading you?

"Working at this job, I have developed my communications skills, my ability to strategize and plan goals. I can conduct a campaign now. In these four- to five-month-long campaigns, you learn to strategize and create changes; you are—quite literally—taking on capitalism.

"I want to be a top-notch organizer, doing better campaigns and building a more militant labor movement."

> **TAKING OFF: EXTRAORDINARY WAYS TO SPEND YOUR FIRST YEAR OUT OF COLLEGE BY LAUREN TARSHIS PROVIDES TIPS AND STRATEGIES FOR GIVING YOURSELF A MEMORABLE EXPERIENCE FOR YOUR FIRST YEAR OR SO OF POST-COLLEGE LIFE.**

70. Labor Union-Organizing Lead

description: The organizing lead of the local chapter of a labor union helps manage that chapter's organizing efforts. In many respects, this job includes the same basic duties as that of a union organizer.

The efforts of an organizing team are directed at campaigns, most often to establish a union presence in workplaces that have no such representation. At other times, organizing efforts will be directed at strengthening existing chapters.

Organizing leads work with union members and labor organizers, providing resources for them as they talk to nonmembers about the benefits of joining a union, or about the problems in their shop. Organizing leads will find that their job duties and those of organizers will overlap; leads will do their fair share of talking to nonmembers as well. Much of that work consists of knocking on doors and talking to people.

The work is high in stress and long in hours. Union organizers face a lot of resistance to their efforts from management, and fear from workers. Though it is legal to organize and form a union, one out of every four workers who attempts to organize a union is fired from his or her job. The goal of the union organizer is to help workers of a particular company band together in order to address their grievances and better their working conditions.

salary: Leaders of labor union organizing teams can expect to make from $18,000 to $30,000 a year. The amount they make will be largely dependent on the union they're working for—on its size and level of funding.

prospects: Labor unions are always looking for good people who are committed to their cause. For many, union organizing is the first taste of labor union work—this is an excellent entry-level opportunity.

qualifications: The main qualifications for directing a union's organizing team are prior organizing experience and a desire to help workers. Proficiency in a foreign language, particularly Spanish, will likewise make your resume shine.

characteristics: Directors of labor union organizing teams should be capable of managing groups of people. They should be easy to talk to, good listeners, persuasive speakers, and committed to the labor movement's cause.

Vanessa Surowiecki *is a union organizer in Grand Rapids, Michigan.*

How did you get this job?

"I heard about the AFL-CIO Organizing Institute, and I gave them a call. I went through their program, and I have been a union organizer now for five years.

"When you go through the Organizing Institute's internship and apprenticeship program, that's where you learn the nuts and bolts of organizing. It's a four- to six-month process that involves three steps. The first step is the application process. If you're accepted, then you attend what they call a three-day training, which gives you a chance to look at the program and at what's involved in being an organizer.

"The next step is the apprenticeship/internship program. The internship is three weeks long," Vanessa says. In a typical internship, 6 to 12 interns who have attended the three-day training are assigned in a group to ongoing organizing campaigns. "You spend three weeks talking to workers who don't have representation about organizing," she says.

> **OUR JOB IS TO EDUCATE WORKERS, TO CHALLENGE THEM TO CHANGE THEIR WORKING LIFE**

"Then you go on to the apprenticeship, where you take on more responsibility." Apprentices typically will be given responsibility for all or most of an ongoing campaign.

"The Institute helps with job placement," Vanessa says. "I worked with the American Federation of Teachers, and organized workers in hospitals. Then I took this job a couple of months ago."

What do you do all day?

"The United Food and Commercial Workers Union has about one million workers nationwide; there are about 30,000 members in our local," Vanessa says.

"People without unions take a lot that's illegal—abuse, low wages, and worse.

"We organize in retail operations, we find a target. We look at stores, or workers in grocery stores themselves approach us about helping them organize. We do research, checking out leads and seeing how many workers are at the store, checking to see if there has ever been an attempt to organize a union there before. We work with our contacts at the store, and put together a list of workers. Then we start contacting those workers. We work 10- to 12-hour days for a week or more doing that. We call people, but mostly we do home visits.

"Our goal in that initial bout of organizing is to build a committee, the foundation of the union at that shop. Once that is done, we continue working with the committee, to get out petitions to the other store workers, and build the union. If a majority of the workers in the store wants a union, they go to the boss, who legally has to hold an election, to see if the store will become unionized.

"You usually have to fight to recognize the union. Before the election, there will be a couple of months for the boss to urge the workers, to vote against unionization. The boss will always find out what's going on in the store—you can't build a union in secret. And it's just not natural for people to stand up to their boss.

"This is frustrating work because it can seem that everything is stacked against you. The times you win and a store signs a union contract—that is the upside. But I think we win elections only about 45 percent of the time, and only in 50 percent of those wins do workers sign a contract with their employers. The number one reason a contract isn't signed is because of an employer campaign to bust the union."

Where do you see this job leading you?

"Organizers and organizing leads go on to other jobs in the labor movement," Vanessa says, "but this isn't really career track kind of work.

"If you want to organize, this is it. Either you do it or you don't. I guess you could go into research, but for me, union organizing is the cutting edge of social change, and I believe I'll stay here."

71. Corporate Foundation Worker

description: Many major corporations have established foundations to support projects that the corporation wants to support, and that fit its overall mission.

Workers at a corporate foundation screen inquiries to see which program proposals fit their employer's mission; they represent the corporation in meetings with nonprofit organizations and other prospective funding recipients; and they manage the budgets of and help design the programs that they choose to fund. They give speeches and interviews, representing the philanthropic arm of their employer to the public.

In corporate philanthropy, areas of sponsorship will likely be more narrowly targeted than they are for privately-endowed foundations. As an employee of a corporation, program officers will be able to call on different tools and resources—the expertise of corporation employees, and the products and services produced by the corporation—than would an employee at another type of foundation.

salary: Annual salaries for corporate philanthropic foundation employees could range from $40,000 to $100,000 or more. Salaries will be dependent on experience, education, where employees fall in their corporation's hierarchy, and how much emphasis the corporation puts on its philanthropic work.

prospects: Most major corporations have philanthropic arms, but the investment they make in their philanthropic efforts can depend on the overall economic health of the corporation, and on the business climate in which it finds itself.

Competition will be fierce for any openings that occur in this field. Corporations will be able to draw from their own employees, as well as from a pool of applicants from the outside, and there will be no lack of qualified applicants for these jobs.

qualifications: People who hope to work for a corporation's philanthropic arm should possess a solid grounding in a substantive field that the corporation specializes in—fields such as the arts, education, or human services issues, for example. Corporate foundations usually won't consider someone lacking a recognized level of experience. A college degree (most typically a master's or above) is important, but experience is the most significant factor in determining who gets hired.

characteristics: People working for the philanthropic arm of a corporation will need to be creative and innovative. They will be called on to come up with ways that a corporation's business goals can be matched with philanthropic programs.

Strong "people" skills are necessary for this type of work. Workers will have to negotiate with the highest-level officers in their corporation, and with nonprofit organization leaders as well. They will find themselves in the position of having to turn down organizations who come to them for funding, and whose officers might not understand why their mission doesn't mesh with the corporation's. Corporate foundation employees have to leave the impression with everyone they encounter that they have been dealt with fairly.

Milton Little *is the vice president of a health and human services program at a large corporation in New York City.*

How did you get the job?

Milton Little began his work in the public policy arena while attending Moorehouse College in Atlanta. He worked part-time at the Institute for the Black Family while going to school, and picked up experience working on issues affecting poor families.

After college, Milton went to graduate school at Columbia University, where he studied urban sociology and social policy. He picked up more public policy experience at New York University, where he attended a program in public administration.

"Through that program, I ended up getting a job under [New York] Mayor Ed Koch, looking at transportation policy in the city. That experience strengthened my public policy skills."

Milton left the mayor's office, and went to work for a New York City-based nonprofit organization called Interface,

THE CORPORATE PHILANTHROPY REPORT CAN PROVIDE A GOOD CLUE TO CORPORATE PHILANTHROPIC ACTIVITY.

which he describes as a public policy firm. He specialized in education and social service issues there, until he was hired by Manpower Demonstration Research Organization.

"MDRO specializes in education, training, and welfare issues," Milton says. "The AT&T Foundation was one of our supporters. I had spent eight years at MDRO, and began looking for other opportunities. When this position came open at the AT&T Foundation, I applied for it.

"The AT&T Foundation is the central institution for AT&T-sponsored philanthropy around the world," Milton says. "We provide cash grants to nonprofit organizations for work in the health, human services, arts and culture, and public policy arenas."

What do you do all day?

"My job is to utilize the strengths of this company as we try to identify effective solutions to social issues," Milton says. "Keeping in mind that AT&T is an information and communications company enables me to target the areas of our philanthropy to take advantage of the strengths of this company.

"During a typical week, I answer calls from prospective grantees. In any given year, I receive maybe 1,000 or 1,500 unsolicited requests for funding. My job entails a lot of phone time, a lot of meetings, and a lot of reading.

"I respond to contacts about AT&T's philanthropy. I deal with shareholders and customers with specific questions. I talk to AT&T executives and employees about our products and services, and the notion of philanthropy; I try to create marriages between [our products and services and philanthropy]."

"I have to design programs that take our projects and services and use them to help solve social issues. My budget is at about $12.5 million per year, so budgeting skills come into play. I have to manage resources and manage the staff members working under me."

Where do you see this job leading you?

Corporate foundation workers can move from jobs at one corporate foundation to another, or can go into work at other, different types of foundations. They can also get into nonprofit organization work, or into work in fields in which they specialize, becoming the administrator of an art museum, for example, or getting involved in the public policy arena.

72. Development Department Staffer

description: An organization's development office is its fund-raising arm. This fund-raising can take the form of applying for grants, corporate fund-raising, and individual-giving campaigns. Individual-giving campaigns are those that target noninstitutional sources of fund-raising. Direct-mail, workplace-giving campaigns, special event fund-raisers, and phone solicitation are all examples of individual-giving campaigns.

People doing development work conceive of and implement these campaigns. Their work will be project-based, where they see one campaign through and then move on to the next, or they juggle several different campaigns at the same time.

Development staff may work with an outside agency that specializes in this type of fund-raising, or they may work with another organization or business in developing a specific fund-raising event. Development staffers try to line up talent, vendors, and other needed items for such promotions. Or they may be in charge of organizing an annual event—a family-day event or a Renaissance fair, for example.

salary: Work in the development department of a nonprofit organization is traditionally among the highest paid of nonprofit positions. Development staffers can expect to make from $25,000 to $100,000 or more per year, depending on their experience and reputation, and on the financial stability and size of the organization for which they work.

prospects: The prospects for finding work in the development department of nonprofit organizations are perhaps better than for those in any other nonprofit position. Even in times of slow or suspended growth, nonprofits will need to raise money; and they will need people to help them raise that money.

qualifications: Someone hoping to work in the development office of an organization should have some marketing experience, preferably in the fund-raising arena. Workers with mass-marketing experience—working with print, television, or direct-mail campaigns—will have a leg up on other applicants, as will those who have experience in executing a fund-raising campaign or event.

For a managerial position, five to 10 years of experience in the field will usually be required, along with some management or supervisory experience.

characteristics: People who want to work in the development department of a nonprofit organization should be creative—they will be called on to come up with innovative and effective plans for fund-raising campaigns and for approaching individual donors. The job calls for strong communication skills—interpersonal as well as writing and speaking. Someone with research skills, who can ferret out potential financial donors or sources of income, will do well at this sort of work. Fund-raising is typically a collaborative effort, so someone who works well with others can expect to do well in development work.

Brenda Mendoza *works in the development office of Teach for America, based in New York City.*

- -

How did you get the job?

Brenda Mendoza majored in English at the University of Connecticut. After graduation, she was working as a substitute teacher when she read a magazine article about Teach for America; that article prompted her to write to TFA requesting an application.

Once accepted into TFA, applicants go through a one and a half month training session before they are sent to their teaching post, where they remain for two years.

Brenda was posted in Houston. She describes her experience as a teacher in Houston as a "wonderful but extremely challenging one. Teach for America can be a very trying experience, because you are removed from your support network, and have to walk into situations that you are unfamiliar with. On the other hand, in the classroom, you are placed in a situation where you are in total control. Very few people just out of college get to feel that. That gives you a chance to boost your problem-solving skills."

She says she enjoyed her experience but, as the end of her first two year posting drew to a close, she wasn't sure that she wanted to remain in the field. She received a letter in the mail from Teach for America, outlining an opening in the organization's development department. Six months after her initial application, Brenda was hired for the position.

What do you do all day?

Brenda's day is spent working on ongoing fund-raising campaigns or preparing for upcoming campaigns. She writes letters to or phones current or potential donors. She works with con-

> THE NATIONAL SOCIETY OF FUND-RAISING EXECUTIVES, WITH HEADQUARTERS IN ALEXANDRIA, VIRGINIA, CAN BE AN EXCELLENT RESOURCE FOR INFORMATION ON THIS ASPECT OF THE NONPROFIT WORLD.
> - - - - - - - - - -

sultants to plan campaigns and carry them out. She works with donor groups to see how TFA can meet their needs and answer their questions. She meets with her organization's management team to strategically plan the campaigns.

"Right now, we're working on our major donor campaign," she says. "I've got to go to the data we have from past campaigns and other sources and figure potential targets. Then I'll put that information together, sort it by year, and then take some time to acclimate to it. I'll put together a master list, and figure out how to structure different people in a 'gift table.' For instance, there are a handful of people who might contribute $100,000 or more to our organization. I will put together a donor portfolio for those people, a strategy for each person."

Where do you see this job leading you?

"This sort of work could easily segue into work in direct-mail marketing, general marketing, advertising, or public relations," Brenda says. Some people will pursue a career in the development field.

"You could always go into consulting," she says. "Some people specialize in a very specific area or in cause-based marketing. You could segue into the for-profit world, or you could stay in the nonprofit world and still be very comfortable."

Brenda, however, intends to head to business school.

73. Grant Writer

description: As a grant writer, only part of your duties will entail the writing of grants. People—workers in your organization or people your organization works with—will come to you with an idea for which they need funding.

You will need to do research—research on both the subject of the grant and possible sources of funding. You will write proposals for these funding agencies. You will work to bring together the various parties involved in the grant proposal—possible donors as well as those individuals and organizations looking for funding—so they can discuss each other's needs and desires. You will also work with your organization's board of directors, supplying them with reports about outlining the money you have raised and its sources.

salary: Beginning grant writers can expect their salary to range from $30,000 to $40,000 per year. As they gain experience and achieve success, that salary can rise to $60,000 per year or even more.

prospects: Nonprofit organizations are always looking for people who can bring in more money. Applicants who know how to write grant proposals and raise funds should have no problem finding work. Positions in specialized fields, such as higher education, will be harder to come by, unless an applicant has prior experience or training in that particular field.

qualifications: Organizations looking to hire people to write grants for them typically seek those with previous experience in this type of work; they also look for evidence of success—documentation of how much money you have raised for other organizations. Perhaps the best way to get such experience is through an internship or volunteer position. (You could pick up some experience by presenting yourself to a nonprofit organization, and volunteering to research and write a grant proposal for a project in which they might be interested.) Research and writing skills are important, as is the ability to work collaboratively.

characteristics: Since grant writers can work on proposals for months only to find them rejected, workers should be full of self-confidence. Grant writers should be extroverts, comfortable dealing with the CEOs of companies as well as with organization workers and clients. They must also be able to handle pressure.

Kimberly Allen *is the program manager for grant activities for a university system in Minneapolis, Minnesota.*

- -

How did you get the job?

"In graduate school, I got an internship with the Minnesota Community College system, and became their development intern. After I was there four months, the development coordinator left to go to one of our 21 campuses. The system chancellor asked me to step into the position.

"I later applied for this position—the program manager for grant activities. I didn't think I would get this job, but I knew how to write well and research well."

What do you do all day?

"My job is one deadline after another," Kimberly says. "That's all it is.

"My job involves lots of meetings. For instance, there are 59 campuses. And I'll often be dealing with projects of system-

MOST CITIES WILL HAVE A FOUNDATION CENTER, WHICH CAN CLUE YOU IN TO GRANT-FUNDING POSSIBILITIES IN YOUR AREA AND TO POSSIBLE EMPLOYMENT OPPORTUNITIES WITH THOSE FOUNDATIONS. CHECK WITH YOUR LOCAL CITY COUNCIL OR CHAMBER OF COMMERCE FOR THE PHONE NUMBER OR LOCATION OF A FOUNDATION CENTER NEAR YOU.

- -

wide import. I sent in one grant proposal for a nursing work-force development project that saw us partnered with 64 other organizations in the state.

"I also serve in a service capacity to our campuses. Almost all of our campuses—community colleges, technical colleges, and state universities—have grant writers or fund-raisers on their staffs, but their fund-raisers are on different levels, so I'll work with them, do workshops for them, proofread their proposals.

"Our board also wants reports on how much money has been raised, systemwide and at each campus. It's my responsibility to prepare those reports.

"Once I've attended any meetings I have to get to, it's back to my office to write," she says. "It will take six to nine months to put some proposals together. I would say it's a 50-50 split between grants like that and ones where we have a month to get everything together and get our proposal out. Foundation proposals will typically have short-term deadlines. Government grants are annual or biannual; you know when those deadlines are coming due.

"There's very little downtime in this job. You're faced with project after project, and deadline after deadline. It can be very stressful. I've got a lot of gray hairs at 26."

Where do you see this job leading you?

"I want to stay in higher education," Kimberly says, "and hope to become the president of a community college. With the positive reputation that I have made for myself in this system, I think it is very possible for me to move from this position to a position on one of our campuses. My goal is to end up as a dean, and to move on from there to the presidency. I have skill as an administrator, and have developed a good working relationship with other administrators in our system.

"From this position, I could go on to a campus and direct a foundation there, or I could go into nonprofit work and assume a leadership position."

74. Nonprofit Fund-Raiser

description: As the fund-raiser (or part of the fund-raising department) for a nonprofit organization, you will work to develop and implement strategies and campaigns aimed at bringing in donations to your organization. You will work on annual campaigns as well as special fund-raising projects.

Donations will typically come from four sources: individuals, corporations, foundations, or the government. Fund-raisers write grant proposals for foundation and government sources of funding. Approaches to corporations will usually take the form of proposals as well, though proposals aimed at these sources will take decidedly different forms. Foundation and governmental proposals will be very analytic in nature, with programs and their effects laid out in intricate detail. Corporations will be concerned about how a donation to a specific organization will advance their bottom line, or further business objectives.

Efforts aimed at individuals take a more personal approach. Direct-mail campaigns are one tool of the nonprofit fund-raiser. Prospect mail—where the organization's materials are sent to individuals whose names are garnered from lists provided by other like-minded organizations—is another method of fund-raising. Seasonal activities and special events—house parties that bring organization staffers and contributors together, for example—are other fund-raising initiatives that might be attempted.

Part of the job of the fund-raiser will be to educate workers in other departments of the organization about their role in the fund-raising process, to show how they can contribute ideas and effort toward raising money for the organization for which they work.

salary: Salaries for organization fund-raisers can be wide-ranging indeed, starting at $17,000 per year or so for entry-level positions, and rising to $150,000 or more for experienced fund-raisers working with the largest agencies. Some fund-raisers will work on commission, though the National Society of Fundraising Executives frowns on that practice. The highest-paying fund-raising jobs are typically in the university and hospital sectors.

prospects: Fund-raising is perhaps the most important aspect of nonprofit work, for the money fund-raisers bring in supports all of the organization's endeavors. These are popular jobs in the nonprofit sector, but turnover is fairly high. Job-seekers with appropriate experience should be able to find work in this field.

qualifications: The first thing most employers look for in their prospective fund-raising staff members is previous fund-raising experience. Employers will also look for management and supervisory experience, and experience working with the boards of directors of nonprofits. Strong writing skills are required. A bachelor's degree is recommended, and an M.B.A. will give prospective fund-raisers a grounding in the financial aspects of the job.

characteristics: Fund-raisers should have a good sense of ego—they shouldn't take it personally when proposals they have worked on get rejected. They need to develop good listening skills, and learn to persevere in the face of rejection (just because they're told "no" doesn't mean that their proposal will ultimately be rejected). They need to be able to work with a wide variety of people, from corporate types to individual donors, and to respond to their different needs.

Elizabeth H. Coit *is the director of planning and development for a legal defense organization based in New York City.*

- -

How did you get the job?

"I used to be a program director for the Unitarian Universalist Service Committee, working on international program development.

"After 10 years of doing that, over a five-year period of transition, I parlayed my ability to raise foundation grants into my current position.

"I attended the Fund-Raising School at Indiana University's Center for Philanthropy in Indianapolis. The Fund-Raising School offers two- and three-day workshops throughout the country. The introductions to fund-raising sessions usually include something about developing your own annual campaign, management skills, working with volunteer leadership, and raising money from foundations, corporations, and individuals.

"I took courses at the New School for Social Research in New York. I began doing free-lance fund-raising work. I landed a mentor, who was on the staff at the Fund-Raising School.

"My mentor preceded me to the NOW Legal Defense and Education Fund; he pulled me

IF YOU'RE INTERESTED IN TAKING COURSES ON FUND-RAISING FOR NONPROFIT ORGANIZATIONS, GET IN TOUCH WITH THE NEW SCHOOL FOR SOCIAL RESEARCH IN NEW YORK CITY OR THE FUND-RAISING SCHOOL AT THE CENTER FOR PHILANTHROPY AT INDIANA UNIVERSITY. THE NATIONAL SOCIETY FOR FUND-RAISING EXECUTIVES IN ALEXANDRIA, VIRGINIA, CAN PROVIDE YOU WITH INFORMATION ON CONVENTIONS AND OTHER CAREER-BUILDING ACTIVITIES. (SEE RESOURCES.)

- -

in here. I started as the deputy director of planning and development and was promoted. I have been here four years."

Started by the National Organization of Women but separate from that organization, the NOW Legal Defense and Education Fund engages in high-impact litigation aimed at bringing about social change.

What do you do all day?

"My work has a supervisory role, an educational role, and a fund-raising role," Elizabeth says.

"I supervise a staff of three, plus work with three outside consultants. I supervise our annual campaign. Our budget is based on one-third individual

support, one-third corporate funding, and one-third foundation support. I feel very fortunate that we have developed a diversified, balanced funding base. I manage the team that works with our program staff—lawyers, primarily—and craft what they do into proposals for corporations and foundations.

"I have a frenetic schedule," Elizabeth says. For instance, part of my time is spent inputting our database information on who has made contributions to us, so we can organize our acknowledgments of those contributions. I am currently organizing meetings with our program staff so we can frame a new grant proposal. I am working with our president to set up

a planned giving committee, a system whereby people will leave us money in their will. My work also consists of drafting proposals."

Where do you see this job leading you?

"I would say that with the experience you could acquire working for a nonprofit organization's development department, you could start your own consulting firm," Elizabeth says. "You could start a fund-raising firm, and have nonprofit organizations as your clients. You could provide services to foundations, helping them to spend their money better. You could help organizations with their organizational development and strategic planning. This work provides a good background for entrepreneurial work, for setting up your own business, because you come to understand the overlay of the profit motive with the goals of a nonprofit organization.

"You could also move on to become the executive director or top officer of a nonprofit organization. Or you may want to go on to further your education. Dealing with public interest law as we do, some of our program staff go on to law school."

75. Program Officer

AT A GRANT-GIVING/PHILANTHROPIC
FOUNDATION

description: Program officers at philanthropic foundations determine whether or not a funding proposal will be considered by the board of the foundation they work for. They make the first cut of the proposals that come into their office.

The process usually begins with an agency, nonprofit organization, or individual submitting a letter of inquiry to the foundation. Program officers read these letters to see if the proposal outlined by the letter fits within the parameters of the foundation. If it meets the foundation's stipulations, the program officer will invite the submitting organization or individual to submit a full proposal for review.

At this point, or shortly after the proposal is received, the program officer will begin to investigate the proposal, visiting the site of the submitting nonprofit, talking to people there and to the people the organization works with, and getting familiar with the program and the proposal. The officer will also research the proposal to see if there is a need for the program the proposal will create.

Program officers also oversee grants that have been given out, to see how the programs are progressing and whether they are meeting the requirements of the grant.

salary: The salaries of program officers at philanthropic foundations can vary greatly, depending on the nature of the foundation, and the experience and duties of the officer. Salaries can range from $30,000 per year up to $80,000, with senior program officers and supervisors earning slightly more pay.

prospects: This is a very tight field. Positions are highly sought, and there are very few openings. People with the best chances for obtaining a position with a foundation will have an extensive nonprofit or political background, as well as experience in areas in which the foundation specializes.

qualifications: Specific qualifications for a foundation program officer will vary, depending on the nature of the foundation and where it puts its emphasis. A general interest foundation like the United Way might require more general budgetary and money management skills, while a foundation specializing in medical research will most likely require some sort of medical knowledge and experience. Applicants should be familiar with the types of programs to which the foundation supplies money. They should be knowledgeable of grant-making strategies, be able to develop contacts and resources in their chosen specialty, and possess good communications skills.

characteristics: Foundation program officers should be nonjudgmental; they will be determining (or helping to determine) which projects get funded and which ones don't, so they need an ability to sift through and check out all the facts in order to come to an objective decision.

Jocelyn Ancheta *is a program officer at a grant-giving/philanthropic foundation in Minneapolis, Minnesota.*

How did you get the job?

"I worked for the state of Minnesota for four and a half years, administering traffic safety grants—'Do not drink and drive' programs and that sort of thing. I found government work to be very narrowly focused. The grant money we would get would only address part of a person or a problem, never touching on the fact that there are other things that lead young people to take risks, for example. Our grants wouldn't address the multiple causes of some problems. I felt that I needed to get involved in more broad-based activities. Plus, it is easy to be a lifelong state employee, and I didn't want that to happen to me.

"I saw a job posting for a trainer position at Piper-Jeffery, a local investment firm. They were just starting up their foundation there. When I went there to interview, I found out that they had hired someone from the McKnight Foundation. So I

thought, 'Aha! There will be an opening at the McKnight Foundation.'

"I always thought I would be the director of a nonprofit organization, not in philanthropy. Yet I've been here two years."

What do you do all day?

The Minneapolis-based McKnight Foundation, with assets of $1.2 billion, gives grants to human services, arts, and environmental programs and agencies, as well as those in the international field and those doing eating-disorders research.

> **THINK LONG-TERM. AS YOU PURSUE YOUR JOB SEARCH, KEEP THE QUESTIONS "WILL THIS JOB GET ME WHERE I WANT TO GO?" AND "WILL THIS JOB PROVIDE ME WITH AN OPPORTUNITY TO LEARN NEW SKILLS?" IN THE BACK OF YOUR MIND.**

"We work on quarterly grant cycles," says Jocelyn. "We give out money four times a year. So, we have to turn every grant proposal around every three months. My job involves a lot of site visits and a lot of writing.

"We receive a 30-page grant proposal, and have to distill the information down to a two-page summary for our board. So much of what I do is writing and analysis. We also plan where we want to put our money—the McKnight Foundation looks at system advocacy change.

"Our Mondays start with a 9 A.M. staff meeting. Then I go into writing or on to a site visit. Right now, I am organizing a trip to Arizona and to Stanford, where some of the eating-disorder research we underwrite goes on. I need to prepare an itinerary for that trip, and also plan out the questions I need to ask. Or, for instance, if we get capital requests to fix a building, it is much more powerful to see that building in person to see where the money will go.

"I have to synthesize how each request fits into the larger picture of aid. How many other programs provide similar solutions? I'm always looking at the issue of duplication."

Where do you see this job leading you?

"I enjoy the work I am doing," says Jocelyn. "The one sacrifice I have had to make is that, because of potential conflicts of interest, I have had to give up my board memberships on community organizations. To some, that is a relief. To others, that is frustrating because sitting on boards is how you build up community contacts.

"I can see myself going on to become an executive director of a foundation or the vice president of programs at a foundation—getting into more of a supervisory role.

"People have left the McKnight Foundation to go on to program officer positions at other foundations—operating foundations, community foundations, or other family foundations. Some go on to open their own consulting agencies," Jocelyn says.

76. Coordinator

OF COMMUNITY AND GOVERNMENT OUTREACH FOR PUBLIC TELEVISION

description: Public television stations often plan outreach activities to coincide with programs either that will be airing on their stations, or that the station staff is putting together. Not all PBS stations have outreach programs, but those that do usually include some sort of public service component in that outreach effort. If you work in the outreach arm of a broadcast entity, those programs will be your responsibility.

You will be implementing projects given to you by your supervisor or by the station's board of directors, and will have to coordinate your efforts with the programming arm of the station.

Your duties will include writing proposals for outreach efforts, researching those proposals, and implementing them. Your duties will change with every project. Those duties are likely to include researching, writing, coordinating efforts among large numbers of people, and overseeing the implementation of your station's outreach efforts.

salary: Coordinating outreach efforts is more likely to be a contract or part-time job rather than a full-time position. Outreach coordinators can expect to command anywhere from $15 to $40 an hour. That wage level will depend on your writing and research skills, experience, and education, but the nature of the project on which you're working, the source of funding for the project, and the size of the station you're doing the project for will also factor into the equation.

prospects: Despite the oft-discussed cutbacks in government funding for public broadcasting, the prospects for consulting and contract work for public television are better than might be expected. As stations make cutbacks, they will be forced to rely more on part-time and contract labor. If you can demonstrate that you have the experience needed to get the job done, then this sort of consulting work might be something you would be interested in exploring.

qualifications: People who coordinate outreach projects should have a thorough understanding of public policy. Writing and research skills are essential.

A background of work that corresponds to the type of outreach you'll be doing is another important prerequisite. Outreach coordinators should have a knowledge of those organizations—both national and local—that can aid them in creating their outreach effort.

characteristics: The abilities to work with others, to take direction, to take a project from its formulation stages and see it through to completion, and to instill in others trust in what you can accomplish are all tools of the outreach trade.

Maryam S. Roberts *is a consultant to a San Francisco, California, PBS affiliate.*

How did you get the job?

Maryam Roberts had worked with public television lobbyists when she had worked in various positions in Washington, D.C. and, when a part-time position doing development work at KQED came open, her Washington contacts recommended her for the job.

What do you do all day?

Maryam is currently consulting with KQED on a part-time basis, working with the public television station on a number of projects that correspond with its broadcast mission.

"I'm creating a women's health directory for northern California," she says. "This will be a whole yellow pages of women's health issues—where women can go for treatment and things of that nature.

CONSIDER DEVELOPING A PORTFOLIO OF YOUR WORK. IT COULD CONSIST OF CLASS PROJECTS OR PAPERS THAT YOU ARE ESPECIALLY PROUD OF, OR OF LETTERS OF PRAISE OR RECOMMENDATION FROM FORMER SUPERVISORS OR EMPLOYERS. IF YOU HAVE MATERIAL DOCUMENTING A VOLUNTEER PROJECT OR PROGRAM YOU WERE A PART OF—A NEWSPAPER CLIPPING ABOUT THE EVENT, A PROGRAM FROM THE ACTUAL EVENT—BE SURE TO INCLUDE THAT IN YOUR PORTFOLIO.

"I've written a proposal for an outreach effort centering around a population growth documentary that the station is preparing—that documentary should air in September or October, and the outreach effort will coincide with that," Maryam says. "I'm compiling and writing a manual for distribution to local communities so that people can participate in the population growth debate. This manual will include a section on internships, a section on what people can do nationally and locally to get involved in the debate, a section on government with a congressional update."

Funding for these projects comes from different sources. The funding for the women's health directory came from Blue Shield, while the money for the population growth project came from a variety of foundations.

Where do you see this job leading you?

Maryam says her priorities don't really center on her career at this point in her life. "I've just had a baby, and that's where my priorities are right now. I enjoy the work I'm doing. I enjoy the people I'm working with. This job right now meets my sense of balance—it's part-time, so I can spend time at home and also do valuable work."

There are many places a job like this can lead someone, however. Someone working in community and government outreach could easily bounce back into the public policy arena, into the private sector, or into work with the government. There are also consulting firms that deal with public policy—another possible career path.

77. Editor

OF AN OPINION JOURNAL/MAGAZINE OF POLITICAL COMMENTARY

description: As the editor of an opinion journal or magazine of political commentary, you will have responsibility for determining the editorial focus of the magazine and for guiding it through its production phases.

First, you'll have to plan the magazine's editorial calendar, determining the themes of the magazine's upcoming issues. You'll have to solicit articles for the journal, either from staff writers or (more probably) from a pool of freelance writers. One of your responsibilities will be to develop that pool of freelancers, soliciting articles via academic or other contacts, advertisements, or via the Internet.

Once articles come in, it will be your responsibility to cull through the submissions, choosing the essays or articles you want to or can use for your magazine. Then you'll have to edit those manuscripts, returning some to authors with notes for rewriting, and moving others along through the editorial pipeline.

You could find yourself writing captions, putting together calendars of events, and conducting tours of the office for visitors. You'll also no doubt have to come up with creative strategies for dealing with the limited funds and resources so typical of alternative journals.

Depending on how your magazine is funded—if it is primarily donation- or grant-driven, for instance—you could find yourself cast in the role of fund-raiser.

salary: Editors of "advocacy" magazines and opinion journals shouldn't expect to get rich. A salary in the $30,000- to $40,000-per-year range is about what you should expect.

prospects: Oddly enough, prospects for work in alternative journalism might be even better than for jobs in the mainstream media. While mainstream newspapers are experiencing a decline in circulation and revenue, the growth cycle for alternative publications continues. Though you might have to be willing to move to a new location or work with minimal job security or benefits, even to work a part-time job when you first start out, if you've got the experience, you should be able to find work in the field.

qualifications: Though a college degree of some sort will prove helpful, it is not necessarily required. What will prove essential to landing a job is demonstrated writing and editing ability, which can be verifiable in the form of clips—copies of stories you have worked on, either from your college paper or from other experiences. Quality references will also prove helpful in your quest for employment.

characteristics: An editor of an alternative magazine advises that would-be journalists should possess, "a tough skin, but should be sensitive to the issues, and sensitive to the needs of the people they're dealing with. They should cultivate persistence in the face of criticism. They should push editors, push them to make them see the value of a story. They should be flexible— be prepared to chase a firetruck one moment, and then stand at a grieving widow's side the next."

Jennifer Juarez Robles *is an editor for an alternative publication based in Minneapolis, Minnesota.*

How did you get the job?

"My background is in mainstream newspaper reporting and in alternative journalism," says Jennifer Juarez Robles. "I've been involved in journalism since I was about 15.

"Throughout the past nine years, all my work has been geared toward communities of color, working to increase the fair and accurate coverage of communities of color. I have written freelance pieces for weekly alternative newspapers," Jennifer says. "I have written for the gay press, I have worked on television documentaries.

"I got a job working for the *Chicago Reporter,* an investigative monthly journal that focuses on race and poverty issues.

"I was recruited by the editorial department of the *Minneapolis Star-Tribune* [a Minneapolis daily paper]. I worked for three years as an editorial writer at the paper. What I wrote was geared toward government and political candidates.

"An editorial writer at the *Star-Tribune* founded *Colors* magazine. He left *Colors* to start an organization for writers of color." Jennifer then picked up the editorial reins of the magazine.

What do you do all day?

Colors is published six times a year. "We have a small staff, approximately six people. We don't have any full-time staff writers. We do have paid interns, mostly from the college environment," Jennifer says.

"I edit all the magazine's contents, including our departments, calendar, a section called 'Dates of Celebration'—a historical guide to important dates throughout the month. I supervise our interns and our art director. I write captions. I edit essays.

"I am responsible for the editorial budget of our 64-page magazine. I choose the essays we will run from submissions we receive, or I find special essays to be written. We feature 12 essays per issue, in three main sections—essays on any topic, a theme section, and a section on arts and cultural criticism.

"I usually put in more than 40 hours a week, though the exact amount of time I put in depends on where we are in the throes of the editorial cycle.

"One of my first priorities is connecting with our writers. I need to know each essay well enough to decide whether to reject it, accept it, or to ask for changes. I try to go over each thoroughly." Jennifer says she tries to go over the essays at home or at least out of the office, so she is not interrupted by ringing telephones or other requests for her attention.

"There's not a lot of time left over for editorial planning," she says, "but that's crucial for the type of magazine we're trying to put out. We're a nonprofit magazine, dependent on foundation support. Our publisher does a lot of the foundation work. I deal with site visits."

Where do you see this job leading you?

"Our publication lives on the financial edge," Jennifer says, "but I hope by the fall that I can take a crack at becoming financially self-sufficient. I think it will take one or two years for us to get to that level. That would be one of my priorities.

"I think I will end up back in daily journalism, as an editor or as an editorial writer. I may move again—the great thing about journalism is that you can move to great cities.

"I might like to teach, so maybe I'll go back to school and get a master's degree. I may get involved with online publishing.

"Whatever I do, however, I think my work will always entail coverage of communities of color."

> **FIND AND CULTIVATE MENTORS. A GOOD MENTOR WILL BE SOMEONE WITH EXPERIENCE IN THE FIELD YOU WANT TO GET INTO, SOMEONE YOU RESPECT, AND SOMEONE WHO IS WILLING TO SHARE THEIR EXPERTISE WITH YOU.**

78. General Manager

OF A COMMUNITY RADIO STATION

description: Community radio can perhaps best be defined as public radio not affiliated with the organization National Public Radio.

Managers of community radio stations are responsible for the day-to-day operations of their radio station. The core workers—or at least the vast majority of workers—at community radio stations will be volunteers, and the GM is in charge of leading and collaborating with the station's volunteer workers, which could number 200 or more. General managers have to oversee all aspects of their station—programming, fund-raising, public relations, business operations, and development. They have to negotiate with public radio networks. They have to plan and implement the station's budget. They are in charge of hiring full-time staff for the station. They're responsible for enforcing policy set by the station's board of directors.

This is a job that is strenuous and demanding—both on a person's time and his or her psyche. Workers at community radio stations are intricately involved in the act of bringing disparate ideas and voices—the voices of the community to which they belong—to the airwaves, in itself a dynamic process. They are challenged by new ways of thinking, and are presented with new ideas on a regular basis. Of course, that also means they have to negotiate among all those voices, all of which are likely to have different ideas about what "community radio" means and should be.

salary: The salary of a community radio station manager can vary greatly, depending on the level of support and funding the station has been able to achieve, and on the size of the station. Some stations pay their general manager a small stipend augmented by a commission on the underwriting that he or she is able to bring in. Salaries can range from this situation—with stipends of less than $1,000 a month—up to $40,000 a year at the very largest stations.

prospects: Every city is likely to have at least one community radio station, so the positions are out there. However, each station is going to have a large pool of volunteers that have worked for the station, in most instances, for many years, and stations are able to pull paid employees from that pool. Breaking into a top spot at a community radio station will be difficult if you haven't worked in a volunteer capacity for that station before. Getting hired in one of the support positions might not be quite so difficult.

qualifications: General managers will need some past supervisory experience. Communication skills, fund-raising experience, and experience putting together a budget are all likely requirements for a general manager. Radio experience—either at a college radio station or with community or public radio—is going to be looked upon highly.

characteristics: To succeed in this position, you'll have to be good at building consensus. It will be up to you, after all, to foster a sense of community among your volunteers in order to get a large number of people working together to keep the station moving forward. You also must have, or develop, a business sense to be responsible for the day-to-day operation of the station. You'll find that you will have to be good at juggling a lot of duties and tasks as well.

Jenny Wong *is the general manager of a community radio station in San Diego, California.*

- -

How did you get the job?

Jenny Wong earned a liberal arts degree in college, and worked as a disc jockey at the college radio station while she was there. She was also heavily involved in print journalism. She worked for the student magazine and started volunteering at a political journal. She started out doing office work there, then began writing articles for them. She eventually became the journal's capital correspondent.

"Through that job, I also became the capital correspondent for community radio station KPFT." She attended a community radio conference that summer, and did a story on the fight between the college radio station and a nascent cooperative radio station, over her city's last available FM frequency.

After graduating from college, Jenny spent a year working and studying in Taiwan. Upon returning home, she found out that the two stations had negotiated an agreement—they would share frequencies, with the student station broadcasting at night and the co-op station, called KOOP, taking the daytime hours.

Now the problem was getting a station organized and on the air.

Jenny began attending co-op meetings. "It was apparent that there was a need for someone to coordinate things and pull things together," she says. "I volunteered to do that. Almost immediately, it became a full-time job."

What do you do all day?

Just because the station is now broadcasting doesn't mean that Jenny's work has stopped.

"There's been a complete change of focus with this job every few months," she says. "When I started out in this position, we had absolutely nothing. We had the promise of a construction permit and we had a bank account. But we needed a studio; we needed everything. We were a loosely organized group of 12 to 24 people. I began doing phone calls from my house, figuring out who could do what, sched-

uling meetings, building a base from which we could then start delegating responsibilities."

Currently, Jenny is working with station volunteers toward setting up a satellite downlink with the Pacifica radio network. She's helping out with office duties—insurance, appraisals, budget projections. She's working with volunteers on the station's first program guide. She attends board meetings and meetings with volunteers, whether they be the station's program staff or the station's

volunteer accountant.

"My goal is to become a true general manager, where I can help maintain what we've already got in place, where this becomes more of a delegating job."

Where do you see this job leading you?

"Making this position a career goes against my idea of what community radio should be—giving as many people as possible broadcast training and experience. I don't want to leave this job in a situation where there will be serious problems, but I don't intend to stay here forever."

Jenny says that she knows of the manager of a community radio station in Boulder, Colorado, that left that position after 15 years to take a job as the membership director with the National Federation of Community Broadcasters. She says that general managers can go on to specialize in certain aspects of community radio, by going on to a position as a program director for a larger station, for instance. She adds that this position is excellent experience for any sort of nonprofit management position.

> **CONFERENCES CAN BE AN EXCELLENT SOURCE FOR MAKING CONTACTS AND FOR MEETING PEOPLE INVOLVED IN A FIELD YOU MIGHT BE INTERESTED IN. MOST TRADE ASSOCIATIONS AND SOCIETIES WILL SPONSOR ONE MAJOR CONFERENCE OR CONVENTION A YEAR, AND MANY OF THEM OFFER STUDENT RATES.**
> - - - - - - - - - -

79. Investigative Journalist

description: Investigative reporting has much in common with most other journalistic reporting in that it is the collection, distillation, and distribution of facts to a wide audience. However, investigative reporters typically attack a certain subject, topic, or story with more depth and ferocity than other reporters.

Perhaps more than any other type of reporting, investigative work has a social change element.

"Investigative reporting is very specialized reporting," says Laura Washington, editor and publisher of *The Chicago Reporter,* a monthly investigative journal. "It is very detail-oriented, very time-consuming. The typical news stories you read are summaries. Investigative reporting tries to get behind the story, to create a new source of information, to shed some light on an issue."

Investigative reporters could be assigned to a specific beat, or their work could be more general in nature. They spend a lot of their time poring over government reports or checking financial data. They do a great deal of first-hand reporting as well.

salary: Salaries for investigative reporters will be in line with those of other reporters of their experience level. Starting reporters can expect to earn from $16,000 to $30,000 per year, while those with three to six years of experience will bring in from $25,000 to $44,000. Workers at a nonprofit enterprise like *The Chicago Reporter* bring in somewhat lower salaries, up to $35,000 or so for most positions.

prospects: Newspapers are not a growth industry at the moment, while the magazine industry is a rapidly fluctuating one. And even in the television arena, where increased channel capacity often leads to more television news coverage, stations and networks are cutting back on the resources they allocate to investigative reporting. Investigative reporting jobs will be tough to find. One avenue of exploration, and possible career opportunity, is the world of "new media"—online services and the Internet.

qualifications: Prospective investigative reporters will typically be culled from the ranks of seasoned television, newspaper, or magazine journalists. "To come here as a reporter," Laura Washington says of her publication, "you need two or three years experience in newspapers or magazines. We have made exceptions to that policy for people who have been here as interns—people have worked their way up from being a senior intern to research assistant to beginning reporter."

characteristics: Investigative reporters need to be part journalist, part detective, and part social activist. Investigative reporters can expect many of their interviews to be confrontational in nature, so prospective investigative journalists should have the stomach for confrontation. Effective investigative journalists tend to be fueled by a commitment to racial, social justice, or environmental issues, and a desire to change the system for the better.

Laura Washington *is editor and publisher of an investigative publication in Chicago, Illinois.*

How did you get the job?

The Chicago Reporter was founded in 1972 by civil rights activist John McDermott as an investigative publication that would, as current editor Laura Washington puts it, "set the record straight on controversial issues." The journal does this primarily through investigative reporting.

"I started here as an intern," she says. "I was attending graduate school at Northwestern University, and when I finished my degree, I started here as a housing reporter. I was here for five years, during which time I worked as the publication's education reporter, and then as assistant managing editor, and finally managing co-editor.

"I left *The Chicago Reporter* to work for then-Mayor Harold Washington, where I worked in the mayor's press office as deputy press secretary.

"I stayed in the mayor's press office two years, and then I went to WBBM-TV, the Chicago CBS affiliate, where I was the producer for the station's investigative news department."

Laura returned to *The Chicago Reporter,* this time as the publication's editor. "At that time, Roy Larson was the editor and publisher of the publication. The publisher's job here is an administrative one, primarily fund-raising, and he wanted a strong editor in the editor position. He retired last year, and the positions were combined again."

What do you do all day?

"I am a policymaker at the *Reporter,*" Laura Washington says. "I help set our direction, and see which stories we want to do. We have around 5,000 subscribers, and that is intentional. We are targeted at the movers and shakers in the city.

"*The Chicago Reporter* employs four full-time reporters, a managing editor, myself, a part-time circulation manager, and a part-time office manager. Interns, though, are the backbone of our publication. We are so research- and data-oriented that we need a lot of people to do 'grunt work.' We have 4 to 15 interns here at any given time. Most of our interns are graduate or undergraduate students.

> FOLLOW UP ON JOB APPLICATIONS YOU HAVE SUBMITTED AND RESUMES YOU HAVE SENT OUT. END YOUR COVER LETTER WITH A LINE LIKE, "I WILL GET IN TOUCH WITH YOU NEXT WEEK TO SEE IF YOU HAVE ANY QUESTIONS ABOUT MY RESUME, OR HAVE ANY QUESTIONS YOU WOULD LIKE TO ASK ME."

"We work on a monthly production cycle," Laura says. "We'll send out an issue at the beginning of the month, and the last week of the month is concerned with finishing up an issue and printing it.

"Early in the month, reporters are in the final reporting stage of their work, or they're out getting interviews. Each reporter publishes a story about every two to three months.

"We take about a week before sending the copy off to the printer to finish the stories and lay out the pages. That's about a 7- to 10-day process.

And that's our most intense time, because everyone reads and writes copy. Everyone reads everything that goes into the stories—every graphic, every photo. We encourage the team process: everyone here is involved in production.

"I'm not heavily involved in the editorial process. The managing editor runs the day-to-day side of things. I spend my time writing grant proposals, meeting people, and trying to raise money for the publication."

Where do you see this job leading you?

"I just took the combined editor-publisher position six months ago, and I am committed to staying here for the next several years," Laura says. "I want to strengthen our fund-raising efforts—that is one of my major goals.

"But who knows? You build tremendous research skills here. I might go on to become an investigator or researcher in private industry, with a law firm or some such organization—our current managing editor was a criminal lawyer for seven years. I could also go on to do media relations, public relations, or corporate relations."

80. Media Trainer or Consultant

description: In its most basic terms, the task of a media trainer is to teach clients how to get the kind of media attention they want, whether it be from traditional print and broadcast media outlets, or from the Internet and other forms of electronic communications. In certain instances, media trainers might act as public relations liaisons for their clients, but more often, they teach their clients how to act as their own public relations specialists by helping them to better their PR efforts.

While media trainers teach their clients how to use the media, media consultants work more closely with their clients to strategize, plan, and implement media campaigns. They help a group draft its message and carry it to the public via press conferences, talk show appearances, advertising campaigns, and other means.

Media consultants might find themselves drafting press releases, putting together press kits, organizing media events or demonstrations, writing speeches, or briefing clients before talk show appearances. Media trainers involve themselves with preparing for and putting on training conferences and with organizing materials that teach people how to do those activities for themselves.

salary: Starting salaries for media trainers or consultants typically range from $18,000 to $22,000 per year. Experienced employees could command salaries in the $30,000 to $35,000 range. Experience and the size of the organization will be the primary salary determinants.

prospects: Communications is a growing field, especially when you add the Internet and the World Wide Web to the equation. Almost every city has media consultants who work with local businesses, politicians, and organizations, helping them to get out their message and to refine their delivery of that message. The number of such consultants working exclusively with nonprofit or community organizations is quite a bit smaller, of course. Opportunities are somewhat better on the East Coast (especially in Washington, D.C.) and on the West Coast.

qualifications: The primary qualification for becoming a media trainer or consultant is experience working successfully with the media, which could come in many forms. Work in the fields of print or broadcast journalism or public relations is perhaps the most common way to get this experience, but such avenues as corporate communications or putting together newsletters should not be overlooked. Educational or training experience might be another prerequisite.

characteristics: Strong communications and writing skills are a must for this type of work. An ability to switch tasks rapidly—from working with an organization's board, to dealing with a press inquiry, to planning a fund-raiser—is also a valuable asset.

Thom Clark *is the president of a media consulting company in Chicago, Illinois.*

How did you get the job?

"My work experience began with a neighborhood-based community organization," Thom says. "For a college internship, I was placed with a housing group called Voice of the People. There, I did tenant group activist work; I did public relations work and put together our newsletter; I revamped our board of directors; and I developed a training program for area youth who wanted to get involved in the building trade.

"Doing this work, I discovered other like-minded groups working in the city. We formed the Chicago Rehabilitation Commission, and we were able to secure a direct contract with HUD, thereby circumventing local politics, and cementing the coalition.

"After three years, I left to become an editor. I went to work for an organization in Chicago called the Center for Neighborhood Technology, where I edited a publication called *Neighborhood Works*.

"I left that job six years later and began running a freelance photography and newsletter editorial support services business with my wife.

"Hank DeZutter was a journalist I had followed for many years. Hank and I formed a partnership, and began to provide two to three media trainings per year to community groups—training them how to use the media more effectively. We did some spot media work, and published a guide to talk shows.

> ONE OF IVAN R. MISNER'S TEN COMMANDMENTS OF NETWORKING: PROVIDE OTHERS WITH A LEAD OR REFERRAL WHENEVER POSSIBLE. THE MORE YOU HELP OUT OTHER PEOPLE, THE MORE WILLING THEY WILL BE TO HELP YOU OUT.

"For our first four years, our funding was almost entirely grant-based, but now grant support is beginning to funnel out. Media work is not high on many foundations' priority lists. In response to this trend, we are moving toward more fee-for-service work. We also sell copies of a media guide that we put together—originally 30 pages, now grown to 180—a guide to getting into television and print."

What do you do all day?

"We put on a five-day training course three times a year," Thom says. "Our other training efforts are usually broken out from those five-day sessions. Representatives from some two dozen groups attend. During the first session, we introduce everyone and find out why they need the media. In the second session, we talk about what goes into a good story, and the drama inherent in compelling stories. In the third session, we deal with the basics—what makes up a press release, what goes into a media kit, how you write a talk show pitch letter. In the fourth session, people actually pitch their stories to a panel of reporters from local media outlets. And in our last session, every attendee spends five minutes in front of a video camera engaged in a pseudo-talk show experience.

"I have a radio show where I bring members of the community on the air and provide them with a place to present their stories. I teach a graduate-level course on local government and politics part-time at Columbia College. My partner and I also write a column for a weekly newspaper called *The Chicago Reader*."

Where do you see this job leading you?

"For someone doing this type of work for a nonprofit organization, it could grow from being part of one's job description to being all of one's job description," Thom says. "You could go on to a bigger nonprofit. It could translate to more traditional types of marketing and development work. People can move into corporate PR work, work as community relations officers, freelance writing, or newsletter editing."

169

81. Professional Speaker

description: Professional speakers range from those who give presentations on a volunteer basis to groups and organizations in their hometown and local area, to those who work at professional speaking part-time, using the experience to supplement their income, to those who work full-time as speakers and give presentations or present seminars in front of large groups of people.

Should you choose to pursue speaking as a career, the main aspects of your job will be researching your topic area and potential market, developing your material and honing your presentation, delivering your message, and marketing yourself and your message to potential clients.

If you embark on a career as a professional speaker, you will spend a lot of time traveling to conventions, associations, seminars, and other locations where you'll be delivering your message.

salary: The salary range for speech-givers varies widely, from those of amateur orators who give their presentations to local organizations and community groups, to the fees of celebrity speakers who can bring in $25,000 or more for one engagement. Speakers who are just starting out may charge a couple of hundred dollars per engagement. For established speakers, the typical fees range from $1,500 to $10,000 or so per presentation.

prospects: People who want to speak and who have a message palatable to others' ears will be able to find an audience. But working as a professional speaker full-time is a demanding occupation. With a lot of people hoping to earn a living as professional speakers, the competition can be quite keen.

qualifications: Although a degree is not required of professional speakers, many colleges and universities do offer degree programs in speech communications. It is more important to know your audience, and that typically means gaining experience (through internships, volunteer work, or paid positions) in the area you want to talk about.

characteristics: Professional speakers must feel they have a message that other people should hear, and must enjoy bringing that message to people; they must feel comfortable presenting before audiences, and must be confident enough to deliver speeches that are engaging, and that hold an audience's attention.

Mark Sanborn *is a professional speaker in Denver, Colorado.*

How did you get the job?

"I started out speaking in competitions when I was 10 years old and involved in my local 4H club," says Mark Sanborn. "Typically, there are lots and lots of speech competitions and opportunities for kids to get public speaking experience, whether it be through organizations like 4H or through high school debate teams.

"I became a state and then a national officer in Future Farmers of America. I took a year off from college as president of the FFA, and traveled for 325 days that year; I spoke five or six times a day—to FFA chapters, to teachers, and at banquets. That gave me an incredible amount of public speaking experience at a young age. I worked my way through college doing after-dinner speeches, in fact," he says, "making $150 to $200 a speech.

> THE INTERNET OPENS UP A WEALTH OF OPPORTUNITIES FOR SPREADING YOUR MESSAGE TO GROUPS OF PEOPLE.

"When I graduated from college, I went into corporate America because I believed that I had to get experience in that arena if that was what I was going to talk about and if that was going to be my audience. I did sales and marketing in the publishing business for six years.

"At the age of 27, I started speaking full-time. I did public seminars for Fred Pryor and Career Track, two public-seminar marketing companies. And for the first three years of my career as a professional speaker, I made my living doing that.

"I segued out of that and developed my own business," Mark says. "Today I work with Fortune 500 companies and with large associations—those are my two primary areas."

What do you do all day?

"I speak on four main areas," Mark says, "leadership, teamwork, mastering change, and customer service strategy. I am published in all four areas, in videos, books, and magazine articles. I do 90 to 100 speeches a year. I'm primarily a keynote speaker, where I will talk for up to an hour on a given topic—I would say 90 percent of my business is keynote speaking.

"I spend my time either speaking or preparing to speak. It will take a half-day to fly there; a half-day to fly back; I'll spend one and a half days on site with the client and in giving my presentation.

"I research every client extensively," Mark says, "so I can then tailor my presentation to their needs and concerns. That way, when I give a speech to an organization, they know I haven't given that speech to 100 other organizations before them; the presentation I give is unique to that client. I will typically spend one day to a day-and-a-half researching each client. I work with a research assistant who helps me with that.

"I do a lot of work on the phone, prepping the clients and doing client relations.

"My job consists of preparing for, delivering, and following up on my presentations," he says.

Where do you see this job leading you?

"I'm hoping to get wider exposure through the media," Mark says. "Cable programming has provided opportunities for a lot of people to get their message out, and it will continue to provide those opportunities. There are a lot of audiences out there. I plan on staying in this business for the long haul."

He points out that there is a lot of attrition in the public speaking business. "People tend to go back to whatever they came from."

82. Program Director

FOR A CABLE TELEVISION NETWORK

description: The proliferation of cable- and satellite-based television systems, and the increasing number of channels carried by those systems, have meant an increase in the number of programs and networks to fill those channel slots. From home-shopping networks, to stand-up comedy channels, to cartoon-only channels, there is now a channel for seemingly every interest. A number of the slots on the dial are taken up by public affairs, cultural, or educational programming—examples include C-SPAN, Bravo, and the Discovery channel. And all of these networks have staffs running them.

Program directors for cable television networks are in charge of the programming that goes out over their network. They oversee the production of programming for the network, and may even do some producing themselves. They oversee the budgets of those programs and are generally responsible for everything viewers see—excluding the advertising—on the network they work for.

salary: In this field, the major networks (ABC, CBS, NBC, and Fox) are still where the big money lies. The average salary of a program director for a cable network will range from $50,000 to $75,000, depending on his or her experience and on the resources of the network for which the program director works. Entry-level salaries—which consists of production work—will range from the upper teens to the lower $20,000s.

prospects: The Department of Labor foresees expanded job opportunities in the field over the next decade.

qualifications: A program director will need extensive experience in television programming and production. A broad-based background—with experience in news, live, and entertainment broadcasting—will serve an applicant in good stead.

characteristics: Program directors should be open to new ideas; television is an ever-changing field, and program directors shouldn't discount a suggestion just because it isn't "the way things are done." In fact, part of a program director's job is to encourage and nourish creativity. They should also have a good grasp of technology and an understanding of the technical side of what goes into a television broadcast.

Merlyn Reineke *is the program director for a Washington, D.C.-based political television network.*

How did you get the job?

"I've been in television for about 10 years," Merlyn says. "I had earned a degree in broadcast management, and had started out in programming and production at a station in Los Angeles, KCAL, owned by the Walt Disney Company. I worked my way into straight news production, where I worked for the last three years. I spent about seven or eight years, all told, in Los Angeles.

"I came to Washington, D.C., and got a job as a producer at NET. NET is a political news talk cable network. We feature mostly public affairs programming. We broadcast 24 hours a day, and do about eight hours live per day.

"I came here two years ago as a producer, and rose from there to become senior producer, and then program director," Merlyn says.

IF YOU HAVE ACCESS TO THE WORLD WIDE WEB, CHECK OUT THE "CAREERMOSAIC J.O.B.S." DATABASE. THIS WEB SITE LISTS ALL JOB-RELATED "USENET NEWSGROUPS," WHICH CAN CONTAIN A WEALTH OF INFORMATION FOR THE JOB SEEKER. THE WEB SITE CAN BE FOUND AT "HTTP://WWW.CAREERMOSAIC.COM/CM/".

What do you do all day?

"Here at NET, we've got about 65 to 70 people dedicated to the production end of things. And part of my job is spent responding to the needs of my staffers," Merlyn says. "I try to give them resources, to help them do their jobs better, whether they [are] assisting someone in setting up a remote from the Hill, authorizing the money to do the remote, or putting together video material for a broadcast.

"Some of that material might be controversial—there might be a question as to whether or not it would be appropriate for our audience. I help make those kinds of editorial judgments.

We have a family audience, and I have to take that into account when making my decision.

"We pride ourselves on being the 'tell the truth' network. The traditional networks often take things out of context, and can skew the message. Part of my job is to look at material we are to air, say sound bites from participants at an event, and make sure that we don't use things that were said that weren't indicative of the event as a whole. We don't want to give a false portrayal of anything that we put on the air."

Where do you see this job leading you?

"We're in an interesting time in this industry," Merlyn says. "Television was all I wanted to do as a kid and that's true today. Cable isn't the be-all and end-all of the television industry, though. We now have satellite transmission, and telephone companies are thinking about distributing television programming. It's too early to tell where the television industry is going to end up, especially with the current climate of deregulation.

"But I think there will always be a place for creative people, people who can write and think visually.

"Here at NET, we have an interesting collection of people. There are people like myself, who have a straight television background, and there are people with a straight political background. We have an interesting marriage here of television and public policy work, and people can go from here into either of those arenas.

"Some people can jump from this sort of work onto a campaign and do media work in that context."

83. Public Relations Worker

FOR NONPROFIT GROUPS

description: Public relations work can range from employment on the administrative assistant level, up to the senior account executive level, and even as high as the head of the firm. Administrative assistant work entails standard office management duties, as well as maintaining a media database—a list of reporters and media contacts organized by beat, media market, congressional district, etc. Administrative assistants also help organize media events and put together press kits. Assistant account executives make media calls and pitch stories to reporters. Account executives have more contact with clients (the nonprofit groups that hire your firm to get out their message). Senior account executives help develop communication strategies, meet with clients, and pull together materials for a particular PR campaign.

Most public relations firms work using a team approach, with several agency members working on a single campaign. Crunch times will come as media events, votes on bills, event-driven deadlines, and presentations to clients approach.

salary: Administrative assistants can expect to make from $19,000 to $22,000 a year, assistant account executives in the low $20,000s, account executives in the upper $20,000s to $30,000s, senior account executives from $40,000 to $50,000, and account supervisors from $60,000 to $70,000 a year.

prospects: The public relations firms that concentrate their efforts on the nonprofit sector are few, but the need for nonprofit groups to get out their message is great. While there are opportunities for people willing to do public relations work for these groups, you might have to do this type of work on your own, rather than work for an established firm.

qualifications: People hoping to work in social change public relations should have previous PR campaign experience and should know how to utilize various media tools—print, television, talk radio, cable television, and the Internet. Prospective workers should also have a clear understanding of the issues in which they're going to be involved.

characteristics: If you want to do this type of public relations work, you should be driven by the same issues that drive nonprofit organizations. You should be self-motivated and independent, but also able to contribute to and work effectively as part of a team. Public relations workers should be creative and innovative thinkers as a matter of course.

Diane MacEachern *is the president of a Washington, D.C., public relations firm that works for nonprofit groups.*

How did you get the job?

"I grew up in Michigan and became sensitive to environmental issues at an early age," Diane says. "I was active in church organizations and worked in inner-city Detroit."

Diane earned a master's degree in environmental resource management, moved out to Colorado, and did work on election campaigns and on campaigns to ban underground testing of nuclear weapons.

After that Diane moved to Washington, D.C., where she did grassroots organizing on legislative and referendum campaigns.

"I quickly realized that few activists had communications skills," she says. "So I set up a nonprofit organization to provide communication help to nonprofit issues and groups I was involved in."

Then, she says, she "took a break" and served as communications manager for the Sierra Club.

"Later, I decided to set up a for-profit organization," Diane says, "recognizing that media and communications are an underutilized tool of nonprofit groups. Vanguard Communications provides full-service communications expertise; we develop broad-based education campaigns for nonprofit and activist groups."

What do you do all day?

"My every day is concerned with generating public awareness on issues we choose to concern ourselves with. What tools we choose to use depends on the specific campaign we're involved in. Sometimes, we do communications training, as in the time when we produced a video explaining and identifying signs of mental illness. For Farm Aid, we basically get reporters together and announce the date and location of the next concert.

"One of our campaigns was an attempt to protect six million acres in southern Utah, and for that campaign we put together press releases, press conferences, and press junkets, all to try to make it a national issue.

"We have 25 to 30 employees at any one time. Some of our staff members are seasoned campaign pros, while some have expertise in the issues we involve ourselves in."

Where do you see this job leading you?

"Where this job takes you depends on whether or not you're interested in climbing the corporate ladder or in working on the issues," Diane says. "People have left our organiza-

AMERICA ONLINE FEATURES A SITE CALLED "ACCESS POINT," WHICH PROVIDES ONLINE FORUMS AND JOB SEARCH INFORMATION FOR NONPROFIT GROUPS. FROM ACCESS POINT, YOU CAN CONVERSE WITH NONPROFIT WORKERS FROM ACROSS THE U.S. AND PERUSE POSTINGS OF NONPROFIT JOB OPENINGS.

tion to go back to school. Some have left D.C. You could go on to organization work, to become the communications director of organizations like the Sierra Club or the ACLU. Some people stay in the communications field and go on to positions of more responsibility."

84. Researcher

FOR A RADIO TALK SHOW

description: Radio shows—interview shows, and broadcasts of political and social commentary, all the programs that can fall under the banner of "talk radio"— tend to be personality-driven. As a researcher for a show of this type, you will, in all likelihood, answer to the host of the show that you are working for. And that host's personality and prerogatives will shape the type of work you do. In some instances, your job might be purely research-based. You will gather information on topics the host expresses interest in—or in topics that arouse popular interest—and present that information to your boss. It is much more likely that you will be doing more than that, however. You could be called on to write some, or all, of the scripts for the radio show. You might be in charge of rounding up guests for the program. You could screen the calls of listeners who phone up during the show. You could help produce the show; find yourself gathering music, special effects, and other incidental material that will be used during the show; answer phone calls and respond to inquiries regarding the show; or do promotional work for the show—making calls to stations that could potentially carry your show, preparing media and promotional kits.

salary: A 1992 survey conducted by the National Association of Broadcasters listed the annual median salaries of radio reporters as ranging from $12,000 to $33,500. Researchers for a radio show can expect their salaries to be in that same range.

prospects: It won't be easy to find work as a researcher for a radio talk show—many talk show hosts do not employ researchers, and simply rant about items they pull from the daily paper. In other cases, the research position will be a part-time one. If the current boom in talk radio continues, however, the number of research positions could increase. Advocacy and non-profit organizations often employ researchers, though, and the tasks of those workers are analogous, in many instances, to the work of a researcher for a radio program.

qualifications: Prospective researchers should be well-versed in information gathering, or in the way information is collected. Current emphasis may be on online collecting (and gathering) of information, but a potential researcher should be well-versed in traditional research techniques. A library degree or experience working in a library is excellent preparation for this type of work. A research background, or journalism or investigative experience, will give you a step up on other applicants.

characteristics: Researchers should be meticulous and patient. Successful researchers will be those who are determined to find an answer to whatever question lies before them—someone who is not able to stop until he or she has found the needed information.

Mimi McKay *is a research associate at a radio station in a large Southwestern city.*

How did you get the job?

Mimi McKay began working in her schools' libraries when she went to college, first at Claremont College and then at the University of California at Berkeley. "When I graduated from college, I didn't want to leave Berkeley. I was hired full-time as a library assistant, and basically did library work full-time.

"I liked the public services aspects of those jobs. Part of my duties included setting up exchanges at libraries around the country. I first came here when I helped set up the computer system at the law library, and helped the librarians there learn that system."

While there, she checked out the school's graduate programs and soon began pursuing and obtaining a master's of journalism degree.

She also worked doing publicity for a public television series that broadcasts musical concerts. She also worked as a researcher for an organization called Bat Conservation International.

"I graduated with my library science master's degree, and moved back to Berkeley for the summer, and spent the next

> THE NATIONAL ASSOCIATION OF BROADCASTERS CAN PROVIDE YOU WITH INFORMATION ON JOB OPPORTUNITIES IN THE RADIO FIELD OR RESEARCH OPPORTUNITIES WITH MEDIA OUTLETS. (SEE RESOURCES.)

three months looking for that 'real job.'" By the end of the summer she had two offers in hand: a full-time job with Bat Conservation International, and a job as research associate for Hightower Radio. The previous spring she'd heard that Jim Hightower, the well-known Texas politician, was putting together a radio show, and when she spotted him at a benefit for an environmental organization, "I went up to him and asked him if he would be interested in hiring a freelance researcher. He took down my name, and then I went to Berkeley for the summer." When she got a call from Hightower's research director, who said he was quitting and asked her to interview for the job, she

prepared some presentation and research materials for Hightower, went for an interview, and was hired.

What do you do all day?

"We were supposed to launch a two-minute radio commentary in February 1993," Mimi says.

"In February, we launched with 15 stations, and we were up to 70 within our first year."

Mimi's duties during that portion of her time with Hightower included booking guests and working with writers, as well as research.

In August of that year, Hightower filled in for a talk-show host at an ABC radio affiliate, which so impressed ABC that Hightower and his staff were given the go-ahead for a weekend call-in show (three hours on Saturday and Sunday) on ABC radio.

"I became the producer of the call-in show at that point," McKay says. "Before that I had done special effects, but nothing of this nature.

"In December or January, we realized that we needed to hire a full-time producer for the call-in show," she says. Procuring a producer was another job that fell on her shoulders.

"My duties for the show included going through five newspapers a day, as well as magazines and newsletters, looking for things to bring to Hightower's attention.

"Hightower would get an idea and write it up, and then my job would be to edit it down, to make it short enough to fit into the weekly two-minute commentary format. I would return it for his approval. Then I would pull the special effects we needed, and when we went to the studio once a week to record the shows, I would insert the special effects where they were supposed to go. I would mix commercials, for our union and other advertisers."

Where do you see this job leading you?

Mimi McKay has left Hightower Radio and currently works for Interactive Digital Works. She's part of a team working toward putting her city's daily newspaper on the World Wide Web.

"I was offered high-powered librarian work across the country, but that isn't where I wanted to be. I've become interested in putting media online and was attracted to this project because it was a start-up project, where changes can be made and things aren't entrenched."

85. Art Director

FOR A MULTIMEDIA STUDIO

description: Much of the work done in a multimedia studio involves developing new products and designs—prototyping, testing, and refining new products, releases, or updates to existing products. If the studio is producing a periodical product, another part of the development process will entail establishing a production cycle and methods for turning out new editions of the product on a regular basis.

The art director for a multimedia studio will be in charge of determining the "look-and-feel" for the product or products the studio is working on. Art directors manage the work of other artists and, especially in smaller shops, come up with rough drafts and finished design pieces. They design logos, page design formats, animated characters, backgrounds, and other elements of a multimedia release.

Workers on the art team of a multimedia studio combine their artistic and computer skills to create designs and graphics that are uniquely suited for use in a multimedia environment.

salary: Average starting salaries for graphic designers are in the low $20,000s, with median salaries at around $30,000 to $40,000 a year. But workers for multimedia studios embrace another whole skill set, and their salaries can be expected to be somewhat higher. Beginning computer graphic artists can expect salaries of around $25,000 a year, rising to $45,000 or more for workers with more experience.

prospects: The worlds of multimedia and World Wide Web production have opened up new possibilities for those with an artistic bent. As the tools for production of these products continue to improve, the quality expectations of those products improve as well, and those with professional artistic skills will be called upon more and more often to make multimedia releases and, especially, World Wide Web pages shine. Opportunities for graphic designers to get into the multi-media business are constantly appearing.

qualifications: Proficiency in specific computer programs or software will prove beneficial to someone looking for work in a multimedia studio's art department, but employers will most typically be looking at a prospective employee's artistic talents, not so much her or his computer knowledge. Solid graphic design skills are a prerequisite, and some experience in interface design will be a tremendous boon.

characteristics: Artists in a multimedia studio must be collaborative in nature. Final products will be the result of many contributions other than their own, and artists must be prepared for the give-and-take and the release of the ownership of their ideas that will occur.

Phil Waters *is an art director for a multimedia studio in Denver, Colorado.*

How did you get the job?

"I have been an art director or graphic designer for my entire career," Phil Waters says, "primarily in Los Angeles. I had worked at the *Los Angeles Times* and remained friends with staffers there after I left the newspaper. In 1987, I bought a Macintosh computer. I was customer number 48 of Quark-XPress. [QuarkXPress is a page-layout/desktop publishing program that has become the standard in newspapers and magazines.] My friends at the paper would come over and see what I was doing and say, 'We've got to do this at our newspaper.' So I went to the *L.A. Times* to help introduce them to desktop publishing.

"While I was working at the *L.A. Times*, I began to explore new media on my free time. An opportunity was presented, by having the Super Bowl in Los Angeles, to explore new media and to experiment with ways to re-utilize products. We were an alpha site for the Apple Media Tool. We used it to produce a Super Bowl CD-ROM after the game.

"I left the *L.A. Times* and was recruited by the *San Jose Mercury News.* Then the design director for the *San Jose Mercury News* met the *Ingenius* editor at a conference. That editor articulated the need at *Ingenius* for someone with a news background, design experience, and computer experience for a project they were putting together. The *Mercury News* design director said, 'I've got the perfect guy.'

> ONE OF IVAN R. MISNER'S TEN COMMANDMENTS OF NETWORKING GOES LIKE THIS: TRY TO SPEND LESS THAN 10 MINUTES WITH EVERYONE YOU MEET. DON'T GET STUCK CONVERSING WITH FRIENDS AND ASSOCIATES, WHICH WILL DEFEAT THE REASON FOR YOU ATTENDING WHATEVER EVENT YOU'RE ATTENDING.

"I got a call from Denver and was told that Ingenius was putting together a daily news journal for kids. I wanted to get more fully involved in new media, so this seemed like a perfect opportunity for me."

What do you do all day?

Ingenius produces *What on Earth*, a daily multimedia news journal for children, in partnership with Reuters News Media and Telecommunications, Inc. The service is delivered each weeknight over a school or home's cable line and is downloaded onto a computer's hard drive. What children get when they boot up their computer each morning is a set of six major stories, playing off news events of the day, presented in a multimedia format. Video, animation, audio, and text are used to present the stories and interactive puzzles and games so users can test their knowledge.

"We have a core group of three educators, three journalists, and three multimedia experts who get together every morning with the editors and talk about what stories they want to cover for that particular day," Phil says.

"Our education and journalistic staff make sure our content is edited specifically for kids. Current events are used to launch off onto other topics. And we try to explain the context of certain events.

"By 4:30 P.M., the stories have come together, and we do a walk-through with the editors. The stories are tested on computers, and then compressed and sent out over a cable line.

"I have become part of the management team at Ingenius. I oversee the daily design leader for *What on Earth*.

"I work on strategic positioning of the company, new product development, and on taking what we produce, which is now exclusive to cable modem-users, and moving it to new arenas."

Where do you see this job leading you?

"I haven't really looked ahead at where I will go from here," Phil says.

Art staff in a multimedia studio could go on to other multimedia studios. They could take their skills to other markets—the advertising business, for example, or to Hollywood. As the multimedia business matures, new opportunities will arise.

86. City Universal Access Director

description: Municipal governments and private organizations in many cities have undertaken the task of ensuring that all people in their area have access to the Internet, e-mail, the World Wide Web, and other new media tools. A city freenet or universal access director has the responsibility of bringing that vision to fruition.

Universal access directors will find themselves working with a network of people—people with the tools, technical know-how, and resources to help make "universal access" to the Internet a reality in their area. Much of their time will be spent networking with Internet access providers, equipment donors, technical support providers, city personnel, area businesses, and people working where the universal access stations or centers are installed. They will go out into the community and find out what residents' wants and needs are in regards to universal access. Gathering of resources or fund-raising will take up a good deal of their time. They will help install equipment and set up Internet accounts. They will train people on the use of the tools of the Internet. They will work to develop programs that use the tools of the Internet to benefit their city's residents. And they will serve as troubleshooters when, for instance, a server goes down or a computer program isn't working correctly.

salary: This field is still a new one, and salaries can be widely disparate depending on where and for whom universal access coordinators are working. Workers for nonprofit organizations could start at $18,000 to $20,000 per year. Salaries for city managerial staff members could be higher, rising to $50,000 per year or more.

prospects: There are probably about 65 international freenets established, and another 100 or more in the planning stages. Many of these organizations are volunteer organizations, though, without any paid positions. As the Internet and the World Wide Web become a more pervasive medium, prospects for work of this type will improve. The best opportunities will be for those with experience in electronic media and technology, and in project management.

qualifications: Someone hoping to work as a municipality's universal access coordinator should possess a broad range of qualifications, including a technical background and previous management or coalition-building experience. An understanding of the tools that nonprofit organizations and the public need will also come in handy.

characteristics: Someone hoping to spearhead a project like this will need to be a good communicator and able to portray convincingly his or her ideas to a broad range of people. Universal access managers also need to be good listeners, so they can understand what their city's residents want and need from their Internet connections. Since they will most likely be in charge of their office's efforts (and their office is apt to be a small one), they need to be self-directed, able to initiate projects, and stick to self-imposed deadlines.

Sue Beckwith *is a universal access project manager in Bridgeport, Connecticut.*

How did you get the job?

Sue had earned a bachelor's degree in mathematics, and went to work for a company called Opinion Analysts, doing opinion polls and surveys, and working on direct mailings sent out to her state's registered voters.

Sue next took a job as the information systems manager for her city's environmental department. "I helped design and implement a network there, and streamlined databases and processes for processing energy conservation rebates."

While working for the city, she was tapped by the city manager to co-chair its Internet Task Force. "We looked at what the city needed to do as far as providing interactive services to its residents. And we came up with three things that needed to be done. One, we had to provide interactive information to our residents, and we set about

A COUPLE OF NEWSLETTERS PROVIDE INFORMATION ON JOB OPENINGS IN THE FEDERAL SYSTEM. <u>FEDERAL CAREER OPPORTUNITIES</u>, A BIWEEKLY PUBLICATION, IS AVAILABLE FOR $7.95 PER ISSUE. BASICALLY A LIST OF JOBS, THIS PUBLICATION LISTS JOBS BY DEPARTMENT, AND ALSO TRUMPETS AN ONLINE JOB-HUNTING SERVICE. ANOTHER BIWEEKLY PUBLICATION, <u>FEDERAL JOBS DIGEST</u>, IS AVAILABLE FOR $5.50 PER ISSUE, AND INCLUDES A LISTING OF JOB OPENINGS CATEGORIZED BY STATE, AS WELL AS OVERSEAS JOBS.

doing that by building a city Web site. Two, we needed to get all city staff members e-mail accounts and Web access. Three, we had to work on universal access.

"So the city has dedicated me, as the city universal access project manager, to this project. We have a number of other companies participating in this project, donating everything from equipment to Internet access to office space."

What do you do all day?

"I would say that there isn't a 'typical' day yet," Sue says. "I attend lots of meetings and take lots of phone calls—phone calls to set up meetings, to look at fund-raising, to talk about new program ideas, and to discuss collaborations. For instance, we're working with Big Brothers-Big Sisters in collaboration with the work they are doing at Booker T. Washington."

The Booker T. Washington housing complex is a public

housing center, and is the site of the first Free-Net center, a computer room inside the complex's education center where children and adult residents can access the Internet and e-mail and create their own Web pages.

"My job is pretty fast-paced; it entails a fair amount of running around town. There is an Information and Technology conference coming up; they have chosen to sponsor this Free-Net as their nonprofit of choice. I've been making calls to see how we can get tickets distributed. This job is made up of a wide variety of things."

Where do you see this job leading you?

"I will do this for two years," Sue says. "I've been so focused on the Austin Free-Net that I haven't thought about where I'm going to go next. I might start a small consulting company. We'll see."

87. Developer

OF COMMUNITY-BASED INFORMATION
NETWORKS

description: Working to develop community-based information networks (i.e., helping communities become "wired"), you will find that you wear many hats. You will most likely be part of a small staff; you might even be a staff of one. You will do research-and-development work, testing out new systems that might meet your community's needs, attempting to solve problems that you encounter in your efforts to establish this network.

You will serve a technical support function as well, working to fix "bugs" that develop in the system and frantically striving to get the network or part of the network back online when crashes occur.

You will also have to be one of the main proponents of the network, advertising just what the network is, how people in the community can use it, how it is useful to them, and what they can contribute to it.

You will be a customer service representative as well, answering questions about the network, helping people to find the information they need, and instructing them on how to use the network.

You probably shouldn't expect to work 40-hour weeks either. As with most technical jobs, the hours you work are going to be long ones.

salary: Salaries in this field vary widely, depending on the community you are working for, the needs (perceived and actual) of the market, how in-depth the network will be, what information will be carried over that network, and your specific responsibilities. Working to develop community information networks can net you anywhere from no pay (if you are doing the work on a volunteer basis) to the upper $80,000s for paid systems administrators.

prospects: In the short term, prospects for work in this field are good. As more and more communities go online, there will be a continued need for people to set up and manage those networks.

The telecommunications field is a rapidly changing one, however, and one day's needed commodity can be replaced by automated systems the next. If that should happen, people who run and monitor these networks may be rendered redundant, and will need to look for another line of work.

qualifications: The primary qualifications for someone hoping to be a developer of community-based information networks are a familiarity with the technology and a proven ability to deal with hardware, network administration, software, and memory management issues. A demonstrated commitment to building community networks, through either volunteer labor or previous experience, will also be highly regarded.

characteristics: Network administrators should be mechanically inclined. Because each network will be different from the next, administrators should be people who get a charge out of figuring out the problems and solutions on different systems. Network administrators should be persistent and diligent at solving these problems, and should be creative as well.

Dennis Hoops *is the director of rural information networks for the National Public Telecomputing Network in Solon, Ohio.*

How did you get the job?

"I come from an industrial technology background," Dennis Hoops says. "I was involved in education, and became interested in microcomputers as they began to come out. I'm not the kind of person who likes to build computers; I like the applications of the technology. So I began to use computers in education.

"The National Public Telecomputing Network (NPTN) is a nonprofit organization dedicated to the development of public-access community computer systems," Dennis says.

"I've been indirectly involved with NPTN from the beginning. There was a group of us in Medina County [a rural county south of Cleveland] that thought we needed some kind of community information net-

work in the county. It took three to four years to get that network up and running. All of that work was volunteer time. After three years, we moved the system over to the library, where it remains to this day. It became part of my job description to manage that system; I moved over to the library, and was the first paid position for that freenet.

"We had been in contact with the NPTN throughout that project. They wanted to move into the rural area—setting up rural information networks—and they define rural as any community under 50,000 in population. I came here as the director of the NPTN Rural Information Networks, and I have been here over two years now."

What do you do all day?

"Right now, on a typical day I will come in and check the listserv or my e-mail to see what people are looking for. They might have technical questions, or they might be requesting information on setting up networks of their own, or about our organization.

"I spend part of my time installing servers [computers with full-time connections to the Internet]. I buy software and equipment. When we build a server for someone, it is like a black-box operation; we build the server and test it for 24 hours to see if it is working properly. Then we pack it up and ship it to whoever has requested it. Every system has to be tweaked.

"I set up training schedules. Once we put a system in, we have to train people in how to use it and how to add information to it.

"I answer customer service-type questions, and deal with press inquiries. I receive calls and go out and do speaking engagements.

"I probably put in close to 60 hours a week," Dennis says.

Where do you see this job leading you?

"I will probably continue on with what I am doing," Dennis says. "I do hope to get out of the situation where I am at now, where I am a one-man show. I'm kind of burned out on doing that. I will probably go into the service or marketing area, and concentrate on those things. Or I could manage the NPTN rural information network area, if we grow to that point."

88. Developer of Online Sites

FOR NONPROFIT ORGANIZATIONS

description: The task of putting nonprofit organizations online is really a twofold one. The first aspect of the job is educational: teaching nonprofit workers the basics of using the Internet, why using the net would benefit their organization, and how they can best use the tools of the Internet to help them accomplish their organization's mission. The second aspect of the job is helping those organizations get online. That work might entail building and maintaining a Website for an organization, helping organization workers build a Website of their own, or training workers in how to build their own Website.

The job will probably entail regular use of the Internet and its tools: e-mail, gopher searches, Usenet newsgroups, and the Web. Workers might be called on to give presentations to boards of directors or other interested parties.

salary: Web development work can net people $50 an hour or more. That rate will depend greatly on the skills the developer can bring to the table, and how good a negotiator you are. Internet consultants can bring in from $50 an hour to $100 to $200 an hour working for for-profit organizations. Full-time work in this field can bring in $40,000 a year or more.

prospects: Prospects for work in this field will depend, in large part, on the growth of Internet and World Wide Web use. Since those growth rates are still phenomenal, prospects are quite good for those with the skills this job calls for, and the willingness to seek out these opportunities or to go into business for themselves. Organizations or individuals with previous experience building an online presence for a nonprofit organization or two will probably enjoy the most success.

qualifications: People hoping to help nonprofit organizations get online should have a knowledge of the tools of the Internet, and should probably have some programming background besides. An understanding of the "communications portfolio"—everything from print and broadcast media, to the multi-casting and interactive possibilities the Internet opens up—will prove helpful. They should possess an understanding of how the nonprofit and for-profit business worlds operate.

characteristics: Potential developers of nonprofit organizations' online sites should be good communicators, adept at interpersonal, face-to-face meetings, as well as business correspondence. Persistence and patience are other qualities that successful practitioners of this art will possess.

Cindy Shove *is a director for an online services company based in Palo Alto, California.*

How did you get the job?

"The last experience I had before starting Impact Online was working with nonprofit organizations that were trying to start a for-profit business," Cindy says.

"I had started to use online technology, and had found that there wasn't much information online for nonprofits to use, or even much information online about nonprofits. This was about one and a half years ago.

"And Impact Online was created to give people more information. My partner is Steve Glikbarg, the former publisher of *Who Cares: A Journal of Service and Action. Who Cares* is devoted to chronicling the efforts of people and organizations working to have a positive social impact. We saw Impact Online as taking those efforts to the electronic publishing realm.

"It was difficult, starting a nonprofit organization. Three people joined my partner and me, and we did a feasibility study on what we wanted to do. The problem was that our nonprofit didn't fit any of the existing technologies. But we saw a real opportunity being an online Web developer for non-profit organizations, to help nonprofit organizations figure out how to use this new medium.

"Impact Online uses the Internet to get more people involved. We provide information about issues and nonprofit organizations that deal with those issues. We point people to other nonprofit opportunities, to how they can do virtual volunteering and get involved in hands-on service projects. We keep a FAQ [Frequently Asked Questions] file on our Web Site. Most of our efforts make use of the Web.

"At first, we did a lot of work with nonprofits focused on the

---

CHECK OUT THE IMPACT ONLINE SITE ON THE WORLD WIDE WEB: "HTTP://WEBCOM. COM/~IOL/", OR PARTICIPATE IN ONGOING DISCUSSION OF WHAT THE NONPROFIT WORLD IS FACED WITH VIA THE USENET NEWSGROUP "SOC.ORG. NONPROFIT."

---

homeless," Cindy says, "but now we're going into work with environmental and education groups.

"We do a lot of publishing for nonprofits, to serve as a showcase for what we can do. We've put together a course for nonprofits, answering the question why should they use technology and giving them an introduction to the Internet, focused on the needs of nonprofits."

What do you do all day?

"My partner oversees the day-to-day Web development work that we do," Cindy says. "He spends his time managing our site. We have a group of 50 volunteers building Web pages for us.

"I spend a couple hours a day on e-mail. E-mail messages come from a new advertiser on our site, a potential donor, a consultant for new development, a potential or current volunteer, volunteer coordinators.

"Right now, I'm focused on developing a new board of directors for Impact Online. We're in the process of restructuring and coming up with new bylaws.

"I do some Web development. Right now, I'm working on a survey we want to put up on our site.

"On Friday I'm attending an event that we have helped to present: Cookin' on the Net, an Internet fund-raiser. Five cooks from around the country donated recipes and were paired with five organizations, all related to kids and computers. If people send in $12, they receive the five recipes. All funds collected are distributed to these organizations.

"Technically, I'm not a full-time employee at Impact Online. My partner and I both put in 30 to 40 hours a week as half-time employees, though."

Where do you see this job leading you?

With work experience like Cindy Shove's, you could go into business for yourself, move into commercial Web site development, or get a job in the online or new media departments of newspapers, magazines, cable television stations, or other traditional media businesses. Work in this field could also segue into more traditional marketing, development, or programmatic work in the nonprofit sector.

89. Independent Multimedia Producer

description: Multimedia refers to the use of video, animation, music, sound, and text in an interactive setting. Currently, the most common means of delivering that multimedia content is via a CD-ROM disk inserted into a multimedia computer.

Multimedia producers oversee the entire process of creating a multimedia title, from conceptualizing the project, to distribution of the title. Your duties will include market research, contract negotiation, title acquisition, content development, pre- and postproduction work, graphics- and video-editing, computer programming, and more. If you're not involved in those aspects in a hands-on capacity, you will be involved in at least supervising those tasks.

Working with educational software, you might find yourself dealing with state and national educational boards and associations, negotiating with them to ensure that your multimedia work meets their guidelines and recommendations.

Independent producers have the luxury of pursuing their own projects. The downside is that pursuing your own projects sometimes means no steady income. Once producers are established and have a name for themselves, that can be less of a problem, but part of the job of an independent multimedia producer will always entail securing financing for current or future projects.

salary: Salaries vary widely, depending on location, experience, and how much funding multimedia producers managed to procure for their projects. Salaries can start at around $30,000 per year, and that figure can go as high as $90,000 per year or more for producers working on the coasts.

prospects: Like all aspects of the multimedia industry, educational multimedia will continue to grow, although perhaps not as quickly as entertainment and home applications. In this industry, experience is invaluable, so the more experience you have—especially in technical areas and in educational fields—the better.

qualifications: Experience with computers is a necessary prerequisite for someone who hopes to become a multimedia producer. Sub-specializing in one of the aspects of this work—such as graphics or the budgetary-planning side of things—can give you a foot in the door. You won't come into the field as a multimedia producer, but by getting a start in the industry and by learning everything you can about the field, you will be preparing yourself for a producing role.

characteristics: The chief virtues of any multimedia producer are tenacity and patience. You have to be tenacious because people you're working with are going to have something you want, and you'll have to get at them to get it. You'll have to be patient to deal with all the snags and delays projects like this inevitably entail.

Dewey Winburne *is an independent multimedia producer in Seattle, Washington.*

How did you get the job?

Dewey earned a teaching certificate, and went to work in a public school system.

"My real passion was working with kids that had been kicked out of traditional schools or with kids that were in detention centers here in town," he says.

He began working at the American Institute for Learning, an alternative education center for students who had fallen through the cracks in public schools. He says, "I settled on the idea of project-based learning—learning by doing. And I began working with students on a variety of media-based projects." His students interviewed and shadowed newspaper reporters, and created their own newspaper. They also produced their own community access television show.

> ONLINE JOB FORUMS CAN BE A BOON TO YOUR JOB SEARCH. THE MAJOR ONLINE SERVICES—AMERICA ONLINE, COMPUSERVE, AND PRODIGY—ALL HAVE JOB FORUMS OF THEIR OWN, WHERE JOB SEEKERS CAN EXCHANGE RESUME TIPS, NEWS OF JOB OPENINGS, AND OTHER ADVICE.

With a focus group of 12 students, Dewey helped evaluate 75 adult educational software titles for IBM. This work led to a grant from his state's Department of Drug and Alcohol Abuse that allowed Dewey to put together two award-winning multimedia laser disc titles, *Addiction and Its Processes* and *Lifemoves: The Processes of Recovery,* with the help of former and current Institute students.

What do you do all day?

"It can take two months to a year to produce a piece of multimedia software," Dewey says, "depending on the scope of the project."

"I deal in contract negotiation," Dewey says, "and marketing. Part of what I do is team management. I deal in pre-production work and in systems integration—video, graphics, and music production. And then you get into post-production work—the heart of multimedia—which is implementing interactivity into your design, making the elements sing to the message, so to speak.

"Graphics editing, video editing, computer programming—you have to oversee those teams or do that work yourself."

Where do you see this job leading you?

"We don't see any multimedia titles on the market that deal with critical social problems. I want to do that," he says.

He hopes to form a publishing company to help develop an industry niche with topics related to self-help and social responsibility.

He is also advising and consulting with a statewide multimedia incubator, which has plans to facilitate dozens of multimedia projects.

As the multimedia field grows, Dewey sees ever more opportunity for socially-conscious multimedia projects to become a reality. For instance, Amnesty International and some of the environmental organizations have already produced multimedia titles.

90. Internet Services Marketer

description: Computers. The Internet. Digital transmission and storage of data. The convergence of computers with broadcast and telephony technology. All of these things are poised to make a tremendous difference in how we receive information, and even how we interact with each other. Getting in on the early stages of this technological transformation can allow workers in this field to have a say in how this transformation will affect society.

Marketing new technology is much the same as marketing any other product. You might have to learn some specialized lingo, but your main focus will be on promoting this new technology.

Working with the Net will give you the thrill that comes from feeling that you're on the cresting wave of something new, something that could bring about societal change, anticipated or unanticipated, premeditated or not. Though salaries can be quite impressive in this field, hours are likely to be long and arduous.

salary: In large part, salary can depend on where you are located and whether your knowledge is in demand. Some areas of the country will be booming high-tech centers with a shortage of knowledgeable people; other places (such as Silicon Valley) may have more skilled workers than there are jobs available. Salaries will typically start at around $30,000 annually, and can rise as high as $100,000 or more.

prospects: The technology field is growing, and the outlook is quite good for jobs in all aspects of the high-tech and telecommunications industries. As business on the Net continues to grow, there will be opportunities available.

qualifications: The more technical and computer training you have under your belt, the more attractive you will be to potential employers. In a very real sense, though, just being comfortable with computers and in navigating the Net can put you a step above many other applicants. Tech-support positions—which traditionally suffer from a high turnover rate and are often entry-level jobs—can offer a good way for those without a heavy technical background to get technical training. Marketing experience is also highly recommended.

characteristics: Flexibility and persistence are important traits—flexibility in adapting to the changes that working with any new technology is going to throw your way, persistence in being able to see projects through to completion, and in convincing others that your project is a worthwhile one.

Ed West *is a product manager for an Internet services marketing company in San Francisco, California.*

How did you get the job?

Ed West earned an undergraduate degree in geography. He got an opportunity to sell software for a California geographic information company, and decided to take that opportunity. He stayed with that company for a year. "That's where I learned a lot about marketing and demographics," he says. He heard about his present employer, ISDN*tek, and was impressed by their focus. "They presented an opportunity to be on the leading edge of technology," he says. It was an opportunity he jumped at.

ISDN*tek is a San Francisco-based company that produces equipment to allow people to work from home, to do tele-communications types of jobs from a home environment, or to set up a home office situation. ISDN*tek's technology links the phone lines of a business with those of its home-based workers and sets up a business-to-home computer network.

CHECK OUT THE INSTITUTE FOR GLOBAL COMMUNICATIONS' PROGRESSIVE DIRECTORY. IT CAN BE FOUND BY SENDING YOUR WEB-BROWSER IN SEARCH OF: "HTTP://GOPHER.IGC.APC.ORG/". THE IGC DIRECTORY CAN PROVIDE YOU WITH INFORMATION ON PROGRESSIVE PUBLICATIONS AND NEWS SERVICES AND A DIRECTORY OF ORGANIZATIONS, AND IT CONTAINS "LINKS" TO OTHER AREAS, SUCH AS THE IGC'S PEACENET AND LABORNET INFORMATION AREAS.

What do you do all day?

Ed says that, especially when he first took the position, his main job was to learn his way around the Internet to get familiar with the technology the company was using.

Now the company's focus is on bringing their technology to the market. Ed spends a lot of time educating people about the product, traveling to trade shows and manning a booth, meeting with potential customers or sellers of the equipment, handing out and collecting business cards. He's on the phone quite a bit, developing contacts and promoting his company's equipment. He puts together the company's marketing materials as well.

"I use the Net quite a bit," Ed says, "to keep in contact with all the people I do business with. I do work from home [he says he's in the company's offices about two or three days per week], so I am using the technology that we're trying to promote."

ISDN*tek is a small company, and so Ed often finds himself answering the phone for technical support calls, and writing letters.

Despite the fact that Ed is able to work from home most of the time, he still puts in long hours—10- to 12-hour days are the rule rather than the exception. "Still, that's the rule in the high-tech business as a whole," he says.

Where do you see this job leading you?

Ed seems to have staked his immediate fortune on this company. His marketing skills are assets he brought to his current job, and could import to jobs he takes in the future.

Ed feels that the growth in the Internet will bring about tremendous opportunities, "especially for people coming out of school," Ed says. "There's a real need for people to do graphic arts. What you see now from the Internet is graphics, it's two-dimensional. But silicon graphics can probably turn the World Wide Web into a 3-D environment. You've got to realize that this is the worst it's ever going to be. We're in the Model-T era. I see opportunities in tech support, training, and developing content on the Internet."

91. Online Activist

description: Though the Internet is still a relatively new tool for use in the activist struggle, it is becoming an ever more popular one. Nonprofit groups are now beginning to use the Internet and online services to spread the word about their activities and about issues they think deserve the attention of like-minded individuals.

If you're in charge of a group's online activities, your duties will likely include maintaining the group's World Wide Web pages and Gopher sites. You could be charged with putting together an online newsletter, updating readers on the organization's activities and on issues with which the organization is concerned, and with distributing electronic petitions and action alerts.

You'll be in charge of the group's online correspondence, responding to the e-mail messages and requests for assistance your organization might receive.

salary: You can expect to make from $15,000 to $40,000 per year, depending on the size of the agency you work for, its funding sources, and where it is located. Those who perform full systems and network administration duties can expect higher salaries.

prospects: As more and more nonprofit groups are seeing the value of online activism, the opportunities for those with the skills to help organizations get online should only improve.

qualifications: Managers of online services should have strong Internet skills, html-writing experience, and knowledge of UNIX and one or more personal computer systems. They should have experience running a bulletin board service or other online forum, building and maintaining World Wide Web pages and archive sights, and doing some scripting and programming.

characteristics: Managers of online services should have good organizational skills so that they can sort information and deal with data efficiently. You should have a good sense of how to word things, because if you word something incorrectly or violate any of the rules of "Netiquette," it may generate bad publicity for your group. You should be able to think on your feet.

Stanton McCandlish *is a manager of online services for a foundation in San Francisco.*

- -

How did you get the job?

"I began programming BASIC in junior high," Stanton McCandlish says, "and took computer courses through my first year of college. Then I got out of computing for a while, but when I moved to a new college, I got an Internet account and found the world of the Net both exciting and liberating."

The Electronic Frontier Foundation (EFF) describes itself as "a nonprofit organization dedicated to protecting and promoting the civil liberties of the users of online technology."

"I had been following the EFF from the time it started, and was on the periphery of the organization until the advent of the Chipper Clip controversy," Stanton says. "The Chipper Clip was an encryption microchip meant for installation in phones; the National Security Agency would be able to break that encryption at any time. There were civil liberties problems associated with the Chipper Clip, and this organization opposed it.

"I was a private bulletin board system (BBS) operator at the time, working at the University of New Mexico CIRT Lab, doing computer consulting, and running my BBS as a free board, running it as sort of a hobby from home. I used my board to disseminate information on the Chipper Clip and the EFF's efforts. By that time, I was in close contact with the organization.

"Soon after, this job became available at the EFF, and I applied for it. There were 50 other applicants, but I was sure this job was mine. I think a lot of people can sympathize with that idea, people feeling that they found a mission and then the mission found them."

What do you do all day?

"I officially work from 9:30 A.M. to 6 P.M. weekdays, but most people here work quite late," Stanton says. "The workload can shoot up to the point where it's pretty smothering, when you're dealing with certain 'public eye' issues. During those times, you can expect even more work, more bills, more state-level actions.

"I answer lots and lots of e-mail. E-mail is integral to what we do. I do online librarianship, organizing files on our public server. I put out the organization's online newsletter. I do online research, scouring the Net for new bills, notices of BBS raids by police, things relevant to what we do.

"Right now, we're tracking 50 bills. We're also in a funding crunch; I need to take time out from my other activities to do fund-raising.

"I maintain an archive of activism," Stanton says, "which includes a Congressional Representative list and a list of hands-on grassroots lobbying techniques.

"I put out action alerts when bills are about to be voted on, letting people know what they can do to affect the outcome of legislation—calling your senator and things like that.

"I stay in constant contact with other organizations. I have frequent meetings—often not held in physical space, though; I would say that 90 percent of the dialogue I have with these groups is via e-mail. I help other Electronic Frontier organizations get started—EF-Norway, EF-New Hampshire, and EF-Ireland, for instance."

Where do you see this job leading you?

"I think I'll be here for a long while," Stanton says, "though the job skills I've picked up here make me very employable. I could be (and have been, on the side) a World Wide Web consultant or operator. I could do BBS consulting types of things. The person who had my equivalent position in the EFF's other office is now doing custom Internet consulting and design.

"There's lots of online activism going on right now, but very few paid positions available. But there is an increasing demand for work on the information management side of things."

> **ONLINE ACTIVISTS SHOULD HAVE THE COMPUTER NETWORKING SKILLS THAT MATCH WHAT THE ORGANIZATION NEEDS.**
> - - - - - - - - - -

92. World Wide Web Publishing

FOR NONPROFIT ORGANIZATIONS

description: A person who creates pages or documents for the World Wide Web can go by many titles: Web master is perhaps the most frequently used. And in very broad terms, the responsibility of a Web master is to build and maintain documents for that medium, fashioning text, graphics, photos, audio, video, and animation into an appealing and powerful method of communication.

Of course, the details of the job are a bit more involved. A Web publisher will have to work constantly to keep up-to-date on applications, plug-ins, and extensions to the Web and hypertext markup language (html), the language on which the Web is built.

Once a page is built, it must be attended to—maintained on an Internet server (a system with a connection to the Internet), and updated as information changes, or simply to keep the page looking fresh. The responsibility for overseeing the interactive aspects of a Web site— e-mail responses, bulletin board comments, and other feedback—will likely fall to the Web master as well. He or she might be responsible for solving any technical problems that crop up with the software, hardware, or applications in use.

Many Web masters also find themselves in the role of company spokesperson (many times the Web master is the entire company!).

salary: Salaries for those working on finessing this new medium are all over the map. Salaries of self-employed Web publishers will depend on how many clients they can attract, and how much they find they can charge those clients. Workers in this medium can expect to make anywhere from $20,000 to $100,000 or more per year, with the majority of salaries in the $20,000 to $40,000 range.

prospects: The World Wide Web is a fast-changing medium, and prospects for Web publishing change just as quickly. However, the Web is a growing medium, so positions and prospects are ever-increasing. In many locales, organizations will be in place that are putting up that information for free, and on a voluntary basis, which could make prospects harder for someone hoping to make a living doing this sort of work.

qualifications: Individuals hoping to build World Wide Web sites for nonprofit organizations should be familiar with both Macintosh and IBM PC-based computers. They should probably be at least nominally familiar with UNIX and other programming languages.

characteristics: A Web publisher needs to be a good communicator—someone who not only can communicate ideas graphically by designing an effective Web page, but can interact successfully with clients and prospects, some of whom may be technically illiterate. He or she should be persuasive, as it is sometimes harder to convince clients of the value of the technology than it is to build the Web pages. Marketing skills or acumen will also help. The Web publisher should be able to master change, as next month's "killer application" that clients want added to their Web pages could be less than a murmur this month, and supplanted by another killer application the month after that.

Gina Faber *is the owner/operator of a Web publishing service in Santa Clara, California.*

How did you get the job?

"I started OneEarth so that I could support organizations by putting them on the net," says Gina Faber. "My goal is to increase the exposure of companies in line with my own vision.

"I worked as a computer programmer and software engineer for six years," she says. "I had gotten a degree in math education, but I discovered that I hated teaching. That was a psychological blow to me because I am very service oriented. I went into computers because they were something I had always had fun with, and were more lucrative than a career in something I disliked.

"That work, however, wasn't very satisfying. I was also not satisfied with the way the world was going. A book I read, *Zen and the Art of Making a Living,* by Laurence Boldt, helped me decide to blow off the corporate world. I searched and have found a way to use my computer skills in a social way.

"During my first year in college, I got an Internet account and have been on the net ever since. My first experience with the Web was when I was working in Virginia, about two and a half years ago. I worked as a Web master at a Palo Alto company.

> **GINA RECOMMENDS *ZEN AND THE ART OF MAKING A LIVING* BY LAURENCE G. BOLDT, WHICH PRESENTS AN INTEGRATED, PHILOSOPHICAL APPROACH TO EARNING A LIVING, AND ADDRESSES THE TOPIC OF EARNING A LIVING WHILE MAKING A DIFFERENCE.**

"I've been working on OneEarth since June. Things started out slow, but there is always a new opportunity in this business. It's just getting to the point where it is supporting itself.

"I am not a workaholic—I have a very keen sense of what is a proper balance for me," Gina says. "And I am now at the point where I can decide when I do not want to take a new job. Now, I really have to think carefully when I take on new projects."

What do you do all day?

"I would say that 25 percent of this job is marketing," Gina says. "I always have my eyes open for companies I might want to promote. As an example, the Seventh Generation catalog sells recycled goods—whenever I run into a company like that, I try to solicit them for business.

"I set aside a day every two weeks to follow up on leads I have generated. That is not much time.

"There is also the work of developing a World Wide Web site. I begin that process by meeting with the customer. I get information from them—the electronic text and graphics and other material they might want put on their Web site. I work on a Macintosh Powerbook to design the pages. Then I take them to the client, who approves the designs. Then I have to put the pages onto a World Wide Web server. I use a virtual server, so I don't have www.1earth.com [Gina's Web site] running on just one computer. Some of my clients maintain their own pages. I maintain clients' pages for $5 per month.

"About half of the clients I have worked with are local," she says, "but I have just put up pages for a German transportation company, and I've put together pages for a blue-green algae provider in Pennsylvania.

If a client has a phone, e-mail address, and a fax number, I can work with them.

"I maintain my own Web page, which includes a gallery that I update every two days. I spend most of my time keeping the OneEarth site up to date, adding material to it. I add 12 to 15 sites to my gallery every two weeks, and am continually making improvements to my site."

Where do you see this job leading you?

"I don't have a clear vision of where this will take me," Gina says. "This industry changes so fast that I am not counting on anything. I'm not even sure where the Web will be in a year.

"And I keep running into opportunities that could consume me. There is a possibility of a book deal, for instance. Or I could go on to help with a start-up organization or any of the organizations I'm working with in this business. I've gotten involved in a network of people in their 30s with business experience, who want to use the Web to turn the country around in the direction they want to see it go. That would be an exciting opportunity, and it would allow me to leverage my experience in something I couldn't do on my own."

93. International Educational Researcher and Developer

description: Educational research and development work in the international arena has many similarities to the sort of work done inside the United States. Workers in this field conduct research and synthesize information that will help the various users of educational systems increase the effectiveness of their efforts. They visit schools to see where the problems and needs are, and then work with government officials, school administrators, and educators to solve those problems.

But since workers will be crossing borders and dealing with other countries' governments in the course of their job, work on an international scale like this can entail more political finessing than might be necessary working inside the United States. Other countries have different educational systems, expectations, and cultures—just a few of the factors that have to be taken into consideration when doing this type of work.

Part of the work involves communicating—coordinating with international agencies, governments, and foundations, as well as documenting the projects undertaken and their results.

salary: Salaries for international educational researchers and developers vary depending on the agency for which they work, how well funded it is, and the priority it places on educational research and development. Experience and education factor into salary discussions as well. In general, workers in this field can expect to make from $30,000 to $70,000 per year.

prospects: Prospects for finding work in this field depend on the international situation. When a crisis arises or attention is focused on a certain area of the world, more money will be funneled into groups operating in those countries, and more jobs will become available. Many private volunteer organizations—such as CARE and the Christian Children's Fund—have educational components, and jobs can be found in those organizations.

Though the creation of new jobs in this field can be a rare occurrence, openings occur as workers leave their positions—to go on to further schooling or to take a position "in the field."

qualifications: Education specialists working on research and development in the international arena should possess Ph.D.-level academic training, international experience, and multilingual skills.

Says Fred Wood, director of education and early childhood development for Save the Children, "We look for people who can communicate well and who are self-programming, since we are a small team in a big program. As an educational specialist in this arena, you need to understand cultures and the differences between cultures, so you can argue from their starting point and not your own."

characteristics: Applicants for international educational research and development jobs should be physically fit and willing to endure less-than-ideal conditions.

Applicants should also be persuasive; they will be called upon to sell their ideas—to funders, to their board, to officials in the countries in which they work—and so good communications skills are a must.

Fred Wood *is the director of education and early childhood development for Save the Children in Westport, Connecticut.*

How did you get the job?

"Initially, I spent five years in the field, doing basic education work in Africa, and traveling throughout Africa and the Caribbean," Fred says. "I was working with the Ugandan government, which at the time was recruiting people like me straight out of school.

"I went back to school, to do postgraduate work in London, and then I decided to try and combine my postgraduate work with actual work, and was hired as a research associate with a development organization.

"For 20 years, I was the head of programs, the chief program officer at the Bernard Van Leer Foundation, the largest educational foundation in the world, located in the Netherlands. We worked with the educationally disadvantaged in 40 countries in Africa and Asia.

"Nineteen ninety-one was my sabbatical year," he says, "which I spent at Harvard University. I was supposed to go back to the Van Leer Foundation at the end of that year, but

Save the Children tapped me on the shoulder. Here was a chance to do something different.

"I set up the Strong Beginnings program, the 'initial education' initiative of Save the Children. We started out concentrating on early childhood education, then made a transition to primary education and literacy education for mothers. We have programs in 15 countries now, including the United States."

What do you do all day?

"I work with a team of six," Fred says, "and members of the team spend part of their time here and part of the time in the field. For instance, we have someone in Bangladesh right now, and someone coming back

> **ALEX HIAM AND SUSAN ANGLE'S BOOK ADVENTURE CAREERS IS A GOOD SOURCE TO TURN TO FOR INFORMATION ON NON-TRADITIONAL JOBS AND CAREER PATHS.**

from Bangladesh. There's always a lot of coming and going here.

"I recently gave a presentation in Kuala Lumpur [the capital of Malaysia] at the first National Convention on Early Childhood, and when I got back I spent some time reviewing with other members of the team what transpired at that conference.

"We spend our time in planning, project development, writing reports, and presenting information—we go before potential funders and convince them to invest their money in us.

"We're involved in educational projects in the field. In Bangladesh, we're involved in small-scale women's savings groups, groups of 20 to 30 women who get together and pool their savings. Save the Children asked us to develop a program based around these groups. We're working with a UNICEF group to increase these women's understanding of childhood development.

"Other projects we're involved in are more conventional. In Mali and South Africa, for instance, we convinced local communities that

they have to build and maintain schools in order to provide decent education for their children. We identify local people prepared to teach in their communities. We train those people and monitor the situation in the schools. In four years, we've helped build 170 of these schools; our target is, by the end of the century, to have 1400 schools in place."

Where do you see this job leading you?

"We are a great formation ground for the international banks, for UNICEF, for other groups that pay more than we do." People that work in educational research and development tend to move on to organizations and positions doing similar work.

Fred points out that workers will sometimes go back to school to improve their educational qualifications or go into the field to do work in a specific country.

195

94. Peace Corps Volunteer

description: The Peace Corps has been around since the 1960s, sending volunteers on two-year (or longer) tours of duty to help developing countries in such fields as health care, education, engineering, and agriculture. The most common image of Peace Corps service is probably serving in a remote village in Africa, but today's Peace Corps volunteers are sent all over the world, to Latin America and to Eastern Europe, as well as to Asia and Africa.

Each country will request workers in areas that they see the need for; the Peace Corps will then try to fill those positions from its pool of applicants.

Volunteers spend two years in the country to which they have been assigned, with the option, in many cases, of signing up for additional tours of duty. Volunteers will work in schools, medical clinics, and on farms. They will engage in bridge-building, tree-planting, business consulting, or any of a host of other duties, depending on each volunteer's skills and training and the needs of the country to which they are assigned.

The Peace Corps accepts applications from all age groups, from the recent college graduate to the newly retired pediatrician. The Peace Corps proves attractive to many college students: it provides them with two years of overseas experience and can be an excellent "entry-level" position.

salary: At the end of their tour of duty, Peace Corps volunteers are paid $200 for every month they have spent with the program, including training. Volunteers are also paid a living allowance while they are working. That living allowance is based on a survey of the cost of living for the country to which volunteers are posted. Living allowances typically pay for food, clothing, travel, and other expenses. The Peace Corps also provides its volunteers with vacation allowances.

prospects: The Peace Corps is most interested in applicants with degrees in science, engineering, computer programming, math, health, and perhaps graduate-level business. A new crop of Peace Corps candidates is selected every year, so there are near-constant opportunities for qualified applicants, especially for those who are willing to or can afford to wait out the lengthy application process.

The emphasis the Peace Corps places on certain skills or degrees can change over time. For instance, with the fall of communism in Eastern Europe came a corresponding need for people with business experience to help rebuild the infrastructure in former communist countries. When that happened, Peace Corps applicants with that experience were especially valued.

qualifications: Peace Corps volunteers usually need to be college graduates, or need to have a lot of experience in a particular field. Peace Corps admissions officers look for degrees in fields that correspond to the requests the agency receives from the countries in which it places volunteers. They will also look for evidence of previous volunteer work.

characteristics: Peace Corps recruiters will look for someone they think can adapt to the situations they will be thrust into during their tenure with the Peace Corps. They will look for someone with evidence of cultural sensitivity and adaptability.

Gail Gresham *is a Peace Corps volunteer working in the Ivory Coast (Republic of Côte d'Ivoire), Africa.*

How did you get the job?

Gail Gresham filled out her Peace Corps application in the fall of her senior year. "I was earning a bachelor of science in nutrition degree," she says, "and wanted to work outside of the United States. I minored in French, which was another skill I thought I could use overseas."

Gail offers a piece of advice to prospective Peace Corps applicants: "I really think people should apply a year ahead of when they want to go overseas because it takes a really, really long time for your application to be processed.

"First of all, you have to fill out an application and include a statement about why you want to join the Peace Corps. You need recommendations from six people—at least one from a

---

> **GIVE THE PEACE CORPS A CALL AND REQUEST AN APPLICATION PACKET. OR MEET WITH PEACE CORPS RECRUITERS WHEN THEY COME TO VISIT YOUR COLLEGE.**
>
> - - - - - - - - - -

supervisor and one from a school professor. Then you have to go through a legal check and get fingerprinted. Then you have to have a medical test. At each step along the way, you'll receive word from the Peace Corps: 'You passed this but you need this.'

"I had my initial [Peace Corps] interview in February and found out exactly where I was going in July. My group left for Africa in September.

"Orientation and training for us consisted of three days in the United States of what was called 'pre-staging.' The Peace Corps volunteers spent a few days getting to know each other.

"Training for us was three months in Senegal. Recruits with other specialties would train in the States and in-country for different lengths of time.

"In-country training was really intense. We would have language classes all morning, 8 A.M. to noon Monday through Saturday. Afternoons were spent in technical training, mostly in English.

"After the training session, I was sent to the Ivory Coast for two more weeks of training, and then lived for a couple weeks in

the city closest to where I was to be posted, and worked at the main health center there.

"I went out with someone from the health center, who formally introduced me to the village. Then the chiefs, the heads of the village, showed me around."

What do you do all day?

"For the first three months I was in the Ivory Coast, I basically spent my time hanging out with the people in my village, learning their customs and language," Gail says.

"I had problems gaining the respect of people in my village because I was young and a woman," she says. "I could see the health problems immediately. In my village, there were no particular problems with vaccinations, but they did have problems with hygiene, and with weaning children from their mothers. I would ask people in the village what they saw as their health problems, and they would say they needed telephones or they needed running water.

"I would ask people in the village, 'What kind of sicknesses are you getting that you need medication for?' And I would try to get them interested in

building latrines or trying to start health committees. I would try to get the influential people in the community signed onto these projects. The most important thing I did was to get people interested in and aware of their health problems so they could in turn teach their village about them.

"My schedule depended on the schedule of the people in the village. Most people worked in the fields in my village, so there weren't many people around in the afternoon. And during the rainy season, I could hardly work at all because people were in the fields from sunup until sundown."

Where do you see this job leading you?

Many former Peace Corps volunteers follow their experience overseas with graduate school.

Other volunteers will broker their Peace Corps experience into a career working overseas.

"I feel that I gained a lot of managerial and organizational skills during my two-year tenure in the Peace Corps," Gail says.

"I could go on to do program coordination for a nonprofit agency. That's the job that is most like what I did in Africa."

95. Program Director

FOR A PHILANTHROPIC ORGANIZATION

description: Program officers at philanthropic organizations with an international focus will find their job duties similar to those in a philanthropic organization with a domestic focus.

Program officers will typically have a geographic area or a program area (human rights, say, or reproductive issues) that they oversee. Officers search out groups whose goals and initiatives coincide with the funding organizations, or perhaps agencies seek out the funding organization.

Program officers deal with grant management and allocation. They perform site visits and network with their programming partners or grant recipients overseas. They might be involved in fund-raising efforts, both in the United States and overseas. And if the organization has an advocacy component, program officers could engage in those types of activities as well—researching or writing position papers, developing educational materials, giving speeches about the organization and the causes it supports.

salary: Salary levels for program officers can range from approximately $28,000 to $38,000 per year, depending on the nature of the organization the officer works for and the worker's experience and duties.

prospects: While relief and humanitarian aid organizations continue to send workers into other countries, fewer and fewer community development organizations send people overseas, says Shalini Nataraj, the Unitarian Universalist Service Committee's program associate for Asia. The focus is shifting to working cooperatively with indigenous groups. However, domestic agencies that do work overseas will still need liaisons with these indigenous groups, and that is where the best opportunities may lie.

Keep in mind, though, that competition for these sorts of jobs will likely be fierce. More schools than ever before are offering international relations degrees, and those schools are graduating more and more students. These types of jobs will likely be concentrated on the East and West coasts.

qualifications: Successful applicants for international programming positions will have a combination of academic and real world experience. A master's degree is likely to be a requirement for this type of work, though it might be waived for equivalent experience. Employers usually look for someone with field experience in community development, either in overseas communities or in U.S. communities facing analogous conditions. Good communications and writing skills, interpersonal skills, and cross-cultural experience will all be highly regarded.

characteristics: An ability to understand and work with people of other cultures is essential to success in this type of job. Prospective program officers should have (or should labor to acquire) a talent for listening, and for leaving any personal agenda behind when dealing with other groups and agencies.

Shalini Nataraj *is the program associate for Asia for the Unitarian Universalist Service Committee in Cambridge, Massachusetts.*

How did you get the job?

Shalini calls the path that led her to her current position a "convoluted" one. "Originally, I wanted to get into marine biology," she says. "I earned a zoology undergraduate degree.

"I was offered a job directing programs for an environmental organization in India. I was at that position for two and a half years.

"I was interested in strip-mining. While in India, I made contacts with people in the United States, and was invited by an organization in east Tennessee to come to the United States. So I went to Central Appalachia to do environmental work there. I stayed for two months, and then was offered an internship there."

She enrolled in a graduate-level program in New York City, and earned her master's degree through an evening class program structured for United Nations professionals. While she attended school, her "day job" was working for a development organization in New York.

She saw the Unitarian Universalist Service Committee program associate for Asia posi-

tion advertised, applied for the job, and ended up moving to the Boston area when she was hired for that position. She has been in her current job for three years.

The Unitarian Universalist Service Committee grew out of the Unitarian Universalist Church 52 years ago. A secular organization, the UUSC works to advance the causes of human rights around the world, by funding human rights organizations as well as training programs and by working to educate and mobilize its own constituency—the organization's 17,000 members, who are primarily members of the Unitarian Universalist Church.

What do you do all day?

Shalini says she is responsible for the UUSC's Asia program, which includes initiatives in India, the Philippines, and Burma.

"My job entails identifying groups overseas—organizations we want to work with—as well as grant management and allocation.

"In India, our work has a strong human rights focus. We sponsor six or seven women's groups there, groups involved in domestic violence issues, legisla-

> RESEARCH ORGANIZATIONS WITH WHICH YOU HAVE SCHEDULED AN INTERVIEW. LIBRARY REFERENCE SECTIONS CAN BE USEFUL SOURCES OF INFORMATION, AS CAN JOB PLACEMENT CENTERS. THE INTERNET, SHOULD YOU HAVE ACCESS TO IT, CAN BE ANOTHER HELPFUL SOURCE OF DATA.

tive initiatives, groups that monitor existing law and do legal aid counseling, groups that work at consciousness-raising—bringing women into the fold.

"Our initiatives in Burma are relatively new programs for us. Right now I am looking for groups to fund.

"In the Philippines, our efforts take a broader focus. We work with groups that are concerned about native rights, environmental rights, women's health and reproductive rights.

"A typical schedule for me would entail keeping up on the issues.

"I do a lot of networking—calling people, doing whatever needs doing. I work on funding proposals, funding requests. I have ongoing communication with my programming partners. There's also a lot of coordination with other departments in this agency.

"I write op-ed pieces for newspapers and magazines. I do speaking engagements and answer correspondence. And I go to a lot of meetings—a standard feature of most nonprofits. I attend meetings of other nonprofit organizations, departmental meetings, interdepartmental meetings, agency meetings, and board meetings."

Where do you see this job leading you?

"I think three years is a good time to stay in any one position," Shalini says. "The next step for me would be to the senior project associate level, or to the management level. Right now, I am directing a program but I have no final budgeting authority, so I would look for a management position where I would have staff under me, and where I would be directing a budget."

96. USAID Officer

description: USAID stands for United States Agency for International Development, the government agency that handles the portion of the U.S. budget that goes to foreign aid. USAID is an agency independent from the State Department; both organizations maintain their own "foreign service" staff.

USAID has offices (missions) in more than 100 countries throughout the world. Those missions include such divisions as health, education, the environment, democracy, and agriculture, working in cooperation with local governmental and nongovernmental agencies in the distribution of AID funds and the implementation of AID-funded programs.

Officers could be in charge of one of those divisions; they could be project officers, in charge of the design and implementation of a specific AID project; they could be program officers, overseeing the entire mission operation and checking on where the money is going.

salary: The salary of beginning USAID workers is based on what the prospective worker was making before he or she was hired by the government. Starting salaries won't be higher than the low $40,000s per year in any event. Employees get a step increase once per year, and supervisors can recommend salary increases beyond that as well. Benefits are excellent; overseas housing is provided free of charge to employees, and there are good health and retirement programs.

prospects: USAID jobs are tough to get. Thousands of people apply each year, and only 30 to 40 are hired. USAID priorities are set by the U.S. government, and those priorities can change from year to year. What was once a large mission can grow or shrink as congressional and presidential directions change. Election-year changes in the make-up of the House and Senate can result in subsequent changes in AID funding. While the status of the projects you could be working on can be subject to those sorts of whims, your position within USAID is relatively secure. The hard part is getting that position.

qualifications: USAID positions require at least two years of overseas experience, preferably in a developing country. Foreign language proficiency is another prerequisite. And most positions now require a graduate-level degree.

characteristics: Knowledge of the economic and social issues of development is crucial in succeeding in a USAID job. A knowledge of why you want to work in development, and what you want to do in that field, is also important. Two other important characteristics are cultural sensitivity and interpersonal skills. You have to be able to cooperate and work as a team member, and should be sensitive to cross-cultural relationships.

Cynthia Rohl *is a USAID employee in San Salvador, El Salvador.*

How did you get the job?

Cynthia got an undergraduate degree in Japanese from the University of California-Santa Cruz, and spent her first year out of college teaching English in Japan.

She found out about a master's-level program at Stanford University that, as Cynthia puts it, "linked development and education. I had worked in education and had become interested in development work." She earned a master's degree from Stanford in international development education. Through the newsletter of the Society for International Development, she got the lead on a job in Washington, D.C.

She used the Stanford alumni network to provide her with names of people from her old university working in Washington. She set up as many informational interviews with Stanford alumni as she could. She also compiled extensive lists of international development organizations and set up interviews with their staffs. Although she had never been in the Peace Corps, she attended a job fair for returned Peace Corps volunteers and met a recruiter for USAID.

"The recruiter said that if anyone had any questions, they should give him a call," Cynthia says, "and so I did. Through personal contact was how I got my connection at USAID."

After a lengthy application process, Cynthia was accepted into the program.

She entered the new-entry training program as an international development intern (IDI), working in the Asia bureau, the area of the world in which she thought she would be assigned. About eight months into her training program, she was switched to the Latin America bureau. She moved to El Salvador, and spent a year in training there, working in all of the agency's different offices to get a feel for her office's overall mission. And when the deputy director of the education office left, the offices of education and health were combined into one. Now Cynthia serves as the director of the education division in her office.

What do you do all day?

Cynthia says she works closely with her Salvadoran counterparts in the Ministry of Education and local nongovernmental organizations (NGOs). The Salvadoran government sets the priorities for the projects USAID is involved with, and Cynthia works on the implementation of those projects. She works on basic education programs in El Salvador for children in kindergarten through the sixth grade, teacher training, modernizing the administrative system in education, community education, and other projects. She meets with the Ministry of Education, NGOs, teachers unions, think tanks, university organizations, and other groups in her eight- to nine-hour days. Her duties include supervising the staff of 15 in her office (most of the USAID employees in El Salvador are Salvadoran). "A lot of my time is taken up dealing with bureaucracy," she says, "dealing with the local politics of El Salvador, plus dealing with the politics of being an outsider and a representative of the U.S. government."

Where do you see this job leading you?

"This is a career-type job," Cynthia says. "This is a foreign service job, where a lot of time is invested in training you, with the expectation that you'll stay on after the training is over. I've passed through the initial stages, I'm not an intern anymore. I have to get tenure—I need two years overseas with USAID and then I can start bidding on AID jobs anywhere overseas." With free housing and a free trip back to the States every two years, it can be hard to walk away from USAID jobs, especially after investing so much of your own time in the two-year training program (plus the lengthy process of getting hired in the first place).

> THE SOCIETY FOR INTERNATIONAL DEVELOPMENT PUBLISHES A NEWSLETTER THAT INCLUDES A CLASSIFIED SECTION LISTING OF JOB OPENINGS. IT ALSO PUBLICIZES SEMINARS AND CONFERENCES LIKE THE JOB FAIR FOR RETURNED PEACE CORPS VOLUNTEERS THAT LED CYNTHIA, INDIRECTLY, TO HER CURRENT POSITION.

97. Worker in a State Agency

FOR INTERNATIONAL TRADE AND RELATIONS

description: The world is becoming a smaller place, and state governments are learning that it behooves them to establish relations not only with other state governments and the federal government in Washington, D.C., but with other countries' governments as well.

Nowhere is this more true than in the southwestern states that border Mexico, where relations with its southern neighbor can be as important to a state's economy as its relations with Washington, D.C. And so states have created agencies whose job it is to promote and strengthen that state's relationship with Mexico or other foreign countries.

Workers in these offices labor to create policies for dealing with these other countries, policies affecting everything from transportation to education, the environment to industry. They help to plan the agenda of foreign dignitaries visiting their state, and to put together trips for representatives of their state's government and business community to those countries in return. They plan conferences that bring these people together. They help in the promotion of the art and culture of the other country within their state. They might work with the foreign consulate of the country they're aligned with.

These positions allow workers to be on the forefront of policy development, and this work will most likely involve some traveling. Workers are likely to put in long hours, with 10- to 12-hour days not being uncommon.

salary: Project managers or entry-level workers in this field can expect to make from $20,000 to $27,000 working full-time. Supervisory salaries can rise up to $85,000 or perhaps even higher, depending on where you are working and how closely tied the economy of your state is to other countries.

prospects: Although every state that borders Mexico (Arizona, California, New Mexico, and Texas) has a commission to deal with affairs with that country, those commissions are small offices in the governor's, Secretary of State, or Department of Commerce office, with small staffs and few openings. As with any job, though, if you're in the right place at the right time, you could find yourself working in one of these offices. As the world economy becomes ever more closely entwined, expect more of these commissions and agencies to be created.

qualifications: Persons hoping to work in a state governmental agency that deals with foreign trade and relations should speak the mother tongue of the country they will be dealing with. Good communications and problem-solving skills are also a must.

characteristics: Workers in offices such as these should be adept at handling an environment full of rapid change, where they have to juggle, at the least, two or three projects at any one time. They should be able to work well with others, but should possess leadership skills as well.

Ruben Alvarez *is deputy director of the Arizona-Mexico Commission in Phoenix, Arizona.*

How did you get the job?

Ruben earned a political science degree from Arizona State University and says he got his job through "networking. I was pretty well known in the community because of my connections in the community. I had volunteered at organizations while I was going through school, and my leadership positions within those organizations at school allowed me to participate in functions where I met people from the larger community.

"What initially attracted me to this type of work was the whole NAFTA debate," he says. "I met the director of the Arizona-Mexico Commission at a conference—he liked my point of view and offered me an internship here. I interned here for approximately one semester. Then they offered me a part-time project manager position. While I was still in school, I managed different committees, 15 committees including transportation, industry, education, health, the environment, and agriculture; I worked with my counterpart on a commission in Sonora, Mexico—twice a year our members meet with their

members and discuss issues of importance to both our states. I was a project manager for approximately one year.

"I graduated from college, and a few months later, they offered me a job as the commission's deputy director. I served in that position for one and a half years, then took a six-month leave to create another organization. I worked for the Mexican government as the director of the Mexican Culture Center, working here in Phoenix out of the Mexican consulate office. In that job, I networked in the community, did some fund-raising, worked on building the credibility of the organization, did some event programming—basically I helped get the organization going. Once I had done that, I came back to this position."

What do you do all day?

The Arizona-Mexico Commission is an agency in the Arizona governor's office that handles the state's relations with Mexico, dealing with protocol issues, some trade and commerce issues, the formalizing of Arizona's relations with Mexico, and the generation of the governor's policy with regard to Mexico.

> MAKE YOURSELF VISIBLE. IF YOU MOVE TO A NEW COMMUNITY, VOLUNTEER AND GET INVOLVED IN THAT COMMUNITY. ATTEND CHAMBER OF COMMERCE MIXERS. TAKE PART IN COMMUNITY EVENTS. BE AGGRESSIVE AND GET TO KNOW PEOPLE.

"I oversee three project managers," Ruben says. "I also handle projects within the commission, deal with committee work, and have policy and administrative duties. We work on wide-ranging projects and communicate with Mexican officials about those projects. I negotiate projects. I coordinate meetings. I represent the governor at different functions. I travel to Mexico two or three times a month.

"The work I do on any given day varies quite a lot. I'll come in and oversee different projects that we're working on. I'll correspond with the project managers working under me. I'll

take phone calls and make phone calls. I attend a lot of meetings and handle problem-solving with situations that arise. I'll attend meetings of other organizations that deal with international trade. For example, last month the governor of Sinaloa visited our state, and so now we have various projects growing out of that.

"We put on several major events or conferences throughout the year. We help put together the Border Governors Conference each year, which brings together the leaders of all the four United States and the six Mexican border states."

Where do you see this job leading you?

"I'm not too sure where I will go from here," Ruben says. "This job could lead me into the private sector. The experience I am getting is valuable in terms of getting to know Mexico more, getting to know state policies and procedures more, developing contacts. Because of my government experience, it would be easy for me to move on to another government agency."

98. Coordinator
OF A STARTUP ORGANIZATION

description: If you're founding your own organization, you will be creating your own job description just as you'll be creating your own organization.

Your main job will be selling your idea—identifying a need in whatever you define as your community, identifying people or institutions that can help you bring that idea to life, and then convincing those people or institutions that your idea is worth supporting.

You can expect to find yourself doing some or all of the following tasks:

• Developing strategies and programs. You will have to come up with a plan, a business plan so to speak, for what your organization is going to accomplish and how it is going to accomplish those goals.

• Developing your own board of directors. You will have to locate people with the talent and desire to serve on your board. You'll probably be looking for folks with specific skills—accounting, legal expertise, business and governmental experience and connections, and representation from among the community you're hoping to serve.

• Securing funding. You will write grant proposals, meet with boards of directors of various organizations, go before various governmental bodies, meet with businesspeople—all in an effort to secure the money and materials you need to get your idea off the ground.

• Procuring volunteers. Many nonprofits, and especially startup organizations, are volunteer-driven. Even if your goals are fairly modest, you will probably need some help in order to achieve them.

• Follow-through. Once your idea or organization gets rolling, there will be daily crises to solve, fires to put out, miscommunication to set right, and a host of other things to see to.

salary: Once again, the salary you earn as the founder of your organization is going to be dependent on the money you raise and the resources you devote toward that salary. Depending on the sources of funding you're able to find or the established organizations you're able to partner with, you could earn from $15,000 to $30,000 a year.

prospects: If you're attempting to establish a program or organization of your own, in a very real sense, the prospects for success are entirely up to you. If you can identify a need that is not being addressed, and are willing to put in long hours for little pay, you're well on your way to forming an organization of your own.

qualifications: The main qualification for founding your own organization is identifying a need in your community and being willing to work toward addressing that need. You will have to convince others that you and your cause are worthy of support. Dedication to your cause might be the factor that convinces people to support you. But anything that can impress and convince people of your seriousness can only prove helpful.

characteristics: Don't be afraid to take risks. Be creative and a good prioritizer. Be good with people and good at organizing people. If you can spot high-quality people, people who can help you in accomplishing your goals, your job will only prove easier.

Annie Lee *is the coordinator of a nonprofit organization in Saint Paul, Minnesota.*

How did you get the job?

"I was a senior in college, at the College of St. Catherine in Saint Paul, and I attended a two-week seminar in Washington, D.C., on women in public policy," Annie says. "That seminar was sponsored by PLEN—the Public Leadership Education Network, a coalition of women's colleges. At that seminar, I met students from across the United States and we met women who worked in government, women who worked in communications, women who worked in other organizations.

"I returned to Minnesota and realized that of the 70 students who had attended the program, about three of them were from Minnesota. I thought it was a shame that we didn't have a program like that here.

"And in February of my senior year, I started an internship with the Minnesota Women's Consortium, a coalition of about 170 organizations in the state. The consortium is a resource center for all of those groups. The internship provided me with the opportunity to attempt to put a statewide program of this type together.

"Because it is difficult for a new group to become its own organization, we decided the Minnesota Women's Consortium would house LOTT [Leaders of Today and Tomorrow].

"At first, we were basically just getting feedback on the idea. We received positive feedback, and in June first met with people from outside my college and the consortium, people who had expressed interest in the idea.

"After that June meeting, we had a good feeling about things and actually started planning the program.

"We drafted a program schedule. I started writing to foundations, trying to get money for the program. I spent the next eight months trying to secure funding, publicizing Leaders of Today and Tomorrow, which is what we called the program, trying to find students who might be interested in attending the program.

"I started contacting speakers in August. Most speakers, who were mostly public officials, were excited about getting involved.

"As we began to put together a budget, we decided we needed one staff person to work on the program. And that person became me."

What do you do all day?

Annie has helped put together two Leaders of Today and Tomorrow conferences since she founded the program. The process of organizing those conferences differed in each case.

"The first year that we put this conference together, we had no idea of the response we would get," she says. "We made up brochures and sent them out to 50 or 60 colleges, to political science departments, to women's studies departments, to career centers. We didn't have the resources to send brochures out to a lot of places. Forty-five students ended up

> **IF YOU'RE THINKING ABOUT FORMING AN ORGANIZATION TO TACKLE A SPECIFIC ISSUE YOU'RE INTERESTED IN, DO YOUR HOMEWORK. INVESTIGATE THE ISSUE AND THE PROGRAMS THAT HAVE BEEN DEVELOPED TO TACKLE THAT ISSUE.**

attending that first LOTT conference.

"The focus of our efforts changed from year one to year two," Annie says. "The first year, we just wanted to attract enough funding and get enough students to actually put on a seminar. The second year, we wanted to publicize the program more, expand what we offer, and get different colleges and groups involved.

"I spent time working on developing our board of directors and procuring speakers for the seminar.

"This year, we have added two seminars (a conference focusing on community and citizen-driven organizing and another focusing on 'Women, Law, and Public Policy' for female law students), which has increased the workload."

Where do you see this job leading you?

Annie says she intends to work with LOTT for another two years, and is then thinking about going back to school, either to graduate school or to law school. "I always want to be connected to LOTT though," she says, "enough to at least know what's going on, by sitting on the board of directors or something like that."

99. Missionary-at-Large/Church Planner

description: As a missionary-at-large, you will be responsible for laying the groundwork for a new congregation, and spreading the word of your faith to people who have never heard it before, people who have never listened to it, or people who have turned away from it—or the church—for one reason or another.

Your duties will probably not be as structured as those of a pastor for a formal congregation. You might not even be preaching on Sunday. You will also find yourself—at least at first—without much of the support or many of the resources that pastors in established churches can expect—a council of elders, standing committees, or a parsonage (a home for the clergy, provided by the congregation).

You will be planning for the establishment for this new congregation, finding people willing to work with you on this project, and then putting your plans in motion—plans for finding a place to meet, for determining when to meet, for Bible study sessions, for reaching out to the "unchurched." You will work with committees on these issues and more. As a missionary-at-large, you will be responsible for coordinating and presiding over all of these initiatives.

You will be a spiritual leader to members or potential members of your nascent congregation—to many of them, you will be the first spiritual leader they have ever had; for others, your efforts could be the last chance they will take on church-going.

As do other clergy members, you will also find yourself serving as psychological counselor, surrogate family member, marriage counselor, and confessor to a variety of people at various points in their lives.

salary: Missionaries-at-large can expect to make less than clergy members of their equivalent experience level in established churches. Salaries will vary widely depending on the area of the country you're working in, the size of the population where you're working, the denomination of the church you belong to, and the support the regional and national level of your church provides. Salaries could range from $20,000 to $45,000 per year or more.

prospects: Missionary-at-large positions—attempting to form a new congregation with the backing of an established denomination—will be harder to come by than positions in established churches, but those opportunities will arise for the people who are attuned to them and express interest in this type of work.

qualifications: Missionaries-at-large typically have served with an established church before going out and trying to build a congregation, so prior clerical experience is an important qualification for this job. Some missionaries-at-large begin right out of seminary, though. Perhaps the most important qualification is the desire to help build a church and a congregation from the ground up.

characteristics: Prospective pastors and missionaries-at-large should be willing to listen to parishioners in their times of distress, be able to provide advice when needed and a shoulder to cry on, and be a friend to laugh with. Members of the clergy are on call 24 hours a day and should be prepared for the demands that will make on their time. They should be persons of strong faith and good character.

Rex Rinne is a missionary-at-large for a church in a medium-size town in Wisconsin.

How did you get the job?

After earning a bachelor's degree, Rex went on to a Lutheran seminary, spending four years there and leaving with a master's of divinity and an internship with a church in Baltimore. He was in Baltimore for a year, and then was sent to serve as the pastor in two churches in two different cities [Phillips and Kennan] in northern Wisconsin.

"I received calls from 16 different congregations when I was in Phillips and Kennan, churches inquiring whether or not I would want to serve as their pastor. Then I received a call from a small church in Kansas. The Kansas church was a mission congregation that had broken off from another congregation and needed someone to help get it on its feet.

"I was there [Kansas] for two and a half years, helping to get the congregation established, helping to get the church building built. And then I was ready for something else.

"Faith Lutheran Church in Appleton, Wisconsin, was looking for an associate pastor—a second in command. I took the call, and stayed there 11 years.

"I got a call from our district

GOOD WORKS: A GUIDE TO CAREERS IN SOCIAL CHANGE CAN BE AN EXCELLENT JOB HUNTING RESOURCE. THE 600-PLUS PAGE MANUAL, PUBLISHED BY BARRICADE BOOKS, CONTAINS A DIRECTORY OF SOCIAL CHANGE ORGANIZATIONS, WITH NAMES, ADDRESSES, PHONE NUMBERS, AND CONTACT PERSONS LISTED FOR EACH ORGANIZATION, AS WELL AS THE ORGANIZATION'S SIZE, STAFFING LEVEL, ANNUAL BUDGET, NUMBER OF JOB OPENINGS EACH YEAR, AND OTHER PERTINENT DATA. THE MANUAL LISTS THESE ORGANIZATIONS ALPHABETICALLY AS WELL AS BY GEOGRAPHICAL REGION AND TOPIC.

office then, and they said they were interested in targeting, going after people who don't like church. They asked if I would be interested in attempting to do that.

"And so I began this process in March. I took a $23,000 cut in salary and gave up a church where the average Sunday attendance was 1,000, to this experiment, where the average attendance right now is less than 100."

What do you do all day?

"I like the target group I'm going after—people who don't like church. That's a challenge," Rex says. "So many people don't think about the church until things in their lives go bad. It's fun because I go out in the community and I talk to people, and I never know how they're going to react. A large part of my job is making contact with people. My counseling load is pretty high—I've talked to people who didn't want to go to an established church, but realized they had a spiritual emptiness in their lives and wanted to address that. A lot of people are spiritual, but they have no connection to the church.

"Most of my time is spent interacting with people, making follow-up calls. At Faith, I always got one day off a week. Here, I haven't taken a day off since we started this project.

"We have a relaxed, informal service—a whole different mood from an established church. In fact, we weren't even going to start services until the fall, but people wanted to have Sunday services, so we started doing that in May. We get between 60 and 90 people on Sundays. More than half of those people are new."

Where do you see this job leading you?

"I picked up my clinical pastoral education in Kansas," Rex says, "so I could go on to become a therapist, I suppose.

"Sometimes members of the clergy will go on to be insurance salesmen, or they will become personnel directors for corporations—the training we receive prepares us for jobs that involve working with people.

"Other opportunities are serving as the chaplain for a corporation or plant. You could go into a plant and say, 'I will be your chaplain and your therapist.' Hospitals have chaplains as well, and there is typically a lot of turnover in those positions."

100. Pastor

description: Some of the chief duties of a pastor are to lead worship services, to preach a sermon every Sunday, to administer the sacraments—the wine and bread that are part of Christian ritual—and to officiate at weddings, baptisms, funerals, and secular ceremonies. But that isn't all there is to being a pastor.

Pastors are the heads of the churches they're serving, and some of their responsibilities will fall under that banner. Pastors serve as contact persons for leaders of Sunday school services, youth clubs, and other Bible study groups, and can be called on to resolve disputes arising out of those gatherings. A council (or some other designation) of laypeople determines church policy. Pastors are usually in attendance at these council meetings.

Pastors lead Bible study groups, and counsel and instruct prospective church members; they conduct marriage counseling and confirmation classes.

Pastors often serve as counselors for church members in distress, persons facing a terminal illness, suffering through a bad marriage, or experiencing any of a myriad of family problems.

salary: Salaries for pastors can vary quite widely, depending on the denomination of the church and the size and wealth of its congregation. Most postings will include housing or a housing allowance. Salaries could range from $15,000 a year for pastors serving in their first church, on up to $70,000 or more for pastors serving large congregations in metropolitan areas.

prospects: Some denominations have more postings than there are pastors to fill them. Some denominations are in the exact opposite predicament. Overall, though, competition for posting as a pastor should continue, as growth in church membership is expected to be slow and the pool of qualified candidates is not expected to shrink. If candidates are willing and able to move to small or rural churches (or are willing to work as part-time pastors) once they are ordained, their prospects should be good for embarking upon a career as a pastor.

qualifications: The main qualification for work as a pastor is to be someone who feels "called" to the work. Would-be pastors have to be willing to attend four or more years of seminary school. Many denominations require a bachelor's degree of seminary candidates. The process of applying to seminary may take up to two years, and the applications and screening process can be quite rigorous.

characteristics: Strong faith is the dominant characteristic a pastor, or would-be pastor, should possess, of course. Pastors should be people who have their own spiritual life in order. They should be interested in the secular, as well as the spiritual, well-being of their parishioners. Pastors should be willing to put in long hours, and should most definitely be "people people."

Grace Cangialosi *is a pastor at two churches in Virginia.*

How did you get the job?

"I became a pastor through what you might call a midlife course correction," Grace Cangialosi says.

"Our diocese has a rigorous process leading to ordination. I met with the commission of my local church and underwent psychological evaluation for two years before entering the seminary. The diocese's Commission on Ministry evaluated my application. It was finally the decision of the bishop as to whether or not I should attend the seminary.

"I attended the Virginia Theological Seminary in Alexandria, Virginia," she says.

"The primary purpose of the seminary was training men and women for parish work. While I went to school full-time, I also did volunteer work at the Church of the Savior, an ecumenical church in inner-city Washington, D.C., that sponsors a number of programs ranging from medical clinics to housing services, across the bridge from Alexandria."

After completing her seminary work, Grace stayed on in Alexandria, continuing her work with a ministry of the Church of the Savior as a pro-

gram director. She also worked there as the pastoral services facilitator for a summer program that brought seminarians to the Church of the Savior for a program of theological reflection and hands-on ministry.

Grace later left the D.C. area for the Shenandoah Valley area of Virginia, where she took over as pastor for a pair of rural mountain churches.

What do you do all day?

"My churches are part of a string of missions set up in the early 1900s to serve the mountain people of this area," Grace says.

"For me, the gospel is about being in the world, standing in a place without hope and pro-

claiming hope. Being a model for the congregation is important, and so I'm involved in social outreach programs here. We have founded a Habitat for Humanity chapter here, and are building our first house. I serve on a local council on domestic violence. The churches provide emergency shelter for victims of domestic violence.

"A typical week for me involves time preparing sermons and classes, and visiting parishioners. I also do hospital visitations.

"I also attend meetings of clergy. We have 14 churches in our region, and the pastors of those churches meet once a month. I'm also the dean of our region, and I meet with deans from other regions four times a year."

The busiest time of the year for many churches revolves around the big church holidays—Christmas and Easter. That's not really the case at her churches, Grace says. "It's interesting because the rhythm of life here is much more steady. No one goes on vacation for the summer here. If anything, our summer is busier because we have two vacation Bible school programs, and this year we put on a three-day program in conjunction with the local national park."

Where do you see this job leading you?

"This is the kind of ministry I always wanted," Grace says. "There is a lot to be done here. The issue is how long the churches here can afford a full-time person.

"In most church positions, the 'corporate model' is followed. After first graduating from the seminary, people will be posted to a job as an assistant in a medium or large church, or they might be put in charge of a small church. One to three years at that first posting is typical. They keep moving up. By the third call, they will be the head of a large church or the assistant of a very large church. This is not a model I see for myself."

> WHO CARES: A JOURNAL OF SERVICE AND ACTION IS A QUARTERLY MAGAZINE DEVOTED TO SERVING AS "THE COMMUNICATION FORUM FOR A NEW GENERATION OF LEADERS IN THE NONPROFIT SECTOR." THE MAGAZINE COVERS THE EFFORTS OF NONPROFIT GROUPS TOWARD BRINGING ABOUT SOCIAL CHANGE. THE BACK PAGES OF EACH ISSUE ARE A RESOURCE DIRECTORY, WITH ADDRESSES AND CONTACT INFORMATION ABOUT THE GROUPS COVERED IN THE ISSUE.

RESOURCES

Organizations

ACT UP New York
135 W. 29th St.
New York, NY 10001; (212) 564-AIDS

AFL-CIO Organizing Institute
1101 14th St., NW, Suite 320
Washington, DC 20005; (202) 408-0700
or:
AFL-CIO Organizing Institute
519 17th St., Suite 111
Oakland, CA 94612; (510) 832-8765
The AFL-CIO Organizing Institute was established in 1989 "to promote and foster union organizing." The Institute's three-day session provides an intensive look into what being a union organizer involves. Promising participants in that program can go on to internships and apprenticeships with Institute's participating organizations, and from there on to full-time organizing work.

AIDS Treatment Data Network
259 W. 30th St., Ninth Floor
New York, NY 10001; (212) 268-4196

American Friends Service Committee
1501 Cherry St.
Philadelphia, PA 19102; (215) 241-7000
The American Friends Service Committee was founded by the Quakers in 1917 as an independent organization; today it works on social justice and nonviolence issues. With an annual budget of $28 million, a total staff of about 400, and at least 30 area offices in the United States, the AFSC has approximately 80 staff openings per year.

American Health Care Association
1201 L St., NW
Washington, DC 20005; (202) 842-4444

American Society of Association Executives
1575 I St., NW
Washington, DC 20005-1168; (202) 626-2723

Annenberg Institute for School Reform
Brown University
Box 1969
Providence, RI 02912; (401) 863-3384

Association for Community-Based Education
1805 Florida Ave., NW
Washington, DC 20009; (202) 462-6333

Center for Educational Renewal
Box 353600
University of Washington
Seattle, WA 98915; (206) 543-6230

Federal Job Information Center
1900 E St., NW, Room 1416
Washington, DC 20415
The Federal Job Information Center provides information on job openings in the U.S. government or career opportunities on the federal level. The center is operated by the Office of Personnel Management.

Call "Career America Connection," the U.S. government's official employment information service 24-hour hot line at: (202) 606-2700.

Foundation for Hospice and Homecare/
National Certification Program
519 C St., NE
Washington, DC 20002; (202) 547-6586

Fund-Raising School at the Center for Philanthropy
at Indiana University
550 West North St., Suite 301
Indianapolis, IN 46202; (317) 274-4200

International Schools Service
P.O. Box 5910
Princeton, NJ 08543; (609) 452-0990
This service provides information on teaching opportunities abroad.

Meeting Planners International
1950 Stemmons Freeway
Infomart Building, Suite 5018
Dallas, TX 75207-3109; (214) 746-5222

National Alliance for Restructuring Education
700 11th St., NW, Suite 750
Washington, DC 20001; (202) 783-3668

National Association of Broadcasters
1771 N St., NW
Washington, DC 20036; (202) 429-5300
The National Association of Broadcasters can provide you with information on job opportunities in the radio field, or about research opportunities with media outlets. The association sponsors an employment clearinghouse, and holds an annual Radio Convention, which can provide you with a wealth of job leads and potential contacts, should you be able to attend.

National CASA Association
2722 Eastlake Ave. East, Suite 220
Seattle, WA 98102; (206) 328-8588

National Coalition to Abolish the Death Penalty
918 F St., Suite 601
Washington, DC 20004; (202) 347-2411;
fax: (202) 347-2415; e-mail: abolition@igc.apc.org
The national coalition can give you information about activities going on at the state level, as well as who to contact in your area.

National Education Association
1201 16th St., NW
Washington, DC 20036; (202) 833-4000

The National Society of Fund-Raising Executives
1101 King St., Suite 700
Alexandria, VA 22314; (703) 684-0410

RESOURCES

Peace Corps National Headquarters
1990 K St., NW
Washington, DC 20526
Call (800) 424-8580 to get information on applying to the Peace Corps or to find out when a Peace Corps recruiter will be making a stop near you.

Recruiting for Teachers Inc.
This organization can give you information about employment opportunities in teaching. Call them at: 1-800-45-TEACH. Recruiting for Teachers can offer you information on how to become a teacher and will send your name as a prospective teacher to "a network of school districts and teachers' colleges."

Senators and Representatives
Contact those Senators and Representatives with whom you are interested in working. Or get in touch with:
Placement Office
U.S. Senate
Hart Office Building, Room 142B
Washington, DC 20510; (202) 224-9167
or:
U.S. House of Representatives Resume Referral Service
Office of Human Resources
Room 263
Cannon Office Building
Washington, DC 20515-6610; (202) 226-6731;
fax: (202) 226-0098

Teach For America
20 Exchange Pl., Eighth Floor
New York, NY 10005
The general information number for Teach For America is:
(800) 832-1230.
To receive an application package from Teach for America, call (212) 425-9039, or send a 9-inch by 12-inch self-addressed stamped envelope with $1.93 worth of postage to the above address, attn.: Application request.

Toastmasters International
P.O. Box 9052
Mission Viejo, CA 92690; (714) 858-8255
Toastmasters International is an association whose members work to improve their communication and leadership skills.

United States Agency for International Development (USAID)
Recruitment Branch
Room 1026 SA-1
2401 E St., NW
Washington, DC 20523-0116; (202) 663-2296 or
(202) 663-2368
USAID applicants with a graduate degree, two or more years of experience working in a foreign country, and knowledge of a foreign language will have the greatest chances for success.

Publications

Adventure Careers, by Alex Hiam and Susan Angle, is published by Career Press, 3 Tice Rd., P.O. Box 687, Franklin Lakes, NJ 07417; (800) CAREER-1.

The Almanac of American Government Jobs and Careers, by Ronald L. and Caryl Rae Krannich, is published by Impact Publications, 4580 Sunshine Court, Woodbridge, VA 22192; (703) 361-7300.

Impact Publications also offers books with such titles as the *Almanac of International Jobs and Careers, The Complete Guide to Public Employment, Jobs and Careers with Nonprofit Organizations,* and *Mayors and Managers,* any of which may be useful to you, depending on what career field you are exploring.

The American Almanac of Jobs and Salaries, by John W. Wright, is published by Avon Books, a division of the Hearst Corporation, 1350 Avenue of the Americas, New York, NY 10019. For ordering information, call (800) 223-0690.

The Chronicle of Philanthropy, 1255 23rd St., NW, Washington, DC, 20037; (202) 466-1200. Subscriptions to the biweekly newspaper are available for $67.50 per year from P.O. Box 1989, Marion, OH 43305; (800) 347-6969.

This newspaper covers the world of nonprofit organizations and foundations. A classified help wanted section in the back of the newspaper lists job openings at nonprofit organizations and foundations across the country. The newspaper also provides information on a multitude of seminars and workshops.

Community Jobs can be ordered for $5 a copy from Access, 1001 Connecticut Ave., NW, Suite 838, Washington, DC 20036; (202) 785-4233.

Corporate Philanthropy Report is published monthly by Capital Publications, Inc., 1101 King St., Suite 444, Alexandria, VA 22314; (703) 683-4100.

Subscriptions and back issues are expensive ($205 annually, or $20 per issue), but copies should be available in your local college's library or job placement center, or in a nearby foundation center.

The Electronic Job Search Revolution, by Joyce Lain Kennedy and Thomas J. Morrow, is published by John Wiley & Sons Inc., 605 Third Ave., New York, NY 10158-0012; (800) 225-5945.

The Encyclopedia of Associations, published by Gale Research, breaks down organizations by geographical location, membership size, staff size, annual budget, and founding date, and provides a plethora of information on each organization, from addresses and phone numbers, to contact persons within the organization, to newsletters and magazines published by the association. The encyclopedia also includes listings of new associations. A new edition of *The Encyclopedia of Associations* is issued annually.

Federal Career Opportunities is available ($7.95/issue, $39/six issues, $77/12 issues, $175/26 issues) from Federal Research Service, 243 Church St., NW, P.O. Box 1059, Vienna, VA 22183-1059; (703) 281-0200.

RESOURCES

Federal Jobs Digest is available ($5.50/copy, or $125/year) from Breakthrough Publications Inc., 310 N. Highland Ave., Ossining, NY 10562; (914) 762-5111.

Good Works: A Guide to Careers in Social Change, edited by Donna Colvin, is available for $24 from Barricade Books, 61 Fourth Ave., New York, NY 10003; (212) 627-7000 or (800) 413-4888.

The Institute for Global Communications' Progressive Directory can be found at "http://gopher.igc.apc.org/". The networks set up by IGC "serve individuals and organizations working toward peace, environmental protection, human rights, social and economic justice, sustainable and equitable development, health, and nonviolent conflict resolution." The IGC's address is: Institute for Global Communications, 18 De Bloom Street, San Francisco, CA 94107; (415) 974-6177; fax: (415) 546-1794. You can send an e-mail message to IGC at: support@igc.apc.org

The Job Seekers Guide to Socially Responsible Companies by Katherine Jankowski is available from Visible Ink Press (a division of Gale Research Inc.), 835 Penobscot Building, Detroit, MI 48226-4094.

National Business Employment Weekly, P.O. Box 300, Princeton, NJ 01020. Call (800) JOB-HUNT (562-4868) for subscription information. Or check out the *National Business Employment Weekly* online at http://www.enews.com/magazines/nbew. The publication's e-mail address is 75557.1060@CompuServe.com.

The National Directory of Corporate Public Affairs is available from Columbia Books Inc., 1212 New York Ave., NW, Washington, DC 20005; (202) 898-0662.

Nonprofit Times is available for $7.95 an issue or $59 a year from Nonprofit Times, 240 Cedar Knolls Rd., Suite 318, Cedar Knolls, NJ 07927; attn.: Susan; (201) 734-1700.

Nonprofits' Job Finder, by Daniel Lauber, is published by Planning/Communications, 7215 Oak Avenue, River Forest, IL 60305. The 1994–95 edition of the book is its third.

The Washington chapter of the Society for International Development can be reached at (202) 884-8590. The society's newsletter, *SID Development Connections,* can be ordered from the society.

The newsletter contains notices of upcoming conferences, seminars, and employment opportunities of interest to those in the development field, and lists chairs of SID work groups and programs (any of whom could prove to be a valuable connection). Membership dues are $65 annually for regular members and $30 a year for full-time students. Contact the association at: SID-Washington Chapter, 1875 Connecticut Ave., NW, Suite 1020, Washington, DC 20009-5728.

Taking Off: Extraordinary Ways to Spend your First Year Out of College by Lauren Tarshis is available from Fireside Books, a division of Simon and Schuster, 1230 Avenue of the Americas, New York, NY 10020; (800) 223-2336.

Using the Internet in Your Job Search: An Easy Guide to Online Job Seeking and Career Information by Fred E. Jandt and Mary B. Nemnich is available from JIST Works, Inc., 720 North Park Ave., Indianapolis, IN 46202-3431; (317) 264-3720.

Who Cares: A Journal of Service and Action is available via subscription ($15 for four issues) from Who Cares Inc., 1511 K St., NW, Suite 142, Washington DC 20005. Call (800) 628-1692 or (202) 628-1691, or contact the organization via e-mail: info@whocares.org.

Zen and the Art of Making a Living: A Practical Guide to Creative Career Design, by Laurence G. Boldt, was published in 1993 by Viking-Penguin. Call (800) 526-0275 for ordering information.

ABOUT THE AUTHOR

Harley Jebens manages the Web site for the Austin American Statesman
in Austin, Texas.

NOTES

NOTES

NOTES

NOTES

NOTES